David Strong
The Bond of Empathy in Medieval and Early Modern Literature

Research in Medieval
and Early Modern Culture XXXV
Studies in Medieval
and Early Modern Culture LXXXIV

David Strong

The Bond of Empathy in Medieval and Early Modern Literature

—

DE GRUYTER

WESTERN
MICHIGAN
UNIVERSITY

MEDIEVAL
INSTITUTE PUBLICATIONS

ISBN 978-1-5015-2252-9
e-ISBN (PDF) 978-1-5015-1546-0
e-ISBN (EPUB) 978-1-5015-1547-7

Library of Congress Control Number: 2022939605

Bibliographic information published by the Deutsche Nationalbibliothek
The Deutsche Nationalbibliothek lists this publication in the Deutsche Nationalbibliografie;
detailed bibliographic data are available on the internet at http://dnb.dnb.de.

www.degruyter.com

Contents

Introduction

Ever since scientists discovered mirror mechanisms in the human brain during the late twentieth century, "empathy" has become a buzzword in the fields of social psychology and cognitive science. Research indicating that we are physiologically hard-wired to respond pre-reflexively to another's emotional reaction has prompted scientists to write hundreds of articles about the neuroscience of empathy.[1] This critical upsurge has shown little sign of slowing down.[2] Refining our ability to draw closer to another person in a world that is continually expanding and diversifying has a wide-range appeal.[3] In fact, two prominent scholars in the field, Jamil Zaki and Paul Bloom, have recently drawn upon their scientific findings and published general non-fiction books pronouncing or denouncing, respectively, the value of empathy as a prosocial tool. Zaki believes, "Empathy's most important role, though, is to inspire kindness: our tendency to help each other, even at a cost to ourselves."[4] Bloom, on the other hand, notes that many real-world acts of kindness are not prompted by empathic concern. "We sometimes miss these cases because we are too quick to credit an action to empathy when actually something else is going on."[5] Despite the seeming antinomy between these two positions, I submit that they are both accurate because the concept encompasses far more than simply alleviating distress. It requires an assessment of the circumstances impacting the other's well-being, knowing how to

---

1 Jamil Zaki and Kevin Ochsner, "The Neuroscience of Empathy: Progress, Pitfalls and Promise," *Nature Neuroscience* 15 (2012): 675. Mirror neurons, as explained by Vittorio Gallese, "are motor neurons that respond not only to the execution of movements and actions, but also during their perception when executed by others" ("Neoteny and Social Cognition: A Neuroscientific Perspective on Embodiment," in *Embodiment, Enaction, and Culture*, ed. Christoph Durt, Thomas Fuchs, and Christian Tewes [Cambridge, MA: MIT Press, 2017], 318; Giacomo Rizzolatti and Corrado Sinigaglia, "The Functional Role of the Parieto-Frontal Mirror Circuit: Interpretations and Misinterpretations," *Nature Reviews: Neuroscience* 11 [2010]: 264–74; Vittorio Gallese, Christopher Keyes, and Giacomo Rizzolatti, "A Unifying View of the Basis of Social Cognition," *Trends in Cognitive Sciences* 8 [2004]: 396–403).

2 Two articles of note that emphasize imitating the empathized's expressions and bodily gestures are: Tanya L. Chartrand and Jessica L. Lakin, "The Antecedents and Consequences of Human Behavioral Mimicry," *Annual Review of Psychology* 64 (2013): 285–308; Ulf Dimberg and Monika Thunberg, "Rapid Facial Reactions to Emotional Facial Expressions," *Scandinavian Journal of Psychology* 39 (1998): 39–45.

3 Jamil Zaki, *The War for Kindness: Building Empathy in a Fractured World* (New York: Crown Publishing, 2019); Paul Bloom, *Against Empathy: The Case for Rational Compassion* (New York: HarperCollins, 2016).

4 Zaki, *The War for Kindness*, 2.

5 Bloom, *Against Empathy*, 25.

https://doi.org/10.1515/9781501515460-001

attune oneself accordingly to the proper degree of the other's emotional intensity, and actively choosing to pursue this mode of consciousness. It is not autonomic. Like the act of love, empathy cannot be compelled and involves the whole person in grasping a full perception of the other person's motivations, desires, and beliefs.

By itself, feeling what another experiences produces only a superficial connection, but when conjoined with knowing the reasons underlying the other's behavior, the composite alloy enhances the intimacy. Drawn from a confluence of cognitive and affective insight, empathy refines an appreciation of what it means to be human and reinforces the volition to further this connection. It does not terminate upon its initial expression, but regenerates its efforts through an ongoing assessment of the other person's condition. This continuous process highlights the willingness to sustain this commitment. The multidimensional elements of empathy thus serve as a keen hermeneutic in explicating the affinity not just between people, but between literary characters too. When applied specifically to those instances where characters seek a harmonious communion, it shows how their efforts offer far more than emotional support. Even if an impassioned event triggers a reaction, it neither determines nor impedes the desire to privilege this bond. The characters elect to dedicate themselves to the other person in such a way that the exchange of information flows as freely as possible. The distinguishing feature in the texts selected here lies in the characters' cognitive perseverance and savvy to access those areas of seeming inaccessibility. The resultant insight allows them to construct a relationship that flourishes whether the other exists in this world or the next. Empathy thus enhances reason's operation by intensifying their commitment to the other's singular, ineffable good.

With this in mind, my study conducts a detailed examination of those medieval and early modern characters whose actions foster an appreciation for the other's person and instill a greater sense of self. The empathizers in the anonymous Middle English romance *Amis and Amiloun*, Chaucer's *Second Nun's Tale*, William Shakespeare's *The Tragedy of King Lear* and *The Tempest*, John Donne's speaker in *Songs and Sonnets*, and Richard Crashaw's religious heroines actively cultivate a heightened interpersonal awareness that enables them to overcome those political, familial, or religious obstacles subverting their connection. By investing their mental energies in cultivating a positive rapport, they vanquish whatever power distress, melancholy, or sadness wield over the other person. Whether utilizing the information conveyed in that very moment or creating surrogates of another's mental states, their interchange affirms the ability to know the other intimately and cherish each one's distinctiveness.[6] It accounts for why they choose to embrace torturous physical sacrifice for the sake of friendship, transgress age-old caste systems to preserve the other's sanity, or forgo bodily needs to feed an ardor that thrives in an otherworldly realm. The insight exchanged between these characters exceeds conventional interpretations of fellowship, romantic love, or spiritual devotion.

The complexity of amassing the proper information to discern the other's thought process and emotional state requires the use of various approaches. As Daniel Zahavi notes in his study on empathy, "We need multiple complementary accounts in order to cover the variety of abilities, skills, and strategies that we draw on and employ in order to understand and make sense of others."[7] My tools of inquiry involve medieval and modern philosophies that place agency within the observer's faculties and address the tripartite structure of an empathetic response, namely the will, the intellect, and the affective. Before such a response can occur, the individual must actively make a decision to utilize their cognitive efforts in this manner. The choice to initiate, terminate, or sustain this pursuit depends upon the freedom of the will and accords with the voluntarism of John Duns Scotus (ca. 1266–1308). His innovation centers upon the idea that the will is not dependent upon the intellect's dictates. The will, as an affective faculty, heeds its own inclinations towards personal happiness or justice, which he identifies as the *affectio commodi* and *affectio iustitiae*, respectively.[8] Whereas the former affection disposes one to seek out goods that bring pleasure and enjoyment to the self, the latter exerts a tempering influence which ensures that the will operates freely.[9] When they strike an internal bal-

---

6 Alvin Goldman advances the hypothesis that the mind literally creates (or attempts to create) surrogates of another's mental states in order to simulate his or her thought process. By creating similar mental states of their own as proxies of those of the target, the observer can effectively ascertain that person's desires and intentions. See "Theory of Mind," in *The Oxford Handbook of Philosophy of Cognitive Science*, ed. Eric Margolis, Richard Samuels, and Stephen P. Stich (New York: Oxford University Press, 2012), 402–24.
7 Dan Zahavi, *Self & Other: Exploring Subjectivity, Empathy, and Shame* (Oxford: Oxford University Press, 2014), 169.
8 Scotus writes: "the *affectio iustitiae*, which is the first controller of the *affectio commodi* with respect to the fact that the will need not actually will that to which the *affectio commodi* inclines it, or will it to the highest degree, is the innate liberty of the will" (John Duns Scotus, *Ordinatio* II, d. 6, q. 2; *Duns Scotus on the Will and Morality*, ed. and trans. Allan B. Wolter [Washington DC: Catholic University of America, 1986], 468–71).
9 Scotus allows the will to heed its own inclinations either towards personal happiness or justice, the *affectio commodi* and *affectio iustitiae*, respectively. Whereas the former affection disposes one to seek out goods that bring pleasure and enjoyment to the self, the latter exerts a

ance, there is self-control. The will retains the power to refrain from, redirect, or execute the decision-making process at any point. Scotus's views are seminal in late medieval and early modern thought, for an empathy that strives to align itself with another's goodness must spring from a will capable of self-determination.

Whereas Scotistic thought lays the foundation to live a life of meaning and purpose, the twentieth-century philosophies of phenomenology and simulation theory explain how one grasps the other's intentions and attributes the proper mental states to that person's actions. They recast the notion of empathy from a "feeling-based" reaction to one that attaches an epistemic value to the interpersonal reality of that experience. In addition, neuroscientific research provides empirical proof for why humans instinctively mirror another's behavior, which accounts in part for how one can make "pertinent theoretical inferences from the observables—that is, behavior and environmental conditions—to mental states."[10] Each approach prioritizes the asymmetry between the two people. No matter how synchronized one is with the other, the one cannot replicate the original presence of the other's consciousness. Phenomenologist Edmund Husserl notes that another's experiences can never be fully fashioned as one's own because the differences constitute the other's individuality.[11] These differences establishe each one's uniqueness and provide a more global understanding of that person and the situation itself.

As a literary heuristic, these schools of thought illuminate the divers ways in which these characters generate an informed connection that can overcome any outside force—no matter how imposing or seemingly impassable. Each text places them in such a precarious position that the aspiring empathizer must employ rather remarkable efforts to access the other's mind. These interactions produce an inter- and intrapersonal knowledge that exposes the limitations of hyperbole, custom, or unbridled passion to explain what drives that person onward. Poetically divined, the interplay between the empathizer and the other person reveals

---

tempering influence which ensures that the will operates freely (Scotus, *Ordinatio* II, d. 6, q. 2, n. 8 (XII, 353).

10 Alvin I. Goldman, *Simulating Minds* (Oxford: Oxford University Press, 2006), 8. He believes that states of mind are either pieces of overt behavior or dispositions to behave in certain ways (6). Still, the neurophysiological link neither necessitates nor ensures that an empathetic reply will occur. It merely establishes the grounds for the individual to cultivate a positive response.

11 Edmund Husserl, *Zur Phänomenologie der Intersubjektivität: Texte aus dem Nachlass*, vol. 1, *1905–1920*, ed. Iso Kern, Husserliana 13 (The Hague: Martinus Nijhoff, 1973), 347 and 440. Succeeding thinker, Emanuel Levinas notes, "If one could possess, grasp, and know the other, it would not be other" (Levinas, *Time and the Other*, trans. R. A. Cohen [Pittsburgh: Duquesne University Press, 1987], 90).

that the empathizer embraces the diversity of another's being and the joy drawn from this show of individuality. Striving to ensure that this exchange of information flows as freely as possible prompts the empathizer to determine how best to put this knowledge into practice and confirms the authenticity of their concern.

While this book distinguishes itself from other literary studies by showing that empathy is the epistemically central method of gaining knowledge of the other characters' minds, it sets itself apart from philosophical treatises by exploring the positive purposes of empathy. Scholars who describe empathy primarily as a means to alleviate distress diminish its qualitative capacity to foster a mutually beneficial relationship.[12] Even in her acclaimed work, *On the Problem of Empathy*, Edith Stein cites anguish as the impetus to express this mode of consciousness.[13] Upon pointing out that asymmetry underlines the dynamic personalities of each individual person, she notes that another's suffering may be expressed directly and unmediated, but is not the observer's pain.[14] Although such negative emotions may incite one to become mindful of another's condition, these kinds of feelings should not be considered as the sole stimulus. The desire to enhance one's understanding of another's goodness can impel such an endeavor. Jean Decety's neuroscientific findings show that mutual perspectives founded upon either positive or negative emotions coincide in activating the same neural network. This activation "gives rise to shared feelings and affects between self and other on which mature empathy and moral reasoning develop."[15] Attuning oneself with another's emotional state and using this knowledge to cultivate a healthy bond maximizes the innate potential to become

---

12 For an investigation into how empathy applies more readily to matters of distress than those of joy, see Olga Klimecki and Tania Singer, "Empathic Distress Fatigue Rather Than Compassion Fatigue? Integrating Findings from Empathy Research in Psychology and Social Neuroscience," in *Pathological Altruism*, ed. Barbara Oakley et al. (Oxford: Oxford University Press, 2011), 368 – 84; Jean Decety and Claus Lamm, "Empathy versus Personal Distress: Recent Evidence from Social Neuroscience," in *The Social Neuroscience of Empathy*, ed. Jean Decety and William Ickes (Cambridge, MA; MIT Press, 2009), 199 – 214; L. Goubert et al., "Facing Others in Pain: The Effects of Empathy," *Pain* 118 (2005): 285 – 88.

13 Stein cites the example of relating to a friend who has lost a brother to show that the experience itself rather than projecting previous knowledge about these circumstances is the basis of knowledge. See Edith Stein, *On the Problem of Empathy*, trans. Waltraut Stein (Washington, DC: ICS Publications, 1989), 8 – 9.

14 The actual experience centers on the effect, not the source of this feeling. Stein writes that empathy "is an act primordial as present experience though non-primordial in content" (*On the Problem of Empathy*, 10).

15 Jean Decety and Jennifer A. Stevens, "Action Representation and Its Role in Social Interaction," in *Handbook of Imagination and Mental Simulation*, ed. Keith D. Markman, William M. P. Klein, and Julie A. Suhr (New York: Psychology Press, 2015), 14.

a compassionate human. As verified by twenty-first century studies, positive emotions stimulate the urge to interact with others and increase the range of thoughts and actions.[16]

Even though emotional sharing does not in itself constitute a substantive link—volitional and intellectual components are necessary—it highlights the driving force that feelings exert upon an individual's state of mind. Upon ascertaining what these phenomena signify, one can structure one's response accordingly to create a moment of genuine understanding. This vivifies the interrelation between volition, intellect, and the affective. Appreciating this interrelation differs from the current interest in the early modern treatises on emotions, which filled bookshelves to the point of surfeit.[17] A sampling includes Thomas Rogers's *Anatomie of the Minde* (1576), Nicholas Breton's *The Passion of a Discontented Mind* (1601), Robert Burton's *Anatomy of Melancholy* (1621), Nicolas Coeffeteau's *Tableau des Passions Humaines* (1620), and Walter Charleton's *Natural History of the Passions* (1674). The vast spectrum of issues covered by these texts attracts scholars today who investigate, among other topics, physiological determinism, its use as a rhetorical strategy, and how it reflects the Reformation's religious and cultural practices.[18] Despite this diversity of interpretation, these writers consistently address the individual's ability to cope with or negotiate the demands of the world. As Christopher Tilmouth observes, the crux of these studies shows that behind "affectivity's turn from passive suffering to active effusion sits

16 Barbara L. Fredrickson, "The Broaden-and-Build Theory of Positive Emotions," *Philosophical Transactions of the Royal Society of London, Series B, Biological Sciences* 359 (2004): 1367–78.
17 As stated in *Renaissance of Emotion*, its purport in this period "was part of the larger project of understanding the human, accordingly it required insights from all of its philosophical, spiritual and physiological and creative engagements" (Richard Meek and Erin Sullivan, *Renaissance of Emotion* [Manchester: Manchester University Press, 2015], 6).
18 Katherine Craik and Tonya Pollard claim that the early modern descriptions of somatic response to literary texts are accurate descriptions of the readers' bodily sensations. Their critical focus lies upon "the profound impressionability of the humoral, emotional self, while also drawing attention to the ways in which readers and playgoers acted as agents in this process by seeking out the imaginative and sensory experiences offered in contemporary literature and drama" (*Shakespearean Sensations: Experiencing Literature in Early Modern England* [Cambridge: Cambridge University Press, 2013], 5). As a means to unpack contemporaneous rhetorical strategies, consult Lynn Enterline, *Shakespeare's Schoolroom: Rhetoric, Discipline, Emotion* (Philadelphia: University of Pennsylvania Press, 2012) and Wendy Olmsted, *The Imperfect Friend: Emotion and Rhetoric in Sidney, Milton, and Their Contexts* (Toronto: University of Toronto Press, 2008). For its ability to shed light upon the reactions underpinning specific historical developments, review Steven Mullaney, *The Reformation of Emotions in the Age of Shakespeare* (Chicago: University of Chicago Press, 2015) and Susan C. Karant-Nunn, *The Reformation of Feeling: Shaping the Religious Emotions in Early Modern Germany* (Oxford: Oxford University Press, 2010).

an expanding sense of the agency of the individual, one born of the very oppor-
tunities that burgeoning intersubjectivity has yielded."[19] My focus draws from
this emphasis on agency to stress how another's emotion spurs the individual
onward to consider that person's desires and beliefs.

Still, scholarly work on early modern emotions often fixates upon negative
expressions. Richard Strier notes that the most recent work often "presents the
period in dark and dour terms."[20] Consider Bradley Irish's masterful book on
emotion's influence upon political constructs of social interaction.[21] He writes
that although "courtly literature particularly encodes the affective negotiation
between the private and public spheres," the governing impulses are competi-
tion and ambition, which effectively preclude acts of compassion and beneficence.[22] For him, the two predominant emotions are "disgust and dread."[23] In
concert with this line of thought, Louis Montrose observes that striving to
meet the court's expectations accounts for why historical figures or literary representations of this world settled into "an authorized mode of discontent."[24]
Dark emotions, like melancholy, pervade these studies and cause Erin Sullivan
to write that grief and sadness consume scholar's interest so much so that this
type of emotion "has arguably become emblematic of the period."[25] To avoid
slipping into this routine, this study examines only those relationships defined
by an engaging and spirited concern for the other's well-being. Its gravamen

---

19 Christopher Tilmouth, "Passion and Intersubjectivity in Early Modern Literature," in *Passions and Subjectivity in Early Modern Culture*, ed. Brian Cummings and Freya Sierhuis (Burlington, VT: Ashgate, 2013), 31.
20 Richard Strier, *Unrepentant Renaissance* (Chicago: University of Chicago Press, 2011), 17.
21 Bradley J. Irish, *Emotion in the Tudor Court: Literature, History, and Early Modern Feeling*
(Evanston, IL: Northwestern University Press, 2018).
22 Irish, *Emotion in the Tudor Court*, 6.
23 Irish, *Emotion in the Tudor Court*, 16.
24 Louis Adrian Montrose, *The Subject of Elizabeth: Authority, Gender, and Representation* (Chicago: University of Chicago Press, 2006), 427.
25 Erin Sullivan, *Beyond Melancholy: Sadness and Selfhood in Renaissance England* (Oxford: Oxford University Press, 2016), 3. Still, she explains that instead of being strictly a negative attribute which undermines one's physiology, mental balance, and way of life, melancholy can also
"stand for something desirable, be it social distinction, intellectual prowess, political awareness
or religious sensitivity" (125). Other works examining this malady include: Drew Daniel, *The Melancholy Assemblage: Affect and Epistemology in the English Renaissance* (New York: Fordham
University Press, 2013); Angus Gowland, *The Worlds of Renaissance Melancholy: Robert Burton
in Context* (Cambridge: Cambridge University Press, 2006); Mary Ann Lund, *Melancholy, Medicine, and Religion in Early Modern England: Reading The Anatomy of Melancholy* (Cambridge:
Cambridge University Press, 2010); Douglas Trevor, *The Poetics of Melancholy in Early Modern
England* (Cambridge: Cambridge University Press, 2004).

avers that empathy serves a greater purpose when originating from an affirmative impetus. Whether seeking spiritual enlightenment, romantic fulfillment, or fraternal communion, a positively charged empathy produces an affinity between two people that fortifies each one's dignity.

Solicitude, longing, and ecstasy lie at the heart of this study. Learning how to master the information conveyed by the degree of their intensity involves a series of steps that describes a process that stands apart from general definitions of empathy. Striving to cultivate a meaningful connection that does not spring from the fervor of the moment, but from an intimate *kynde knowyng* possesses an import that exceeds lessening another's pain. It empowers the individual to give oneself freely to the other and attain a level of awareness that extends beyond anyone else's purview. To this end, I present a four-pronged criterion to account for the diverse shapes and forms of this knowing and how it vitalizes each one's person. First, the empathizer must use this information to reinforce each one's self-worth. Second, defending this worth supersedes any other obligation —political, religious, or even familial. Third, the observer can neither merge with nor lose themselves within the other's identity; a self-other delineation must be maintained. Finally, in spite of the passion felt, a genuine selflessness directs the empathizer's actions. The effort and concern must remain free from any self-serving agenda. Empathy is both a process and a honed skill. It does not culminate in coalescence, but rather in extolling the other's singularity and forming a bond that prevails over worldly tribulations and whatever sorrows that they may present.

The emphasis upon a positive empathetic expression differs from standard views, such as those of Amy Coplan and Peter Goldie. Although both stress the imperative to safeguard individuality while ascertaining the other's intellectual and emotional states, they do not specify what comprises the "substantial characterization" shared between the two parties.[26] On their own affective matching and experiential knowledge do not guarantee that the resultant bond enriches each one's life. Yet, electing to privilege the bond underlines the fact that the power lies within the individual to effect a mutually beneficial outcome. The observer comes to realize that considering another's intentions and

---

[26] Peter Goldie, *The Emotions: A Philosophical Exploration* (Oxford: Clarendon Press, 2000), 195. Amy Coplan offers a breakdown of the various elements that are commonly associated with definitions of empathy, including affective matching, self- and other-oriented perspective-taking, self-other differentiation, and experiential understanding. See "Understanding Empathy: Its Features and Effects," in *Empathy: Philosophical and Psychological Perspectives*, ed. Amy Coplan and Peter Goldie (Oxford: Oxford University Press, 2014), 3–18.

inclinations allows the observer to express a heartfelt devotion. Such a decision refines the subject's capacity to act justly.

In the literary works examined here, the narrative draws attention to each character's capability to discern the reasons underlying another's actions. Explicating this process reveals a specific epistemology. Whereas one text focuses upon the information acquired from the experience itself, another relies upon the truth culled from trying to put oneself in another's mental shoes. Both *Amis and Amiloun* and *The Second Nun's Tale* bring to light the value of choice in developing and defending the characters' rapport. By defying the strictures imposed by legal mandate or established religious practices, the characters display a zealousness that not only adds depth and purpose to their interactions, but also demonstrates their affection for what is just. In the matter of the Fool and Miranda in *King Lear* and *The Tempest*, respectively, these two empathizers strictly rely upon what the experience itself reveals about the person with whom they empathize.[27] They do not let the lack or utter absence of prior knowledge deter their efforts to know the other's state of mind. That very moment instills a surety of knowing which empowers each one's sense of self. It exposes the transience of what this world offers and affirms the permanence of what the characters provide each other. Finally, within a realm of wildly inventive and sensuous images, Donne's and Crashaw's protagonists seek to know by simulating the other person's thought process. These consummate lovers look inward to assess how they would respond to the situation before them and then project their understanding to access the other's mind. This matching phase empowers a dynamic so insightful that it produces an intimacy that bridges the empirical with the empyrean.

Each empathizer exercises independent thinking that lies in contradistinction to the predetermined role assigned to them by society. Their choices, which exemplify the burgeoning emphasis upon individual agency, are neither clouded nor unduly diminished by convention or custom. They invest their energies into accessing the other's mind and forging a meaningful bond. Whether found in texts written in 1300 or 1650, they all strive towards the same end in their empathic expressions. This consistency of thought and feeling exposes the superficiality of imposing boundaries separating the Middle Ages and the Renaissance as two wholly distinct periods. In accord with James Simpson's position, this study also considers such categorizations as "self-enclosed, self-

---

27 Stein writes that the "two subjects are separate and not joined together . . . by a consciousness of sameness or a continuity of experience" (Stein, *On the Problem of Empathy*, 10 – 11).

explanatory, and petrified in their oppositions one to the other."[28] The medieval world may stress the value in adapting to communal practices, but it also commends the person who stands on his (or her) own. In *The Second Nun's Tale*, Cecilia prioritizes her relationship with her husband above her duties to the Roman state. By cultivating a shared knowledge of one another, the couple reject pagan religion and embrace the sanctified state of their Christian union. Though this devotion results in both of them being put to death, the *Tale*'s dénouement extols Cecilia being mindful of what her husband believes and revealing a truth that supersedes mundane matters. It shows the limitations of A. C. Spearing's claim that "medieval culture tends to take a somewhat low view of man, seeing the human condition as one of separation from its true source of value in God."[29] Whether it is Cecilia and her husband or Amis and Amiloun, these characters' deep-seated desire to attain a mutual understanding both affirms and applauds the individual ability to attain a higher level of knowing. It places them in the same coterie of those early modern figures who brave being marginalized because they prize what they know about each other above all else.

Despite the intensity of their efforts to enter into the other's conscience, grasping how they foster a harmonious bond poses certain challenges. Since the term "empathy" does not come into existence until the turn of the twentieth century, tools of inquiry contemporaneous with the literary texts are limited.[30] Derived from the ancient Greek word ἐμπάθεια, which means "physical affection"

---

28 James Simpson, *Reform and Cultural Revolution*, vol. 2, *1350–1547* (Oxford: Oxford University Press, 2007), 32.

29 A. C. Spearing, *Medieval to Renaissance in English Poetry* (Cambridge: Cambridge University Press, 1985), 2. Of course, the reasons underpinning the actions of these medieval protagonists differ considerably from those of some of their contemporaries, such as Sir Gawain. In his battle with the Green Knight, his realization does not prompt him to appreciate the motivations driving the Green Knight onward. Rather, he lets shame commandeer his train of thought. For a perceptive study of the public use of emotions as expressed by Sir Gawain and in the broader portrayal of knightly virtue in Thomas Malory's *Le Morte D'Arthur*, see Corinne Saunders, "Mind, Body and Affect in Medieval English Arthurian Romance," in *Emotions in Medieval Arthurian Literature*, ed. Frank Brandsma, Carolyne Larrington, and Corinne Saunders (Woodbridge, Suffolk: D. S. Brewer, 2015), 31–46.

30 To chart its historical development, see Susan Lanzoni's work which examines its shifting meanings over the past hundred years. Originating as a translation of *Einfühlung*, a term in German psychological aesthetics that described how spectators projected their own feelings and movements into objects of art and nature. "This burgeoning science of aesthetics centered on the spectator's response to the work of art rather than on the work itself. . . . *Einfühlung* described how the spectator 'felt into' or extended the self into the swirling lines of a design, into a mountain rising upward toward the skies, or into the curving line of an archway" (Lanzoni, *Empathy: A History* [New Haven, CT: Yale University Press, 2018], 23).

or "passion," its contemporary meaning signifies the power of mentally identifying oneself with another and striving to understanding or appreciate him or her.[31] In his study on "medieval empathies," Karl Morrison explains that it "exists only among those who respect the integrity of their friends enough to listen to them, to see through their eyes and walk in their shoes, or at least to try to achieve the harmony of two lives, both distinct and in rhythm."[32] This mode of consciousness incorporates both a cognitive and an emotional element in assessing the other's state of mind, thus distinguishing it from the feeling-based affinity underpinning "sympathy."[33] This book aspires to examine the relationship between those characters that elect to direct their energies towards apprehending and assessing another's mental states. And, even if these efforts are not reciprocated, the process attests to their ability to gain such insight and use it to better that person's well-being.

Empathy reveals a horizon of unfolding of meaning that enlightens the observer of another's state of mind and makes the former an active participant in the experience. This expanding view makes the observer more attuned to what that person values and thus they align their perspective accordingly.[34] Stein claims in her later writings that fostering such harmony is a distinct human power. Human souls are capable of "opening themselves in loving self-giving to one another and of receiving one another into their own selves—never, to be sure, as completely as is the case with a soul that abides in God, but in some greater or smaller measure."[35] This knowing comprehension does not leave the observer standing by themselves at a distance, but forges an intimate bond. Even though this understanding may not be as complete as God's vision, it reveals what is actual and what is possible. Medieval and early modern thought emphasized the divine's omniscience in knowing what lies in another's heart. Scotus states, "Thou art happiness itself, God of resplendent vision, of

---

31 The *Oxford English Dictionary* (*OED*) lists its first usage in 1909 by E. B. Titchener in his *Lectures on the Experimental Psychology of the Thought Processes:* "Not only do I see gravity and modesty and pride . . . but I feel act them in the mind's muscles. This is, I suppose, a simple case of empathy, if we may coin that term as a rendering of *Einfühlung*" (*OED n.* 2a).

32 Karl Morrison, "Framing the Subject: Humanity and the Wounds of Love," in *Studies on Medieval Empathies*, ed. Karl F. Morrison and Rudolph M. Bell (Turnhout: Brepols, 2013), 5.

33 According to the *OED*, "sympathy" is a conformity of feelings, inclinations, or temperament, which makes persons agreeable to each other; a community of feeling (*OED n.* 3a).

34 For a discussion of Stein's view that empathetic acts engender self-knowledge, see Sarah Borden Sharkey, *Thine Own Self: Individuality in Edith Stein's Later Writings* (Washington, DC: Catholic University of America Press, 2010), 121.

35 Edith Stein, *Finite and Eternal Being*, trans. Kurt F. Reinhardt (Washington, DC: ICS Publications, 2002), 514.

most joyful love, self-sufficient yet knowing at one and at the same time all that can be known."[36] Despite reason's limitations, the characters at the heart of this study strive to enter the minds of those people closest to them and fashion a fulfilling rapport.

Realizing such an end, however, begins with the decision to exercise one's faculties and powers in this manner. Scotus's theory of the will's freedom thus proves seminal in explaining the characters' insistence to construct something positive from their interactions. Empathy generates an attentiveness towards others that utilizes different modes of knowing in maximizing one's cognitive and affective potential. The modern tenets of phenomenology, simulation theory, and cognitive science provide the conceptual reasoning necessary to elucidate this epistemic process. Paradoxically, the lack of a semantic history accounts for both the dearth of literary studies on this subject and its need. In its present state, scholarship like that done by Karl Morrison, strives to establish the term's historical origins. His examination locates its philosophical analogues within the writings of Gregory of Nyssa (ca. 335/340–after 394) and Aelred of Rievaulx (ca. 1110–1167), among others. The investigative framework, however, stays confined within an emotional arena that stems from "the creative power that comes from the interplay of tensions between two apparent opposites, cruelty and fellow feeling."[37] Yet, given empathy's complexity, a work that integrates the knowledge generated from both the affective and the intellective propels this field of study beyond its nascent stage.

This book stands at the vanguard in conceiving not only the multifaceted ways to cultivate such a rapport, but also how these literary characters put this knowledge into praxis. The emphasis upon fostering a valued connection contrasts starkly with those studies advocating a reader-response interpretation, which garners the bulk of scholarly attention. Akin to Suzanne Keen's and Brian Reilly's argumentation, Elena Carrera in her work on Miguel de Cervantes's *El cellos extremeño* "invites readers to empathize with the characters' limited em-

---

36 John Duns Scotus, *De Primo Principio*, c. 4, p. 145.
37 Morrison finds that the resulting emotional friction brings to light how these irreconcilable demands tear at charity. On the one hand, there is a love for one's enemies defined by obedience to finite institutions and creeds, and on the other hand, the love stems from a broad and generous understanding of humanism. His edited work examines how medieval philosophers, like Augustine (354–430) and Catherine of Siena (1347–1380) provide a conceptual analogue for empathy's meaning. This focus on its historical rather than literary purport also addresses the writings of philosophers like Anselm, Ramon Lull, and Jan Luis Vives. See Morrison and Bell, *Studies on Medieval Empathies*.

bodied experiences and cognition."[38] Her focus on their defective understanding of each other's position falls in line with the traditional view of its applicability to negative situations. For an approach that coincides with mine, Alina Wyman, who examines the modern Russian novelist, Fyodor Dostoyevsky, maintains that a conscious participation with the other's perspective produces a value-affirming and value-revealing event, for she advocates "an *active* understanding of one's fellow men and women as the most productive way of 'entering' other selves."[39] While she employs the philosophy of phenomenologist Max Scheler and dialogism of Mikhail Bakhtin, her research is grounded in the empathizer's sovereignty and individuality no matter how closely one identifies with the other person.[40]

Though using similar theoretical tools, my study expands to examine how this experience intensifies the empathizer's commitment to the other. As an active force, empathy's momentum is not decelerated by differences, but empowered by the empathizer's choice and their asymmetry with the other to preserve the other's dignity. By grasping what constitutes the other's perspective, the empathizer can decide with surety to defend the other's goodness even if it jeopardizes the empathizer's own sense of well-being. For example, when Amiloun contracts leprosy as punishment for defying the king, Amis recognizes the purity of his friend's intentions and elects to give up what is most precious to him—his children—in order to find a cure. Selflessly trusting in his empathetic knowledge of Amiloun's needs ensures not only Amiloun's survival, but also that of his children. As Susan Lanzoni writes, "an empathic stretch toward the different, the strange, or even the unfathomable awakens us to the actuality of the unique, singular lives of others."[41] Electing to act on a firm belief in another's intrinsic worth valorizes one's own person.

The actions of these medieval and early modern characters expose the constraints of conventional knowledge. Their freedom to prize another's distinctiveness enables them to resist the pressures to conform as imposed by palace or

38 Keen employs a traditional definition of empathy as a "vicarious, spontaneous sharing of affect" while also noting its cognitive component: "we feel what we believe to be the emotion of others" (Suzanne Keen, *Empathy and the Novel* [Oxford: Oxford University Press, 2010], 4–5). Elena Carrera, "Embodied Cognition and Empathy in Miguel de Cervantes's *El celoso extremeño*," *Hispania* 97 (2014): 112–36; Brian Reilly, "Irony and Cognitive Empathy in Chrétien de Troyes's Gettier Problem," *Philosophy and Literature* 41 (2017): 169–84. Also see, Raluca Radulescu, "Tears and Lies: Emotions and the Ideals of Malory's Arthurian World," in *Emotions in Medieval Arthurian Literature*, ed. Brandsma, Larrington, and Saunders, 105–22.
39 Alina Wyman, *The Gift of Active Empathy: Scheler, Bakhtin, and Dostoevsky* (Evanston, IL: Northwestern University Press, 2016), 17.
40 Wyman, *The Gift of Active Empathy*, 17.
41 Lanzoni, *Empathy*, 278.

patriarch. Whether it is Amis or Valerian, the Fool or Miranda, their decisions contrast starkly with what courtly culture dictates. Each learns to operate apart from what Barbara Rosenwein describes as emotional communities in which "people adhere to the same norms of emotional expression and value— or devalue—the same or related emotions."[42] By appreciating the unique abilities and experiences of the other person, their responses inspire a profound yearning to advance this intimate awareness even further. It distinguishes their efforts from those who merely measure the quality of their relationships by adhering to worldly expectations. These select literary figures passionately strive to cultivate a closeness founded upon an affection for what is just. By forgoing personal ambition, they exercise a mode of consciousness that fortifies both the other's sense of self as well as their own. Whether initiated by the experience itself or by simulating another's mental states, empathy interlaces the emotional with the cognitive to help the characters realize their potential as individuals capable of fostering a dynamic understanding.

A précis of the chapters and how they explore the philosophical underpinnings of empathy in these texts follows.

The first chapter examines empathy's evolution from a term that signifies an "inner imitation" of another's feeling at the turn of the twentieth century to a contemporary one that focuses upon its physiological operation.[43] Following this historical discussion, I introduce the definition underpinning this study, which both incorporates elements of and distinguishes itself from these preceding views. The study's innovation lies in championing a positively charged expression that fosters a deeper awareness of the other so that each person can gain a greater sense of self. To show how this conceptual framework draws from different philosophical approaches, an analysis of the relation between the speaker and his beloved in Edmund Spenser's Sonnet 7 brings to light the confluence of the primary tenets of phenomenology and simulation theory. Both emphasize the inextricable tie between the physiological and intellectual,

---

42 Barbara H. Rosenwein, *Emotional Communities in the Early Middle Ages* (Ithaca, NY: Cornell University Press, 2006), 2. For an overview of emotions expressed in hierarchically structured groups during these two time periods, see Barbara Rosenwein, *Generations of Feeling: A History of Emotions, 600–1700* (Cambridge: Cambridge University Press, 2016).

43 Theodor Lipps used the German term "Einfühlung" (or "feeling into") to characterize an aesthetic appreciation of objects. This notion of inner imitation also serves as a basis for recognizing each other as minded beings. Still, Edith Stein conducts a lengthy critique of Lipps's view to emphasize the strict delineation between self and other. See Theodor Lipps, "Einfühlung, Innere Nachahmung und Organempfinung," *Archiv für gesamte Psychologie* (1903): 465–519. Translated as "Empathy, Inner Imitation and Sense-Feelings," in *A Modern Book of Esthetics* (New York: Holt, Rinehart and Winston, 1979), 374–82; also see Stein, *On the Problem of Empathy*, 11–18.

the logical and the emotional in determining how the body itself communicates and provides the necessary means for the observer to ascertain the other's mental state. Whether initiated by the experience itself or by the choice to simulate the other's mental states, the empathy expressed between the literary characters in this study illuminates the ability not only to strike a meaningful connection, but also to recognize the other's intrinsic worth.

The second chapter analyzes two medieval texts that accentuate the altruistic drive of characters who face seemingly insurmountable odds in preserving their rapport, namely the titular protagonists in the romance *Amis and Amiloun* (ca. 1300) and the brothers Valerian and Tiburce in Chaucer's saint's legend, *The Second Nun's Tale*. Their commitment springs from the will's freedom to initiate an empathetic act that allows them to attribute the proper mental states to each other and discloses their particular beliefs and desires. Without it, neither set of characters could sustain a belief in the virtues underpinning each's devotion to the other. Its central role in cultivating this mutual understanding reflects the advances in late medieval thought, specifically the voluntarism of John Duns Scotus. His innovation focuses upon the idea that the will is not dependent upon the intellect's dictates. As a result, it can heed its own inclinations towards happiness or justice. Applying these principles to the texts illuminates the specific motivations guiding each one's decision in determining what is in the best interest of the other.

To appreciate the dedication necessary to acquire such a keen insight into the other's state of mind, the third chapter examines two Shakespearean plays that extol the unwavering commitment of its characters as each one expends all their cognitive energies in forging a bond with a person who either has little regard for them or relatively little knowledge of who they are. In *The Tragedy of King Lear* and *The Tempest*, the epistemic value of the Fool's and Miranda's interaction with Lear and Ferdinand, respectively, establishes each one's dignity and shows that the depth of insight depends upon forgoing a solipsistic point of view. As the experience itself enables them to realize the reasons underpinning the other person's motivations, desires, and needs, a phenomenological hermeneutic most readily explains the understanding gained between these characters. Specifically, the theories of Husserl and Stein inform their strong sense of self and efficacy in cultivating a profound empathy. Both philosophers write seminal treatises that establish the fundamental difference between the observer and the other. As a result, they place the observer in a unique position to grasp the other's state of mind, engender a positive change in their behavior, and foster a relationship that transcends worldly concerns.

The fourth chapter enters into the seventeenth century and investigates select poems from Donne's *Songs and Sonnets* and Crashaw's religious lyrics. It specifically addresses how their speakers/protagonists adopt their beloved's line of reasoning, even when the beloved exists in a supernal realm. The subtle nuances of this emotionally charged imitation gain force through an increased sensory awareness that allows the protagonists to integrate this perspective into their assessment of the other and ascertain his or her thoughts. Consequently, using simulation theory provides the best means to explicate the observers' process of knowing. By putting themselves in the other's shoes, the observers can imagine the world from the other's perspective and then impute specific mental states to that person. It is, in the words of Alvin Goldman, "an extended form of empathy."[44] For example, the speaker in Donne's "A Nocturnal upon St. Lucy's Day" fixates upon the darkness around him and then embodies those emotions most commonly associated with this time of day to establish an intimate knowing with his deceased beloved. For Crashaw's Mary Magdalene and St. Teresa, their imaginative use of the senses traverses bounds of even greater lengths to envision a world "where everything is either liquid or hovering on the brink of dissolution or metamorphosis."[45] The sensuous imagery underlines the fluid movement of aligning and then realigning one's state of being to match the divine's effulgence. Although it is not an exact copy, for His beneficence lies beyond our comprehension, this connection allows the divine to be present to the empathizer. Still, what is given to the empathizers in this empathic expression is original. Hence, no matter how imprecise the act of mirroring may be, they are able to recognize His immediacy, make the appropriate inferences, and construct an undying bond.

Whether it is Mary Magdalene's copious tears or the Fool's pointed repartee, each chooses his or her own method of sharing in the other's perspective. The freedom to choose this path effects a strong connection that can overcome any outside intrusion or interference. Studying the texts under an empathetic lens brings to light the delineated self-other identity and how the force of individuality propels the relationship onward. By constructing this kind of insight, these texts uniformly illustrate a dynamic that intensifies the characters' natural capacity to grasp the mental states of another and better the existence of each one. Even in the case of Donne's speaker whose beloved has been lost to death's embrace, he is able to attune himself to her emotional self, transcend fleshly constraints, and gain surety in the truth binding them together. The underlying drive springs from a desire to exercise an objective assessment to ascertain the

---

44 Goldman, *Simulating Minds*, 4.
45 Robert Ellrodt, *Seven Metaphysical Poets: A Structural Study of the Unchanging Self* (Oxford: Oxford University Press, 2000), 142.

epistemic truth stemming from a mutually shared emotionally charged moment. The comingling of affective and intellective forces culminates in a valorizing movement which ensures that the connection does not stem from impulse, but from a concerted effort to privilege their interpersonal awareness.

Chapter 1 The Philosophical Underpinnings of Empathy

While empathy's universality prevents any era from claiming territorial rights to its transforming power, the late medieval and early modern depictions highlight an evolving emphasis upon the individual and the ability to develop a rapport that surpasses conventional interpretations of romantic ardor or fellowship. In texts, such as Chaucer's *The Second Nun's Tale* and William Shakespeare's *The Tempest*, characters, such as Cecilia and Valerian or Miranda and Ferdinand respectively, elect to align their thoughts and feelings with one another to maximize their potential as caring and compassionate beings. These decisions hone a heartfelt appreciation of what it means to be human and respect for each other's distinctiveness. The resultant closeness empowers them to withstand those unrelenting pressures seeking to compromise their bond. Given the complex factors involved in constructing an empathic connection, this chapter will present a detailed definition of this concept and how it evolves from the one propounded by its historical innovator, Theodor Lipps (1851–1914). An explication of Edmund Spenser's Sonnet 7 from the *Amoretti* illustrates this evolution and the applicability of those philosophies addressed in the introduction, particularly as they distinguish empathy from the related concepts of sympathy and emotional contagion. This foundation provides a seamless basis to realize that an empathic embrace involves far more than a pre-reflexive action or emotional mimicry. Rather, it is a conscious act that requires a keen awareness of the other person's motivations and beliefs as the basis of a meaningful rapport.

Empathy, I assert, involves more than its physiological function; its ramifications prompt one to consider the other's well-being. Martin Hoffman notes that the emotional impact of the moment inclines one towards caring about that person.[1] This inclination leads one to cognize the other person's interior worth and help enrich each one's lives.[2] Still, it does not mean that this act must be mutual, for the other person may not be in a position or too distracted to reciprocate this attentiveness. In the literary texts selected here, characters like Valerian, Miranda, and the Fool in his pointed repartee with King Lear, experience the viewpoint of their respective spouse or friend without losing sight of their own identity. This

---

1 Martin L. Hoffman, *Empathy and Moral Development: Implications for Caring and Justice* (Cambridge: Cambridge University Press, 2000), 198–205. Also see, Peter Goldie, "Anti-Empathy," in *Empathy: Philosophical and Psychological Perspectives*, ed. Amy Coplan and Peter Goldie (Oxford: Oxford University Press, 2014), 302–17.
2 Goldie, *The Emotions*, 195.

https://doi.org/10.1515/9781501515460-002

insight adds depth to their affection expressed and in the process extols the other's dignity. As aforementioned, four specific elements come to light that are necessary or consequent in producing such a bond. First, the response fortifies a fellowship or devoted intimacy. Second, its connection supersedes social expectations or obligation—political, religious, or even familial. Third, the empathizer incorporates knowledge of the other while at the same time maintaining a strict self-other delineation. Finally, in spite of any pre-reflexive reaction to the other person, the choice to cultivate this awareness must be selfless. The concern and support must be genuine, free from any personal agenda. Self-interest compromises the objectivity of assessing the other's well-being. These four factors underline the kind of empathy between those literary figures who prize the subtle nuances of an intimate knowing.

Broadly speaking, literature does not attempt to isolate a particular view of what determines a constructive empathic interaction. Rather, it dramatizes and poeticizes the different ways that foster an attentiveness to another's tone, gestures, or perspective. This book, therefore, employs different critical approaches to explicate this discourse. Phenomenology, simulation theory, and cognitive science examine how the individual can ascertain the psychological states of another, thus illustrating the gravitas of what the interplay reveals about each one. Each one examines the inextricable tie between the physiological and intellectual, the logical and the emotional. Although these fields of study postdate medieval and early modern texts, their investigation into this dynamic readily applies to any era, specifically since the term "empathy" does not come into existence until the turn of the twentieth century.[3] In fact, as these literary depictions pass from the late medieval to the early modern era, empathy's import evolves from championing the will's freedom to lauding a situational and corporeal awareness of what the other person is experiencing. Utilizing distinct yet complementary approaches thus reveals the various methods that the characters use to enhance their understanding of the other. Whether acquired from the experience itself or by putting oneself in the other's mental shoes, the epistemological process reveals the supplemental relationship between affective and intellective. The empathizer's agency draws upon both modes of knowing and the other person, in all his or her individuality, is the basic motive of this action. The focus centers on knowing the totality of the individual. Analyzing these characters in light of this hermeneutic affirms the proper valence between

---

3 To chart its historical development, see Susan Lanzoni's work which examines its shifting meanings over the past hundred years. Originating as a translation of *Einfühlung*, a term in German psychological aesthetics that described how spectators projected their own feelings and movements into objects of art and nature.

thought and feeling and how this mode of consciousness distinguishes their relationships.

As a means of entering into this discussion, I would first like to look at Spenser's Sonnet 7 to ground these theoretical views and show how the beloved's acts allow the speaker to enter into her consciousness. Since Spenser's verse bridges the late medieval and early modern periods, the exchange between these lovers, on the one hand, heeds the standards of Petrarchism and, on the other hand, asserts the singular focus of the speaker's affection. The poem opens with the standard fare of praising the beloved's eyes. Her "Fair eyes" mirror the joy pouring forth from his "mazed heart" (l. 1). Although referencing Sonnet 1, William Oram notes that this kind of visual reaction occurs within the mind: "it's an inner action, not a physical movement."[4] The speaker's observation thus points out the mutual affection and the subtle interplay between beauty and understanding. He grasps that "wondrous virtue" manifests itself in her demeanor, accentuating her appeal (l. 2). While virtue most often connotes goodness, it proves more expansive in this usage, indicating the power that her "lovely hue" exerts upon him (l. 5). This attraction galvanizes his thoughts and yearning to appreciate what she embodies. When she directs her "mighty view" towards him, it emits the life-giving sustenance of her attention, assuring him of love's surety (l. 4). Without it, he would languish.

The information culled from body, brain, and behavior accounts for why he concentrates so intently upon her gaze. Though springing from an interior source, their connection relies upon external features to relay this information.

> For, when ye mildly look with lovely hue,
> Then is my soul with life and love inspired:
> But when ye lower, or look on me askew,
> Then do I die, as one with lightning fired. (ll. 5–8)

Her countenance has an effect upon him both spiritually and physically. As her comely grace reinvigorates his soul, his yearning impacts his emotional response so much that he feels as if he teeters on the precipice between life and death. In spite of this precarious position, the interchange generates a continual flow of communication. It perpetuates the desire to know her more fully, and its immediacy prevents him from being distracted by any matters other than what her actions convey. His response is not merely an act of doing, but one that becomes an expression of "being with." Her gaze speaks a language specific to them and in-

---

4 William A. Oram, "What Happens in the *Amoretti*," *Spenser Review* 50.2.3 (Spring–Summer 2020), http://www.english.cam.ac.uk/spenseronline/review/item/50.2.3

vites him to align his mental states with her, signifying that both of them exist in the other's being as much as in their own. He longs for her to recognize that each of them exists no less in the other's being than their own. Expressing this kind of affection transcends any worldly concerns.

As her beauty and the goodness that it represents incite his desire, the choice to share in this virtue establishes his contribution to their rapport. Each brings something distinct and valuable to the relationship. The truth emanating from her eyes vivifies his understanding, for these "bright beams, of my weak eyes admired,/ May kindle living fire within my breast" (ll. 10–12). Even though the rhetoric of Petrarchan love dictates that he idolizes her person, this hyperbole does not diminish or negate her value. Rather, his commitment underscores a singular focus in enriching this dynamic. By allowing the experience itself to inform him of what defines her person, he becomes more attuned to her affection and what constitutes their bond. As a result, the visual embrace of her beauty sanctifies his devotion: "Such life should be the honor of your light" (l. 13). Her radiant might may wield power over him, but his simulation of her purity attests to an innate ability to respond in a like-minded manner. Whether relying upon the experience itself or the imitation of his beloved's movements, the speaker uses the knowledge conveyed through her person to fortify their bond.

The embodied synchrony between Spenser's lovers proves consonant with empathy's semantic origins. In the early twentieth century, Lipps uses the term *Einfühlung* ("feeling into") to explain the natural inclination to imitate the emotions underlying another's actions.[5] "When I see a gesture, there exists within me a tendency to experience in myself the affect that naturally arises from that gesture. And when there is no obstacle, the tendency is realized."[6] The impulse to duplicate those emotions accompanying a particular gesture or facial movement, particularly when incited by a dramatic event, is a basic fact of human interaction, but its import far surpasses a general transference of feelings. Lipps's analysis asserts that this phenomenon stems from our perceptual response to another's expressions; the visual prompts us to penetrate and suffuse that behavior with our own emotional experience.[7] Since the affect is

---

5 As aforementioned in the Introduction, *Einfühlung* is the word that E. B. Titchener translates into "empathy" (Titchener, *Lectures*, 21).

6 Theodor Lipps, "Das Wissen von Fremden Ichen," *Psychologische Untersuchungen*, vol. 1 (1907), 719. For a study of Lipps's contribution to the term's usage, see Gustav Jahoda, "Theodor Lipps and the Shift from 'Sympathy' to 'Empathy,'" *Journal of the History of the Behavioral Sciences* 41 (2005): 151–63.

7 Theodor Lipps, *Leitfaden der Psychologie* (Leipzig: Verlag von Wilhelm Engelmann, 1909), 224.

being represented by or thought into the perceived gesture, the intellect, not the senses, underlies this response. The psychological mechanisms employ a conflu-ence of affective and cognitive powers, which elevate it above a common, indis-tinct reaction to another's behavior.

Lipps's interest in discerning the emotional state of another via their facial expressions arises from his profession as an aesthetic philosopher. He believes that our response to beauty directs us to experience the felt quality associated with that object or person, not unlike Spenser's speaker.[8] Our perception of an object's beauty stirs within us a resonance phenomenon so that we instinctively project our experiences upon it. He describes the vitality of this moment as "ob-jectified self-enjoyment."[9] Operating from the premise that beauty—whether sen-sual, artistic, or human—rests upon its form and expressivity, Lipps draws an analogous connection between aesthetic appreciation and grasping another's state of being, for the nature of empathy is always the "experience of another human."[10] Both focus upon the object's or person's movement as the basis to shape the response. A visual gestalt of another's thoughts and feelings incites a kinesthetic reaction. As the gesture sparks a desire to experience that affect, our body imitates what we perceive. Imitating another's actions attests to the central role that motor mimicry plays in his theory.[11]

This critical focus upon imitation and inner participation captures the inter-est among the burgeoning school of phenomenologists. Husserl and Stein simi-larly believe that the gestures of the other are imbued with psychological mean-ing and enable the observer to ascertain another's mental states. Yet, both of them are adamant that the interaction between the two people depends upon each one's individuality. Husserl claims that a difference necessarily exists since the observer can never experience the other's life in the exact same man-

---

8 Theodor Lipps, *Aesthetik*, vol. 1 (Hamburg: Voss Verlag, 1903), 120.
9 Theodor Lipps, "Einfühlung und Ästhetischer Genuß," *Die Zukunft* 16 (1906), 100.
10 Theodor Lipps, *Aesthetik*, vol. 2 (Hamburg: Voss Verlag, 1905), 49.
11 Adam Smith makes this observation more than a century earlier.
   When I condole with you for the loss of your son, in order to enter into your grief I do not consider what I, a person of such character and profession, should suffer, if I had a son, and if that son was unfortunately to die: but I consider what I should suffer if I was really you, and I not only change circumstances with you, but I change persons and characters. My grief, therefore, is entirely upon your account, and not in the least upon my own. It is not, therefore, in the least selfish. How can that be regarded as a selfish passion, which does not arise even from the imagination of any things that has befallen, or that relates to myself, in my own proper person and character, but which is entirely occupied about what relates to you? (*The Theory of Moral Sentiments* [1853] [New York: August M. Kelley, 1966], 317)

ner. For the observer, they are shown; for the other, they are lived through.[12] Stein posits that this awareness marks the core meaning of empathy, functioning as "a kind of act of perceiving *sui generis*."[13] Its distinctiveness binds these two thinkers. For them, the individual actively experiences another's state of being and neither imagines nor theorizes about its meaning; the observer understands the motivations and import underlying the other's expression.[14] The difference between one's perception and the other's experience accounts for Stein's critique of Lipps, whom she believes advocates a complete immersion of oneself into the other.

> Lipps says that as long as empathy is complete . . . there is no distinction between our own and the foreign "I," that they are one. For example, I am one with the acrobat and go through his motions inwardly. A distinction only arises when I step out of complete empathy and reflect on my "real 'I'."[15]

Stein disagrees because the empathizer never fully apprehends the original experience as felt by the other.[16] The acrobat's motions and the motivations giving rise to them belong solely to him, not in oneself. Preserving this asymmetry allows one to come face-to-face with an otherness that fosters a dialogue where another's actions prompt one to assess not only that person's state of mind, but also consider their role in this experience. Reality thus incorporates a multiplicity of perspectives that forge a connection between the two people. The qualitative difference attests to the fact that each one is a minded individual who can respond to the other's actions as they present specific thoughts and feelings. The insight generated involves far more than a mere projection of one's previous emotions upon the other. It reveals the actual presence of the other's experience and the psychological inimitability underlying the essence of the phenomenon.

For these phenomenologists, the body performs a much greater function than simply linking self and other at sensorimotor and affective levels. It houses a body of experience that responds to the other's subjectivity. As such, the body's

---

12 Maurice Merleau-Ponty, *Phenomenology of Perception*, trans. Colin Smith (London: Routledge, 1962), 356.
13 Stein, *On the Problem of Empathy*, 11.
14 Edmund Husserl, *Ideas Pertaining to a Pure Phenomenology and to a Phenomenological Philosophy*, trans. R. Rojcewicz and A. Schuwer (Dordrecht: Kluwer Academic Publishers, 1989), 240.
15 Stein, *On the Problem of Empathy*, 16.
16 For a detailed account of Stein's delineation between the two distinct kinds of perspective, see Kris McDaniel, "Edith Stein: On the Problem of Empathy," in *Ten Neglected Philosophical Classics*, ed. Eric Schliessen (Oxford: Oxford University Press, 2014), 204–18.

benefit cannot be reduced to simply copying another's behavior, for the body reveals the distinctiveness not only of the other, but also of oneself. As scholar Matthew Ratcliffe observes, empathy revolves around appreciating the differences more than stressing the similarities.[17] These differences spring from the will as it directs the intellect to use the information expressed in this moment to learn more about that individual. Stein observes that the experience's intelligibility allows the observer to recognize this as a genuinely original phenomenon:

> I experience his every action as proceeding from a will and this, in turn, from a feeling. Simultaneously with this, I am given a level of his person and a range of value in principle experienceable by him. This, in turn, meaningfully motivates the expectation of future possible volitions and actions. Accordingly, a single action and also a single bodily expression, such as a look or a laugh, can give me a glimpse into the kernel of the person.[18]

This "kernel" establishes a distinctiveness that reveals who the other is. It places the power of understanding in the immediate perception of that person's actions, whether physical or verbal, providing the information necessary to cultivate an informed connection. Apprehending the similarity and difference affirms the observer's autonomy to sustain the intensity and scope of the experience.[19]

Empathy is not a simple transference of emotion from self to other, but a concerted effort to distinguish between the two selves. As Wyman notes, this process is the "most productive way of 'entering' other selves . . . and is grounded in the empathizer's sovereignty as an active subject, whose unique individuality is not dissolved in the process of empathizing."[20] This process safeguards against a hollow reproduction of behavior and brings to light the particularities of the other. In the case of Spenser's speaker, the irreducible difference between what is known and unknown, original and perceived, creates a conduit to appreciate the fullness of the beloved's person. While he seemingly heeds Petrarchan idealism, humbly declaring that his "weak eies" admire her "bright beams," he is not chained to the stereotypical submissiveness (l. 11). The speaker's modesty belies the fact that the affection exchanged between him and his beloved kindles a living fire within his breast. This fire vivifies his being and, as such, honors her "light" (l. 13). The action does not refer to an involuntary, sensory reaction, but invites him to participate in her emotional state. Springing from a deep-seated belief in her integrity, the first-personal character of his consciousness produces

---

17 Matthew Ratcliffe, *Experiences of Depression: A Study in Phenomenology* (Oxford: Oxford University Press, 2014), 26 – 35.
18 Stein, *On the Problem of Empathy*, 109.
19 Husserl, *Zur Phänomenologie der Intersubjektivität*, 1:333.
20 Wyman, *The Gift of Active Empathy*, 15.

"the general cognitive and emotive preconditions that enable an empathetic experience."[21]

The connection between mind and body shows that the speaker's beloved is not a demanding, unobtainable woman, but someone who is real and not oblivious to her admirer's attention. Her presence engenders an interpersonal surety that emboldens his conviction to such a degree that the world becomes unto themselves and its inviolability affirms the sanctity of his focus. Her power to effect death is a "sad ensample of your might" proves that their bond, though unrequited, traverses corporeal limitations (l. 14). Not to be taken literally, her power testifies to a heightened awareness of his affection for her and how she enlightens him. The empathy subtending their interplay illustrates the verisimilitude of verse to show that their expressions are not merely a pre-reflexive act, but a conscious effort to become more attuned to the other. In effect, it is a mode of consciousness that assesses another's feelings, desires, and beliefs without losing one's own sense of self.

Sympathy's Value

Despite the fact that writers such as Chaucer and Shakespeare present empathy's force and viability as an indelible facet of the human condition, the lexicon at this time lacks a suitable word to convey this nuanced interaction. Its closest parallel is "sympathy," but even that term does not come into existence until the late sixteenth century.[22] Here, it denotes a strong affinity founded upon a conformity of feelings or inclinations that places people in a harmonious relation. Edmund Spenser introduces this term and its usage in "An Hymn in Honour of Beauty" (1596): "For love is a celestial harmony/ O likely hearts compos'd of stars' concent/ Which join together in sweet sympathy" (ll. 199–201). The ardor between the speaker and beloved grows because each one is affected by the same influence—a transcendent passion. Their corresponding emotions engender a harmony that springs from each other's joy and true contentment. Its accessibility as conveyed by their behavior binds them in "sweet sympathy." While early modern writers occasionally use this term and its cognates to highlight a desired affinity with another, a philosophical discussion of its meaning

---

21 Wyman, *The Gift of Active Empathy*, 44.

22 See *OED n.* 3a. Its earliest usage is found in Edmund Spenser's *Hymne in Honour of Beautie* (1596).

does not realize its fullest explication until the eighteenth century.[23] Here, David Hume and Adam Smith examine how its signification denotes likeness, conformity, and correspondence. As asserted by his poetic progenitor, Hume believes that witnessing another person's actions or condition affects the quality or state of being between two people. It enables one to enter into or share the feelings of another.

> When any affection is infus'd by sympathy, it is at first known only by its effects, and by those external signs in the countenance and conversation, which convey an idea of it. This idea is presently converted into an impression, and acquires such a degree of force and vivacity, as to become the very passion itself, and produce an equal emotion, as any original affection.[24]

Hume uses the term "idea" to describe the same type of imitation that today's scientists see in the neural substrate component of mirroring. This "idea" produces a corresponding likeness of another's gestures and facial expressions. Through this correspondence, one can assess its cause. This form of mental simulation supersedes mere synchronicity; it fashions a connection with another. In the example of lovers, such as between Spenser's speaker and his beloved, each one recognizes that the other's passion is in line with his or her own, intensifying their intimacy.

In *The Theory of Moral Sentiments*, Adam Smith also studies how another's behavior affects the observer. Although he does not identify the underlying cause as "an idea," Smith believes that the circumstances surrounding this emo-

---

23 The word "sympathy" appears intermittently throughout early modern literature. In *Henry VI, part 2* (1591), Shakespeare uses it to highlight King Henry VI's hoped-for affinity with his future wife, Margaret. He says, "A world of earthly blessings to my soul/ if sympathy of love unites our thoughts" (2 Henry VI 1.1.25–26). His words express the need for an emotional and intellectual consonance. However, attaining this kind of harmony is never realized because she places her loyalties behind Suffolk rather than him. Nearly a hundred years later, in John Milton's *Paradise Lost* (1667), Eve also conjoins the word with "love," yet does so with another hoped-for alliance that will never come to pass. She employs it to describe her own reflection:
> A shape within the watery gleam appeared,
> Bending to look on me: I started back,
> It started back; but pleased I soon returned,
> Pleased it returned as soon with answering looks
> Of sympathy and love. (4.461–65)

Being mesmerized by one's own appearance may reveal a likeness, but it does not foster a healthy relationship. Still, Eve's use of the term illustrates a fundamental link to love as a means to foster a harmony of disposition.
24 David Hume, *A Treatise of Human Nature* (1739–1740), ed. L. A. Selby-Bigge and P. H. Nidditch (Oxford: Oxford University Press, 1978), 317.

tional event inform the observer's view of the other. Another's passion, he main-tains, influences one's imagination more than the reality before them. The emphasis thus falls upon considering the factors contributing to that original emotive response.

> [Sympathy] does not arise so much from the view of the passion, as from that of the situation which excites it. We sometimes feel for another, a passion of which he himself seems to be altogether incapable; because, when we put ourselves in his case, that passion arises in our breast from the imagination, though it does not in his from reality.[25]

By immersing oneself in the other's situation, the resultant feelings create a sense of connectedness, even if the other's emotions lie beyond our current knowledge. For example, one can sympathize with someone who has lost a loved one even though one has not yet had such an experience.[26] To gain a clear grasp of the salient feelings, the sympathizer must consider the "situation, fully and in all its parts."[27] Determining the reasons underlying the other person's behavior help one align one's feelings accordingly. For both Hume and Smith, the purpose is to produce a healthy fellow-feeling. Sympathy thrives when we find another's actions and motives reasonable and/or laudable.

Their emphasis upon duplicating another's affective condition pervades Continental thought and, at the turn of the twentieth century, persuades Theodor Lipps to see little difference between this concept and his notion of *Einfühlung*.[28] In his mind, both terms revolve around the tendency to imitate or respond accordingly to another's heightened emotional expression. Even though this imitation, whether external or internal, may occur pre-reflexively, it allows the observer to determine what affects the other's well-being: "Then the idea of the affect in the other's gesture, or the thinking of the affect into the gesture, has then become the experience of the affect, has become fellow-feeling [*Mitfühlen*] or sym-

---

25 Adam Smith, *The Theory of Moral Sentiments*, ed. D. D. Raphael and A. L. Macfie (1759) (Oxford: Clarendon, 1976), 12.
26 Smith ponders this scenario in the passage quoted in note 12 of this chapter. While the grieving parents' suffering exhausts their emotional fortitude, the observer enters into this realm of mourning in spite of never having a child. His selflessness affirms his respect for their situation and care for their well-being. By not attempting to judge their situation from his position, it exhibits a willingness to conform his feelings accordingly.
27 Smith, *The Theory of Moral Sentiments* (1759/1976), 18.
28 Lipps writes, "The word 'sympathy' appears to be only another word for *Einfühlung* in the positive sense . . . i.e., as free inner participation" (Lipps, *Aesthetik*, 1:139).

pathy."[29] Although sharing in this joint feeling asks the observer to consider the conditions giving rise to the other's current emotional state, the other person does not have to be cognizant of this concern. As a result, the sympathy expressed has a passive quality. Moreover, certain circumstances render the sympathizer unable to act on their emotive response. When losing oneself in another's anxiety and worry, the experience may prove incapacitating and preclude any effort to establish a value-affirming rapport.

To prevent one from being overwhelmed by another's situation, Mikhail Bakhtin recasts the notion of sympathy and affords it a more active nature. For him, the sympathizer can neither succumb to the limitations of their own solipsistic point of view nor merge with another's consciousness, effectively forgoing their own sense of self. Rather, the sympathizer must play an interactive role in responding to the other's condition. "It is only from within my participation [in the act of aesthetic contemplation, as in any unitary event that links me with another subject in a responsible way] that the function of each participant can be understood."[30] There cannot be one participant. Both must be integrally involved. This exchange of knowledge enriches each one's understanding of the other. With the emphasis centered upon their interplay, sympathy now transposes the other's "experience to an entirely different axiological plane, into a new category of valuation and affirmation."[31] The emotional and volitional structure of this moment does not fixate upon the other as a stagnant object who is passively observed. Rather, it evolves into a sympathetically co-experienced life that "is given form not in the category of the *I*, but in the category of the *other*, as the life of *another* human being, another *I*."[32]

To realize this heightened state, the sympathizer must not only assess the other's person, but also recognize their own value, their own self. Projecting oneself into the other's psyche is no longer adequate in entering into another's mind. The sympathizer must return to their own person with this newfound knowledge and put together the features central to the experience, which are

---

29 Lipps, "Das Wissen von Fremden Ichen," 719. The closeness in meaning between the two terms prompts Titchener, who translates Lipps's conceptual schema into English, to define *Einfühlung* as "feeling ourselves into them" (E. B. Titchener, *A Textbook of Psychology* [New York: Macmillan, 1910], 417).
30 M. M. Bakhtin, *Toward a Philosophy of the Act*, ed. Vadim Liapunov and Michael Holquist, trans. Vadim Liapunov (Austin: University of Texas Press, 1993), 18.
31 M. M. Bakhtin, "Author and Hero in Aesthetic Activity," in *Art and Answerability*, ed. Michael Holquist and Vadim Liapunov, trans. Vadim Liapunov (Austin: University of Texas Press, 1990), 102.
32 Bakhtin, "Author and Hero in Aesthetic Activity," 82.

"transgredient to the entire object-world" of the other's consciousness.[33] Their import, however, involves far more than conveying information. The feelings expressed are not bound by the other's actions, but rather by how the sympathizer elects to "consummate" them. Bakhtin writes, "I must enframe him, create a consummating environment for him out of this excess of my own seeing, knowing, desiring, and feeling."[34] As a result, one acquires a more complete awareness of the other, oneself, and the situation, for only the viewpoints produced within that co-experienced life exist. As Wyman explains, the sympathizer "penetrates the other's inner world not to usurp the other's identity or to impose his own, but to become enlightened by the invaluable, if inevitably incomplete knowledge of the other's private realm in order to affirm his reality as truly personal."[35]

Despite Bakhtin's revolutionary notion of sympathy—in effect, creating a "sympathetic empathizing"—, a divide arises between the two terms as the century progresses.[36] Sympathy becomes identified with those feelings extended to those mired in misery and empathy signifies a more comprehensive grasp of another's experience whether immersed in negative or positive emotions. In her history of the term, Lanzoni writes, "Today sympathy is usually defined as a distanced feeling of pity for another, whereas empathy is a deeper-going ability to engage with a variety of feelings and to inhabit, sometimes even bodily, the other's perspective."[37]

Sympathy may establish a likeness with another wherein whatever affects one similarly affects the other, though not necessarily to the same degree or feeling, but apprehending what the other thinks lies outside its domain. Its expression centers upon a general concern for that person rather than participating in that specific moment. Peter Goldie points out: "The whole phenomenology of sympathy is different from the phenomenology of the experience which is being sympathized with: your feelings involved *caring* about the other's sufferings, not *sharing* them."[38] An outpouring of feeling can simply be directed towards another's well-being. It does not compel the sympathizer to take action because no direct connection must exist between them and the other. In fact, the sympathizer does not even have to know the other person or what has caused this outburst of emotion. The object of the sympathizer's attention

---

33 Bakhtin, "Author and Hero in Aesthetic Activity," 26–27.

34 Bakhtin, "Author and Hero in Aesthetic Activity," 25.

35 Wyman, *The Gift of Active Empathy*, 26.

36 For a historical account of this semantic change, see Jahoda, "Theodor Lipps and the Shift from 'Sympathy' to 'Empathy,'" 151–63.

37 Lanzoni, *Empathy*, 5–6.

38 Peter Goldie, "How We Think of Others' Emotions," *Mind & Language* 14 (1999): 420.

could be either a familiar relation or a complete stranger. Moreover, the feelings elicited do not have to be identical to the other's condition, but rather appropriate to the situation. For example, one may feel sorrow in regard to the other's anger. Though different, the feelings complement each other and draw attention to the sympathizer's support for the one in need. This expression of sadness may serve a prosocial purpose, but does not ask one to exercise a heartfelt commitment in attuning oneself to the other's state of mind.

Empathy, on the other hand, enhances interpersonal knowledge. Like Bakhtin's sympathy, it takes into account the surrounding circumstances and context to infer the other's emotive and cognitive state of being or ascertain what that moment reveals about that person. More than a reflexive action, it charges one to reflect upon the cause, the other person's condition, the action taken, and the potential outcome. Grasping another's view presupposes a willingness to interpret and sustain the affective responses exchanged between the two people. It is both an innate ability and an acquired skill. Its success, however, depends upon not only the other's openness to this commitment to his or her well-being, but also the observer's earnestness to persevere in this task.

Empathy is not an emotion but a means by which emotions are drawn out and directed. It is not determined by non-conscious automaticity, such as the pangs of sadness which arise instinctively when watching a friend mourn the loss of a loved one, but by assessing what this reaction says about the other person's condition and why its effect is so potent. This sensitivity to another prompts one either to simulate that person's behavior or immerse oneself in that experience. Via these processes, it produces a specific mode of consciousness that fortifies the bond between the two parties. Since this pursuit can never be forced, its volition is paramount in preventing one's individuality from slipping into a self-corrupting fusion.

Empathy Today

Despite empathy's short lexical history, which would seemingly limit the concept's meaning, scholars continually debate its purport. Some heed Lipps's view that a direct perception of another's behavioral expressions evokes similar emotions in the observer without any intervening assessment.[39] Others believe

---

39 Elaine Hatfield, John T. Cacioppo, and Richard L. Rapson, "Emotional Contagion," *Current Directions in Psychological Science* 2 (1993): 96–99; Robert W. Levenson, "Biological Substrates of Empathy and Facial Modulation of Emotion," *Motivation and Emotion* 20 (1996): 185–204.

that the value of imitation rests not upon an emotive kinship as much as a tool for mindreading, "the activity of representing specific mental states of others, for example, their perceptions, goals, beliefs, expectations, and the like."[40] And still others assert that the focus should lie upon the physiological mechanisms involved rather than the individual's response. Stephanie Preston and Frans de Waal focus exclusively upon the brain's perception-action system. They claim that "attended perception of the object's state automatically activates the subject's representation of the state, situation, and object, and that activation of these representations automatically primes or generates the associated autonomic and somatic responses, unless inhibited."[41] While empathy's function may prove expansive, my focus strives to integrate key features of these views, particularly as put forth by phenomenologists and simulation theorists, but also by the insistence of the literary characters under scrutiny to prioritize this rapport above all other matters, social or familial.[42] Whereas studies often discuss empathy in response to a distressing or other negative event, this one understands it as a conscious act that evinces a belief in each person's dignity.[43]

At this point, I would like to discuss how empathy's emphasis upon evaluating another's condition lays the foundation for a commitment that can endure hardship and separation strikingly distinguishes it from emotional contagion. Contagion occurs when two or more people are swept up in the fervor of another. Being consumed by this emotion precludes any intellectual assessment of the event and its underlying cause. Since the observer does not have to be familiar with or invested in the other's well-being, their response generates little, if any, insight. It functions more as an arousal of feeling rather than a substantive interaction. Even if a person is "more likely to catch others' emotions if their attention is riveted on the others than if they are oblivious to others' emotions," this attention should not be construed as a desire to know that person better, much less construct a meaningful bond.[44] Fixated upon facial matters, it does attempt

---

40 Alvin I. Goldman, *Joint Ventures: Mindreading, Mirroring, and Embodied Cognition* (Oxford: Oxford University Press, 2013), 50.

41 Stephanie D. Preston and Frans B. M. de Waal, "Empathy: Its Ultimate and Proximate Bases," *Behavioral and Brain Sciences* 25 (2002): 1–72.

42 For an edited work that presents a wide variety of approaches to the concept, see Amy Coplan and Peter Goldie, eds., *Empathy: Philosophical and Psychological Perspectives* (Oxford: Oxford University Press, 2014).

43 For an example of a study concentrating on the use of empathy specifically to remedy a negative situation, see Decety and Lamm, "Empathy versus Personal Distress," 199–214.

44 Elaine Hatfield, John Cacioppo and Richard L. Rapson, *Emotional Contagion* (New York: Cambridge University Press, 1994), 148.

to acknowledge and support another's interior worth.[45] Empathy, on the other hand, directs one to communicate, either verbally or physically, upon apprehending the other's state of mind with the desire to foster a mutual respect.

While another's affective state informs an empathetic response, it is not the chief instrument of knowing. Emotional contagion, on the other hand, involuntarily reacts to these emotions and often imitates the physical expression.[46] Frédérique de Vignemont observes that most instances of contagion are described in bodily rather than in affective terms:

> [O]ne talks of contagious crying or contagious laughter instead of contagious distress or contagious happiness. Similarly, experiences of contagious pain are vicarious experiences of the most bodily aspects of pain. They involve what is known as the sensory-discriminative component of the pain matrix, which encodes the intensity of pain and its bodily location. Hence, in pain contagion one responds to the perception of another's bodily part subjected to painful stimulation by expecting specific sensorimotor consequences of pain at the same location on one's own body.[47]

Since contagion often reacts to the physical source of the emotion, the cognitive resources exercised in the empathetic process do not come into play, precluding any analysis of these movements. Yet, confusing this emotional reaction with an interpersonal understanding blurs its delineation from empathy.[48] Although bodily sensation plays a vital factor in initiating an action to access another's consciousness, it is neither the sole nor the preferred means of knowing. Making the conscious choice to attune oneself to another's thoughts and feelings requires a concerted effort that is anything but impulsive. Attuning oneself to the other implicitly demonstrates a belief in the other's inherent value, and how this person is important to the empathizer. This conscious act surpasses the general notion of sympathy ameliorating pain or contagion fostering a sense of commonality. By intensifying one's awareness and dedication to the other, empathy enriches the understanding of what it means to be human.

---

45 Stephen Davies, "Infectious Music: Music-Listener Emotional Contagion," in *Empathy: Philosophical and Psychological Perspectives*, ed. Amy Coplan and Peter Goldie (Oxford: Oxford University Press, 2011), 138.
46 For an examination into the physiological processes underlying this response, see Frédérique de Vignemont and Pierre Jacob, "Beyond Empathy for Pain," *Philosophy of Science* 83 (2016): 434–35.
47 Frédérique de Vignemont, *Mind the Body: An Exploration of Bodily Self-Awareness* (Oxford: Oxford University Press, 2018), 129. Also see, Frédérique de Vignemont and Pierre Jacob, "What It's Like to Feel Another's Pain," *Philosophy of Science* 79 (2012): 295–316.
48 See Hiroaki Ishida, Keisuke Suzuki, and Laura Clara Grandi, "Predictive Coding Accounts of Shared Representations in Parieto-insular Networks," *Neuropsychologia* 70 (2015): 442–54.

Whether using simulation or phenomenology, neither approach could flourish without the observer's volition. While exercising the will may appear to be a natural reaction, examining its natural inclination reveals that the process involves far more than sharing an emotional affinity with another. A cognitive element is endemic to the process and, as such, discerning how the will directs the intellect brings to light the will's power to liberate one's choices from the servitude of human nature; expressing a genuine concern for another's welfare thus arises from volition, not a predetermined or dictated action. The will's freedom to initiate an empathetic act validates the integrity of this endeavor, for it does not have to pursue an end perceived as selfless good. If will were to necessarily seek happiness, then it would necessarily "force the intellect to continually consider happiness, which is false."[49] Consider the instance of an elderly father who yearns for a deeper connection with his grown-up children. Yet, because he had consistently prioritized his job before his parental duties, his lack of attentiveness has caused them to treat him with disdain and rarely, if ever, visit. Although he should patiently accept this treatment as a consequence of his selfishness and strive to receive their forgiveness, a willful stubbornness blinds him to this option. Instead, he befriends a colleague at work so that he can vent his familial frustrations to someone. Despite the fact that no blood connection exists between them, this person believes in the dignity of all people and tries to help the father recognize his faults. He wants him to realize the necessity of treating his children with kindness and respect regardless of their disinterest. Although the father does not heed this advice, he does cultivate a healthy respect for his co-worker and elects to align his thoughts with him in order to better grasp this person's motivations and belief system. While pursing an unqualified good would direct him to repairing his relationship with his children, the choice to express empathy towards an unrelated person is something that has value in itself, but offers no guarantee that it will provide happiness as a father.

Scotus's account of the will accords it a power distinct from that of the intellect. Since it is not controlled by a teleological orientation, it targets an object which right reason judges to be meritorious in producing an ethically sound act.[50] This does not mean, however, that empathy necessarily possesses a moral quality, but in the context of a positive expression of interpersonal understanding, it prompts one to recognize the importance of knowing someone as fully as possible. Hence, the decision to develop such an understanding does not stand in opposition to Amy Coplan's twenty-first-century claim that "empa-

---

49 Scotus, *Ordinatio* IV, d. 49; Wolter, *On the Will*, 158.
50 Scotus, *Quodlibeta*, q. 18, n. 12; *Ordinatio* I, d. 17.

thy . . . does not in and of itself involve . . . an impulse [to help the other]."[51] Rather, the will can put a checkrein on personal biases and direct one to enact an empathetic mode of consciousness that privileges the other's needs and concerns. Ultimately, it empowers the individual to put into praxis their desire to strengthen their commitment to recognize the other person's dignity.

The literary characters at the center of this study employ this specific mode of consciousness because they choose to pursue this course of action. They are not passive figures, but individuals who are not indifferent to the situation—a marked feature of contagion. Their willingness to gain a more informed awareness drives them onward. This focus amplifies the strength of the perceptual signal of the others' gestures as well as the eagerness to interpret their significance. These signs serve as a means to grasp the full import of that experience. Although attuning oneself to another's perspective does not always indicate an affinity between the two people, these characters' attempts to explain or predict another's actions affirm the authenticity of their commitment. It generates a moment of genuine interpersonal understanding.

Whether friend, ally, or lover, this empathy establishes their integrity in the narrative. While it possesses a prosocial value that allows the relationship, if so desired, to thrive on a larger, more communal scale, it also generates a full sense of self. It brings to light each one's distinctiveness and a heightened awareness that cannot be forced. Volition is its hallmark. These individuals must determine if the other person is deserving of this emotional and intellectual investment. Without this assessment, their ensuing expression runs the risk of simply being reactionary. Their decisions, however, do not always manifest in predictable, prescribed ways. A striking feature of these characters' choices is that neither custom nor duty accounts for the extreme sacrifices they make for one another. Whether Amiloun rejects angelic counsel to preserve his friendship with Amis or the Fool forgoes personal safety to support Lear, the dramatic force of their commitment both defies expectation and elevates their empathy to a transcendent plane. Being attentive to the most subtle nuances of the other's behavior hones their perception of that person's condition, allowing them to adapt seamlessly to the situation. These efforts throw into relief that biology or, more precisely, shared neural networks, do not control their choices. Frédérique de Vignemont's research proves that an "empathic response is not directly and

---

51 Amy Coplan, "Empathic Engagement with Narrative Fictions," *Journal of Aesthetics and Art Criticism* 62 (2004): 146.

automatically activated by the perception of an emotional cue."[52] Rather, a sincere belief in another's dignity supplements the knowledge gained.

Empathy accords a fullness of being that imprints its distinctiveness upon the observer's consciousness. As a literary heuristic, it illuminates the complexities of exercising one's capabilities to establish a substantive connection with another. The characters' interplay culminates in an affective knowing that becomes mindful of the other's unique value. That they exert all their energy into fashioning a thoughtful, caring bond demonstrates a mental flexibility in grasping the various causes underlying the other's emotive well-being. This state of knowing strengthens the relationship and the sanctity of its inviolate trust, qualities which far supersede an impulsive reaction. The choice to structure such a bond underscores not only a need to utilize as many different means as possible to determine the other's motivations, desires, and belief system, but also a resolute desire to succeed in this endeavor. These different uses of the mind reveal a keen insight into that character and validate using varied approaches to assess the epistemic import of this *kynde knowyng*.

---

52 Frédérique de Vignemont and Tania Singer, "The Empathic Brain: How, When and Why?," *Trends in Cognitive Sciences* 10 (2006): 438.

Chapter 2 Empathy's Volition in Preserving a Medieval Fraternal Bond

Since the discovery of mirror neurons in macaque monkeys in the mid-1990s, which revealed why they instinctively copied the behavior and seemingly grasped the intentional actions of other monkeys, researchers have tried to draw a direct line between pre-reflexively imitating another's behavior and interpersonal understanding. Scientists like Vittorio Gallese believe that our capacity to connect with others relies upon the basic information conveyed through these neurons. They assert that the internal motor knowledge produced by these responses enables one to translate it "into something that the observer is able to understand."[1] Christian Keysers takes it one step further, claiming that social cognition is ultimately rooted in the "machinery of motor control."[2] Some researchers, however, question the existence and contribution that these neurons provide for emotional understanding, widening their focus upon the neurobiological architecture as a whole in motivating prosocial behavior.[3] Despite these disparate views, their impact upon scientific thought is irreversible, leading scholars to conclude that "by now, hundreds of studies have examined the neural mechanisms underlying human empathy."[4] While the search for scientific proof to explain the biological processes underlying the imitation of another's actions continues, one inviolate fact remains—an empathetic act cannot be truly realized without making the choice to cultivate these pre-reflexive responses into a meaningful bond with that person.

Copying another's gestures or even expressing a kindred emotion fails to provide the kind of insight into another's state of mind that would lay the foundation for a valued rapport. One must take into account the factors contributing to this situation and why that person is affected so much by them. The decision to pursue this end and, upon establishing an informed understanding, protect it

---

[1] Vittorio Gallese, "Mirror Neurons, Embodied Simulation, and the Neural Basis of Social Identification," *Psychoanalytic Dialogues* 19 (2009): 520.

[2] Christian Keysers, *The Empathic Brain: How the Discovery of Mirror Neurons Changes Our Understanding of Human Nature* (Los Gatos, CA: Smashwoods Editions, 2011), 17.

[3] Jean Decety et al., "Empathy as a Driver of Prosocial Behaviour: Highly Conserved Neurobehavioral Mechanisms Across Species," *Philosophical Transactions Royal Society B* 371 (2016), http://dx.doi.org/10.1098/rstb.2015.0077; Remy Debes, "Which Empathy? Limitations in the Mirrored 'Understanding' of Emotion," *Synthese* 175 (2010): 219–39; L. Pierno, "Mirror Neurons in Humans: Consisting or Confounding Evidence?," *Brain and Languages* 108 (2009): 10–20.

[4] Zaki and Ochsner, "The Neuroscience of Empathy," 675.

https://doi.org/10.1515/9781501515460-003

from any third-party interference springs from the power of the will. When used in a positive manner, it inclines one towards goodness and to forgo selfish ambitions. If not, we limit its freedom for it becomes bound by individual desires. We must prioritize this initiative and do so selflessly in order to grasp that person's condition without bias or indifference. If not, the connection will merely dissolve into a transient reaction. A keen attentiveness allows us to assess another's behavior thoughtfully and, upon affirming its accuracy, we can embrace this knowledge as a means of fortifying the relationship. Apprehending another's thoughts and beliefs helps us realize our potential to express an affectionate understanding. This choice underscores the will's capacity for self-movement and its purport in initiating an empathetic act.

This chapter analyzes two medieval texts that highlight the altruism of characters who face incredible odds in preserving their bond, namely the titular protagonists in the romance *Amis and Amiloun* (ca. 1300) and the married couple, Cecilia and Valerian, along with the brother, Tiburce, in the saint's legend, *The Second Nun's Tale*. The strength of their conviction springs from the will's freedom to recognize each one's distinctive value. Without its impetus, neither set of characters could sustain their devotion. The decision to cherish another's goodness and to cultivate this understanding reflects the advances in late medieval thought, specifically the voluntarism of John Duns Scotus (ca. 1265/6–1308). His innovation focuses upon the idea that the will is not dependent upon the intellect's dictates. As a result, it can heed its own inclinations towards happiness or justice. Applying these philosophical insights to the texts illuminates the specific motivations guiding each one's resolve to maintain an affectionate commitment to the other.

Amis and Amiloun: The Choice to Care

The Middle English romance *Amis and Amiloun* presents two protagonists who are identical in appearance and demeanor. "Bothe thai weren as liche, ywis/ As was Sir Amiloun and Sir Amis" (ll. 250–51).[5] As doppelgangers to one another, their interplay reveals an indissoluble connection that supersedes any demands placed upon them by social obligation. Regardless of what kinds of difficulties they encounter, they consistently prize their friendship above all else and invest their energies into knowing each other as fully as possible. Since

---

5 All quotations from the Middle English text are from *Amis and Amiloun, Robert of Cisyle, and Sir Amadace*, ed. Edward E. Foster (Kalamazoo, MI: Medieval Institute Publications, 2007).

the lack of individuating features lessens the body's ability to convey vital information through its gestures and facial movements, they must assess the other's state of mind to determine how best to better their relationship. The other person thus serves as the basic motive of action. This selflessness differentiates their acts from stock portrayals of friendship and shows how an attentive knowledge of each other's motivations and beliefs is an essential facet of our existence. Indeed, the main principle undergirding Amis and Amiloun's bond is to lead a fulfilling life via grasping the thoughts and feelings of the other. Seeking knowledge that lies in the most intimate recesses of the other person emphasizes the will's power to align oneself with that person.

Empathy's epistemic surety enables Amis and Amiloun to pledge themselves to one another with conviction: "they were trouth plyght" (l. 20). Such an oath of loyalty establishes a kind of "brotherhed," which attests to the deepest bond of friendship (l. 362). Its genuineness requires more than its recitation. It depends upon each one realizing their potential as a thinking individual who is attentive to the other's state of mind. The efforts to enrich their mutual understanding create a connection founded upon the freedom to place the other's needs above their own. Without this conviction, the commitment would slowly diminish and ultimately cease to be. When Leah Haught writes that "the poem is an exploration of total devotion, not to a condition or an experience, but to an oath as an imperishable bond," she glosses over the complex processes underlying their decision to support the other.[6] The narrative focuses upon those specific situations in which each one attunes himself to the other's person and utilizes this knowledge—at great risk to his own safety—to preserve their bond. The reasons driving each one onward surpass a conventional agreement to satisfy a social need or knightly duty. Rather, they stems from a passionate belief in their interior worth. The efforts that each one takes to maintain this connection testifies to the will's freedom to choose and forge an active empathy.

Amis and Amiloun's interactions not only reveal how a heightened awareness of the other's motivations and intentions structure the narrative, but also delineate this version of the story from its predecessors. The medieval legend of these friends exists in nearly every European language as well as a variety of genres, including epic, romance, hagiography, miracle play, and prose history. The earliest version appears in the Latin verse epistle "Ad Bernardum," written

---

6 Leah Haught, "In Pursuit of 'Trewth': Ambiguity and Meaning in *Amis and Amiloun*," *Journal of English and Germanic Philology* 114 (2015): 245.

by Rodulfus Tortarius at the end of the eleventh century.[7] While each account emphasizes the sworn brotherhood between the eponymous characters, the portrayal of this bond varies dramatically, "no one of the romantic versions is the direct source of another."[8] Despite these differences, the story is predicated upon the identical portrayal of its two heroes. This twinning causes external events or authority figures to govern the course of action and, as a result, diminishes the heroes' distinct importance. Although consistent in depicting these physical similarities, *Amis and Amiloun* sets itself apart by highlighting the radical choices of each one as a means to establish their unique identity and empathy for one another.[9] For example, whereas their counterparts in the Anglo-Norman *Amys e Amillyoun* (ca. 1200) passively obey the instructions of a disembodied voice, Amis and Amiloun actively debate the merit of any proffered counsel and determine on their own volition which path best serves the relationship.[10] Their choices establish the will's primacy, distinguish their person, and reflect the seminal changes in the intellectual milieu. Portraying the will as being able to initiate an ethically informed act parallels Scotistic voluntarism. Hence, this chapter contends that Scotus's theory of the will provides a learned base to distinguish these friends and appreciate the profundity of their choices,

---

7 *Rodulfi Tortarii Carmina*, ed. Marbury B. Ogle and Dorothy M. Schullian (Rome: American Academy in Rome, 1933), 266–67. An English translation may be found in Appendix A of *Amis and Amiloun*, ed. MacEdward Leach, EETS, os 203 (London: Oxford University Press, 1937, repr. 1960), 101–5.

8 Leach, *Amis and Amiloun*, xiv. For a study of the Middle English text's indebtedness to previous versions and generic predecessors, see Susan Dannenbaum, "Insular Tradition in the Story of Amis and Amiloun," *Neophilologus* 67 (1983), 611–22; Dean Baldwin, "*Amis and Amiloun*: The Testing of *Treuthe*," *Papers on Language and Literature* 16 (1980), 353–65; Kathryn Hume, "*Amis and Amiloun* and the Aesthetics of Middle English Romance," *Studies in Philology* 70 (1973), 19–41.

9 The earliest extant text of this Middle English romance is found in the Auchinleck Manuscript (ca. 1330), Edinburgh, National Library of Scotland, MS Auchinleck, fols. 49r–61v, and can be accessed via the following link: https://auchinleck.nls.uk/mss/amiloun.html, ed. David Burnley and Alison Wiggins. Three later copies also preserve this Middle English romance. Their codicological information is as follows: London, British Library MS Egerton 2862, fols. 135r–147v (ca. 1400); London, British Library MS Harley 2386, fols. 131r–137v (ca. 1500); and Oxford, Bodleian Library, Douce 326 (Bodleian 21900), fols. 1r–13v (ca. 1500). Notably, the Auchinleck manuscript is the most complete since it lacks only the first 100 and the final 177 lines. For a discussion of each edition's variants, see Leach, *Amis and Amiloun* and Françoise Le Saux, *Amys and Amylion* (Exeter: University of Exeter Press, 1993).

10 Dannenbaum, "Insular Tradition," 611. Leach observes that the Anglo-Norman and Middle English versions "must be considered as a unit, an important member of the romantic family of the *Amis and Amiloun* story" (*Amis and Amiloun*, xcvii).

particularly in relation to their predecessors in the nearest romances, *Amys e Amillyoun* and the French *Ami et Amile* (ca. 1200).

The issue before these heroes is not sustaining a friendship in accord with either social or religious standards of probity, but relying upon their sense of justice to decide which action best insulates them from outside forces and reinforces their closeness. This personally grounded justice drives each to align his interests with the other so that their emotional link can withstand any external pressure, no matter how divinely enforced or socially accepted. For instance, Amiloun elects to ignore an angel's warning and deceive the duke to champion Amis's virtue. Although Amis slept with Belisaunt, the duke's daughter, out of wedlock, his freedom of choice had been compromised by her demands and the resultant action has little bearing on his inner goodness. By rejecting the strictures of positive law and focusing upon Amis's genuine care for Belisaunt, Amiloun exercises the will's affection for what is just. Prioritizing the will over the intellect's dictates affirms each friend's value and champions the advances propounded by Scotus. Scotus allows the will to heed its own inclinations towards either personal happiness or justice, the *affectio commodi* and *affectio iustitiae*, respectively. Whereas the former affection disposes one to seek out goods that bring pleasure and enjoyment to the self, the latter exerts a tempering influence which ensures that the will operates freely.[11] This liberty is a positive inclination to love things objectively and align itself with right reason. Defending Amis is not a generalized depiction of altruism or misplaced loyalty, but a choice founded upon a belief in his intrinsic goodness. Scotist thought, therefore, illuminates the motivations guiding both friends to determine what best secures the fellowship and maintain their attentiveness to the other.

Scotus stands alongside Thomas Aquinas as one of the most influential thinkers in medieval thought and "certainly the one who inspired the most interest in the centuries after his death."[12] His views on the freedom of the will are seminal, for they accord the will the innate capacity of human beings to choose whether or not to love a person's objective goodness. Despite the paucity of writers who actually mention a late medieval philosopher or text, the salience of a Scotist perspective is well-documented in late medieval British poetry, such as Chaucer's *Canterbury Tales* and William Langland's *Piers Plowman*.[13] Scotus in-

---

11 Scotus, *Ordinatio* II, d. 6, q. 2, n. 8 (XII, 353).

12 Richard Cross, *Duns Scotus* (Oxford: Oxford University Press, 1999), 3.

13 Richard J. Utz, "Negotiating the Paradigm: Literary Nominalism and the Theory and Practice of Rereading Late Medieval Text," in *Literary Nominalism*, ed. Richard Utz (Lewiston, NY: Edwin Mellen Press, 1995), 10. For a sampling of those literary studies examining the intersection between Scotus's thought and late medieval poetry, see James I. Wimsatt, "John Duns Scotus,

spires a school of thought, but its influence upon the milieu is unique. As opposed to other schools, it does not serve a particular system of beliefs. For example, Thomas Aquinas's writings were required readings for the Dominican Order; the Austin friars were to follow those of Giles of Rome.[14] As scholar Maarten Hoenen observes, "Scotism, by contrast, emerged and established itself more or less spontaneously, having its origins in the efforts of individuals rather than in the promptings of ecclesiastical or educational institutions."[15] Free from any dependence upon external forces, its ideas attract those thinkers who yearn to understand the internal processes of cognition and volition. Scotus's views on the freedom of the will became publicly available through his disputations, most notably his renowned set of quodlibetal questions circa Advent 1306 or Lent 1307. The theories of what constitute cerebral powers establish his originality, particularly in relation to the will's freedom. In fact, modern philosophers, such as Francisco Suárez and Gottfried Leibniz, view Scotus's doctrine of individuality as superior to those of his contemporaries.[16] This conceptual ingenuity influenced coeval writers and elucidates the ideas central to *Amis and Amiloun*.

In his study of the interconnection between poetry and late medieval thought, Ullrich Langer observes that the literary and philosophical elements within a text operate as related but separate cultural phenomena:

> Yet an emphasis on certain concepts, rather than on the impact of an individual's or a school's entire thought, seems heuristically more valid and more faithful to what literature

Charles Sanders Peirce, and Chaucer's Portrayal of the Canterbury Pilgrims," *Speculum* 71 (1996), 633–45; Lois Roney, *Chaucer's Knight's Tale and Theories of Scholastic Psychology* (Tampa: University of Southern Florida Press, 1990); Janet Coleman, *Piers Plowman and the Moderni* (Rome: Letture di Pensiero e d'Arte, 1981).

14 William J. Courtenay, *Schools and Scholars in Fourteenth-Century England* (Princeton, NJ: Princeton University Press, 1987), 175–78; Maarten J. F. M. Hoenen, "Late Medieval Schools of Thought in the Mirror University Textbooks: The *Promptuarium Argumentorum* (Cologne 1492)," in *Philosophy and Learning: Universities in the Middle Ages*, ed. Martin J. F. M. Hoenen, J. H. Josef Schneider, and Georg Wieland (Leiden: Brill, 1995), 329–69.

15 Maarten J. F. M. Hoenen, "Scotus and the Scotist School: The Tradition of Scotist Thought in the Medieval and Early Modern Period," in *John Duns Scotus: Renewal of Philosophy*, Acts of the Third Symposium Organized by the Dutch Society for Medieval Philosophy Medium Aevum, May 23 and 24, 1996, ed. Egbert P. Bos (Amsterdam: Rodopi, 1998), 198.

16 Francisco Suárez, *Über die Individualität und das Individuationsprinzi*, ed. Rainer Specht (Berlin: Akademie Verlag, 2013), 9; Gottfried Wilhelm Leibniz, *De principio individui*, in *Sämtliche Schriften und Briefe* (Berlin: Akademie Verlag, 2004), 11–19. See also Ignacio Angelelli, "The Scholastic Background of Modern Philosophy: Entitas and Indivduation in Leibniz," in *Individuation in Scholasticism: The Later Middle Ages and the Counter-Reformation, 1150–1650*, ed. Jorge J. E. Gracia (Albany: State University of New York Press, 1994), 535–42.

is about. A literary text does not attempt to represent truthfully contemporary figures or their thought, but reworks key attitudes, experiences, sensation, and concepts into an imaginative whole that is in a sense incommensurable with the initial givens (though not unrelated to them).[17]

Literary discourse does not seek to posit a definitive statement of or resolution to a philosophical question. Rather, it dramatizes the issues presented, deepening the meaning underpinning its structure. A nuanced awareness of the relation between the two discourses illuminates the romance's design and thematic import. The "certain concepts" applicable to the text are those that explain the will's self-determining ability to put into praxis a moral judgment. For Scotus, the will is a power that can move itself from potentiality to actuality without any prior cause. Virtue finds its provenance in the direct control of the agent, which lies only in the free will. A Scotistic will assigns an inimitable quality to each person. Subsequently, neither Amis nor Amiloun necessarily follows the dictates upheld by knightly or religious duty. Rather, each remains free to defend the other's dignity even if such a choice runs counter to established practices. Hence, those decisions exclusive to the Middle English redaction, for all of its poetic sublimity, can be accessed most readily through the interdiscursive light shed by Scotist thought.

Scotus's Dual Affections

Since no text, literary or otherwise, originates in a vacuum, the friends' choices bring to light contemporaneous discussions of the will's power. The freedom to embrace the tenets of friendship before society's logic reflects the principles underpinning the late medieval theory of voluntarism. As stated earlier, this theory privileges the will over the intellect and, in the hands of Scotus, signifies the belief that the will is free to act against reason's dictates and can order the other powers of the mind, vindicating itself as the principle of justice and rectitude. He presents a sophisticated notion of the will's freedom to exercise an action founded upon personal happiness, a desire to cherish the intrinsic value of a person regardless of whether it happens to be good for oneself or not, or a properly ordered combination of the two. People find fulfillment when they "bring

---

17 Ullrich Langer, *Divine and Poetic Freedom in the Renaissance: Nominalist Theology and Literature in France and Italy* (Princeton, NJ: Princeton University Press, 1990), 10.

love for the self into harmony with love for the good" of another.[18] While these inclinations should lead one to the divine font of charity, they preserve the individual's freedom to pursue what one deems most desirable. To account for the will's ability to draw these distinctions, Scotus posits a theory of dual affections—the *affectio commodi* (the affection for the advantageous) and the *affectio iustitiae* (the affection for justice). Because the *affectio commodi* does not consider possibilities other than its own wants, such as self-perfection and happiness, it cannot govern the other affection. The moderating force exerted by the affection for justice empowers the will with an ethical dimension since it seeks to perform another-centered act, whose goal is not possession or use, but benevolence and charity. Scotus writes: "the *affectio iustitiae*, which is the first controller of the *affectio commodi* with respect to the fact that the will need not actually will that to which the *affectio commodi* inclines it, or will it to the highest degree, is the innate liberty of the will."[19] Their interaction shows that the will, in its capacity for self-control, is a *sui generis* cause, distinct from any other cause. Determining how best to balance these affections produces a liberty that supersedes a dependence upon the intellect's commands.

Whereas some thinkers may grant the will the power to move the intellect as to the exercise of the act, they still make it subject to reason's judgment. Thomas Aquinas (1225–1274) contends that every moral agent necessarily acts for an intellectually determined end: "First there is the apprehension of the end; then the desire for the end; then the counsel about the means; then the desire of the means."[20] Scotus, on the other hand, disputes that the will's act is determined (or necessitated) by an act of cognition. For him, the will remains formally separate from the intellect. The intellect can then determine whether or not to heed the will's affections. Once making this division, he focuses exclusively upon the will's twofold structure. Its dual inclinations generate a self-determining power, which frees it from the intellect's commands. The *affectio commodi*, if understood by itself, "is more like a form that inclines one to act in a determinate way than like an act or an operation."[21] The *affectio iustitiae*, on the other hand, seeks out what is most just and reaches its fruition in seeking out

---

18 Mary Beth Ingham, "John Duns Scotus: Retrieving a Medieval Thinker for Contemporary Theology," in *The Franciscan Intellectual Tradition*, ed. Elise Saggau (St. Bonaventure, NY: Franciscan Institute Publications, 2002), 101.

19 Scotus, *Ordinatio* II, d. 6, q. 2; Wolter, *On the Will*, 468–71.

20 Thomas Aquinas, *Summa Theologica* I–II, 15.3, http://www.newadvent.org/summa. Also see, *Summa Theologica* I–II, 9.1. Hereafter, cited as *ST*.

21 Cruz González-Ayesta, "Scotus's Interpretation of the Difference between *Voluntas ut Natura* and *Voluntas ut Voluntas*," *Franciscan Studies* 66 (2008), 387.

goods intrinsically worthy of love, not for self-preservation. This affection directs one to love someone for their interior good because it is a freer act than simply seeking out that person to satisfy one's desires.[22] The interaction between the two affections proves it to be a faculty capable of moral choice.

This progression of thought testifies to a late thirteenth-century metaphysical exploration into what constitutes free choice. Historiographers traditionally draw a bold line of demarcation between the scholastic Aristotelianism indicative of Aquinas's thought and the voluntarism that arose afterwards, but a "growing chorus among scholars" questions its absoluteness.[23] Applying it too broadly "would rob [Scotus's] work in moral psychology of the accolade of originality it so richly deserves."[24] His distinctiveness arises when he differentiates between two orders of causality: nature and will. The intellect acts naturally. "Natural" in this sense means that the intellect is unable to restrain itself. The will, on the other hand, acts "freely" or "rationally."

> [I]t is clear that a rational potency, such as the will is said to be, does not have to perform opposites simultaneously, but can determine itself to either alternative, which is something the intellect cannot do.[25]

The term "rational" does not mean "practical rationality, practical reason, or practical wisdom, but rather the contingency of will as a free power different from nature."[26] The will remains indeterminate with respect to its action, for at that very instant of choosing, it could will the contrary. The ability to embrace, reject, or not act at all establishes it as a truly free power.

While scholars debate if the interaction between the affections or the sole provenance of the *affectio iustitiae* determines free will, no one disputes the regulating power of this latter affection to produce a more noble inclination.

---

22 Scotus, *Ordinatio* III, d. 26; Wolter, *On the Will*, 400–421.

23 Steven P. Marrone, "Aristotle, Augustine and the Identity of Philosophy in Late Thirteenth-Century Paris: The Case of Some Theologians," in *After the Condemnation of 1277*, ed. Jan A. Aertsen, Kent Emery, Jr., and Andreas Speer, Miscellanea Mediaevalia 28 (Berlin: Walter de Gruyter, 2001), 278.

24 Martin W. F. Stone, "Moral Psychology after 1277: Did the Parisian Condemnation Make a Difference to Philosophical Discussions of Human Agency?," in *After the Condemnation of 1277*, ed. Jan A. Aertsen, Kent Emery, Jr., and Andreas Speer, Miscellanea Mediaevalia 28 (Berlin: Walter de Gruyter, 2001), 825.

25 Scotus, *Questions on the Metaphysics* IX, q. 15, in *Opera Omnia*, vol. 7, ed. Ludovicum Vives (Paris, 1891); Wolter, *On the Will*, 168: "Ad primum argumentum principale patet quod potential rationalis, prout dicitur esse coluntas, est contrariorum non simul fiendorum, sed potest se determinare ad alterutrum; non sic intellectus."

26 González-Ayesta, "Scotus's Interpretation," 383.

The affection for justice is nobler than the affection for the advantageous, understanding by "justice" not only acquired or infused justice, but also innate justice, which is the will's congenital liberty by reason of which it is able to will some good not oriented to self. According to the affection for what is advantageous, however, nothing can be willed save with reference to self.[27]

The *affectio iustitiae* is the efficient cause in making it possible to love another for who they are rather than what they can do for the lover. This kind of love directs one to seek what is best for the beloved. The inclination towards this good, however, does not coerce or control the will. Allan Wolter maintains that it is the "native liberty or root freedom of the will" and results in "a freedom *from* nature and a freedom *for* values."[28] Each person can decenter themselves from a self-oriented state to an other-oriented one. By fostering a closeness through the *affectio iustitiae*, the will perfects the self through loving the other's intrinsic goodness.

The Self-Determining Properties of Amis and Amiloun's Will

In *Amis and Amiloun*, prizing the other's virtue underlies the *treuthe* of their bond. Scholars concur that *treuthe* connotes "both fidelity to a vow and the personal integrity and moral courage necessary to fulfill a pledge."[29] Yet, whereas the French and Anglo-Norman romances rely upon an admixture of familial and social tenets to inform this idea, such as Amy's blissful marriage and Amillyoun's martial prowess, the Middle English version locates this truth within each one's person and the willingness of the other to cherish it. Amis and Amiloun heed the inclinations of the *affectio iustitiae* to refine their friendship and exert control over the impulses for personal gain. Scotus's dual *affectiones* thus function as a conceptual paradigm that explains why this *treuthe* springs from the volition to defend the other's integrity rather than a rigid adherence to an oath.

---

27 Scotus, *Ordinatio* III, suppl. d. 26; Wolter, *On the Will*, 178: "Nobilior est affectio iustitiae quam commodi, non solum intelligendo de acquisita et infusa, sed de innata, quae est ingenita libertas secundum quam potest velle aliquod bonum non ordinaturm ad se."
28 Allan B. Wolter, "Native Freedom of the Will as a Key to the Ethics of Scotus," in *The Philosophical Theology of John Duns Scotus*, ed. Marilyn McCord Adams (Ithaca, NY: Cornell University Press, 1990), 152.
29 Baldwin, "*Amis and Amiloun*," 355; also see, Ojar Kratins, "The Middle English *Amis and Amiloun*: Chivalric Romance or Chivalric Romance or Secular Hagiography?," *PMLA* 81 (1966), 347–54.

Although their "plight" states that they will come to each other's aid, they must choose to exercise their knowledge of one another to hold true to its tenets.

> Where that thai were in lond,
> Fro that day forward never mo
> Failen other for wele no wo:
> Therto thai held up her hond (ll. 153–56).

Vowing to never let the other down demands that each one must discern what drives the other onward or the oath would merely become a dictate denying their ability to decide how best to maintain their bond. The will's affection for justice liberates their servitude to the basic constraints of human nature—that is, heeding a socially imposed duty. A true empathizer must assess the unique factors surrounding the event and how they affect the other person. Only by exercising this initiative can one gain an informed awareness of the other's value in that specific time and place. For example, when Amis faces life-threatening accusations by the evil steward, Amiloun seeks out Amis to discover the circumstances leading up to the disputed act. He knows first-hand that Amis is someone who aspires to foster a meaningful rapport with those who are similarly virtuous. Any claim suggesting otherwise would be suspect. Amiloun's efforts to discern Amis's character prove far more expansive than a pledge to act with honor.[30] Whereas scholar MacEdward Leach believes that the truth underpinning their bond equates with "the testing of friendship, not the exposition of Christian character or Christian virtue,"[31] Ken Eckert maintains a friendship founded upon free choice "*is* Christian virtue, in distinction to the proud and cold legalism of exclusive oaths."[32] I submit that both emphases are applicable, but ultimately depend upon an empathic rapport. The loyalty and virtue behind Amiloun's choices stem from a keen insight into Amis's person. He realizes that dangerous foes seek to slander Amis "with wrake/ To sle with sorwe and care" (ll. 1025–26). Amiloun shuns the self-serving attitude that he should avoid or detach himself from Amis's reality. Instead, he inserts himself into this situation regardless of the consequences. Striving to perfect this affection for justice displays a consciousness that embraces the harsh conditions affecting their com-

---

30 For a detailed study of its medieval meaning and its etymological origins, see Richard Firth Green, *A Crisis of Truth: Literature and Law in Ricardian England* (Philadelphia: University of Pennsylvania Press, 1999), 10–11.

31 Leach, *Amis and Amiloun*, xxvi.

32 Ken Eckert, "*Amis and Amiloun*: A Spiritual Journey and the Failure of *Treuþe*," *Literature & Theology* 27 (2013): 286.

mitment to one another and prioritizes the chance for Amiloun to hone his interpersonal awareness.

While this example explains the will's integral function in empowering Amiloun to act justly, the will's self-determining properties come to light even more strikingly when he elects to ignore an angel's warning. To appreciate its dramatic import, an outline of the events leading up to this dispute is required. Upon hearing of his father's death, Amiloun leaves the court to manage his ancestral demesne. At this time, Amis finds himself alone with Belisaunt. She threatens him with an accusation of rape if he does not give into her sexual advances. He acquiesces. The steward, who spies on them, informs the duke of their tryst, but misrepresents Amis's reasons. He denounces Amis as "a traitour strong" (l. 790). Although Amis protests his innocence, the duke decides that a duel between the accuser and accused will determine who speaks truthfully. Amis seeks out and asks Amiloun to take his place in the duel. Since he is innocent of the offense and, therefore, sure to win, Amiloun agrees. Before the joust commences, "a voice fram heven adoun" warns him that if he pursues this course of action, then he will become a leper and suffer other miseries within three years (l. 1250). Among these miseries include being shunned by "thos that be thine best frende" and then forsaken by "thi wiif and alle thik inne" (ll. 1268, 1270). Despite the possibility of contracting such a debilitating disease and being ostracized, Amiloun stands firm in his defense of Amis's name. Acceding to the angel's injunction may appeal to the *affectio commodi*'s desire for survival, but electing to aid his friend demonstrates a pronounced empathetic expression. He knows that Amis would never be a traitor, nor unfairly seduce a young woman. The decision to joust against and ultimately conquer the steward epitomizes the tempering ability of the *affectio iustitiae* to subdue the concern for self-preservation and exercise a loyalty informed by an understanding of Amis's intentions and beliefs. This native *indeterminatio* of the will establishes the preeminence of Amiloun's freedom and instantiates his individuality.

As opposed to *Amis and Amiloun*'s generic predecessors, only the Middle English romance places the angel's admonition before rather than after the joust. This repositioning highlights Amiloun's volition. Neither religious nor intellectual expectations dictate his action. The affection for justice is always operative within the will, ensuring that the two affections work together to provide an initial moral determination for the rational appetite. By directing his love outward, he brings love for the self, *affectio commodi*, into harmony with this higher inclination. Their interplay ensures the betterment of both his and Amis's person. The text stresses the difficulty of balancing these affections by specifying the other miseries that will arise if he does not defer to the heavenly power: "thos that be thine best frende" will shun him and "thi wiif and alle thik inne" will forsake him (ll. 1268, 1270). Despite the instinctive desire to preserve his happiness, he remains free to take whichever action he deems most appropriate. He acts with but is not determined by this knowledge. The counsel is not condemnatory, merely cautionary: "Jhesu sent the bode bi me,/ To warn the anon" (ll. 1262–63).[33] Its neutrality ensures that the decision is not made under duress. As Jill Mann points out, it does not indicate "divine disapproval of the proposed deception, but rather a way of adding an extra layer to Amiloun's act of self-sacrifice for his friend: even if he wins the battle, he knows he will be obliged to endure further suffering."[34] Welcoming such affliction emphasizes the nobility of his will to seek out the love within another, for that is an "eventour strong" (l. 1256). While a knight's adventure traditionally entails momentous battles replete with otherworldly challenges, his singular worth centers upon a distinctive exercise of the will.

Amiloun disregards the angel because "Yif y beknowe mi name,/ Than schal mi brother go to schame,/ With sorwe thai shul him spille" (ll. 279–81). This is not merely a selfless act, but one that places Amis's dignity above spiritual and legal mores. He forgoes heavenly advice, violates positive law by perpetuating a fraud, and neglects personal safety. To prevent Amis from being shamed, he states, "for drede of care/ To hold mi treuthe schal y nought spare" (l. 1283). This "treuthe" references the oath sworn earlier to Amis upon learning of the steward's treachery. If he met this wicked man, he vowed that would with "mi brond, that is so bright,/ Y schal sen his hert blode!" (ll. 1115–16). The justification, though violent, springs from a devotion to a truth that outweighs any other moral arbiter as the basis of his choice. He may conclude his speech with the idiomatic phrase "Lete God don alle His wille" but the motivations underpinning his decision belong to his will alone (l. 1284).

Realizing one's freedom through seeking out the goodness in another separates this version from the French and Anglo-Norman romances. Neither one allows the friends to make their own decisions, depicting them instead as passively submitting to an external authority. In *Ami et Amile*, the angel tells Ami only after he has impersonated Amile in the joust that he will become "a loathsome leper" if he does not confess to the deception.[35] The only possible reply is the one

---

33 See Kratins, The Middle English *Amis and Amiloun*," 351; Baldwin, "*Amis and Amiloun*," 360; Dannenbaum, "Insular Tradition," 620.

34 Jill Mann, "Messianic Chivalry in *Amis and Amiloun*," *New Medieval Literatures* 10 (2008): 154.

35 *Ami and Amile: A Medieval Tale of Friendship*, ed. Samuel N. Rosenberg and Samuel Danon (Ann Arbor: University of Michigan Press, 1996), 82. For the French critical edition, see *Ami et Amile*, ed. Peter R. Dembowski, Classiques Français du Moyen Âge 97 (Paris: Champion, 1969).

given, "There is nothing more I can do, good creature; be off now."[36] Ami is correct. He must accept the punishment for his deception. Confessing would change nothing that has transpired. Hardret, the steward, is already dead, and Ami is innocent of the charge for the simple reason that he is not the one accused. If he revealed that he impersonated Amile, then the friendship would not stay true to its moral purport. As a result, he has no option but to accept becoming a leper.

Such passivity becomes even more pronounced in the Anglo-Norman version. Here, Amillyoun only hears "a voice, which nobody heard but him."[37] No angel messengers of God appear in this version. Although it also speaks about the leprotic consequences, it lacks the authority to prompt self-reflection. In the absence of celestial credibility, this voice does not urge him to assess the moral implications of his impending decision. Rather, the narrator flatly states that even though Amillyoun heard this warning, he "would not stop."[38] His lack of concern for the gravity of the situation attests to a belief in fate rather than freedom of choice. While these earlier versions effectively avoid any ethical conundrum, the Middle English redaction highlights the will's liberty as it springs from the interaction between the two affections to accept or reject the inclination toward the object presented by the intellect. Electing to act contrary to the angel's words shows that Amiloun's choice is necessitated by neither heavenly nor social strictures. Rather, the desire to defend his friend's virtue underlies Amiloun's empathy and proves his uniqueness.

Putting into Praxis the Will's Choice

Amis and Amiloun exalts an empathy founded upon the will's ability to initiate a morally just act. Unlike the intellect, which according to Scotus has no choice but to grasp or understand an object, the will has the capacity, when all conditions for acting are present, either to act or deliberately refuse to act.[39] The intel-

36 Rosenberg and Danon, *Ami and Amile*, 82.

37 *The Birth of Romance in England: The Romance of Horn, The Folle Tristan, The Lai of Haveloc and Amis and Amilun*, ed. Judith Weiss (Tempe: Arizona Center for Medieval and Renaissance Studies, 2010), 181. For the Anglo-Norman edition, see *Amys e Amillyoun*, ed. Hideka Fukui, ANTS Plain Texts Series 7 (London: Anglo-Norman Text Society, 1990).

38 Weiss, *Birth of Romance*, 181.

39 Scotus, *Questions on the Metaphysics* IX, q. 15, n. 7, p. 611; Wolter, *On the Will*, 157: "[T]he will is properly rational, and has to do with opposites, both as to its own act as well as the acts of subordinate powers, and it does not act towards these after the manner of nature, like the in-

lect is not free to affirm or deny in the face of contrary evidence. For Scotus, the interaction between the will's *affectiones* proves that contingency always exists when confronting a dilemma. Seeking the good in the other may epitomize a just act, but the will remains free not to follow this disposition. And, even if it does, the text shows that the resultant act may not instill the kind of trust one expects. The romance does not rely upon a conventional portrayal of selflessness to characterize the friendship, but extols the radical choices of each hero to display their commitment to the other. Three scenes in particular underscore the will's primacy in deciding what is just: the blossoming of their friendship at court, Amiloun confiding in his wife about impersonating Amis, and Amis's decision to slay his children in order to save Amiloun.

In contrast with the previous romances, this one depicts the friendship as dependent upon freely elicited choices, which eliminates any notion that the bond is implicit or predestined. Unlike that of their counterparts, Amis and Amiloun's bond must be cultivated in court where "thei become frend" (l. 17). Having to undergo this process proves that certain actions must be taken in order to establish their mutual devotion. In the Anglo-Norman version, it is understood from the outset that the two heroes are bound to one another: "They loved each other so dearly that they swore to be brothers."[40] And, in *Ami et Amile*, their connection is preordained by the angel who "told of their great friendship and fidelity."[41] It then relates how each one, without ever meeting each other, seeks out the other. Their actions occur through a belief in destiny rather than a kindred love fortified by personal commitment to the other. When they finally do meet, they exchange a vow of loyalty, but the text offers little insight into its import: "They made a pledge of lasting friendship. Then they saddled their mounts."[42] The pledge bears no witness to any consideration about the demands of sustaining the other's virtue in the face of great odds.

Amis and Amiloun, however, elaborates upon the circumstances surrounding their "trouth plight" (l. 20).[43] First, despite being "twel winter olde," they are

---

tellect but does so freely, and is able to determine itself, and therefore it is a potency, because it is able to do something, for it can determine itself."

40 Weiss, *Birth of Romance*, 171.

41 Rosenberg and Danon, *Ami and Amile*, 31.

42 Rosenberg and Danon, *Ami and Amile*, 37.

43 This *trouth plyght* recollects the kind of vows exchanged between bride and groom. See John C. Ford, "Merry Married Brothers: Wedded Friendship, Lovers' Language and Male Matrimonial in Two Middle English Romances," *Medieval Forum* 3 (2003), http://www.sfsu.edu/~medieval/volume3.html. Anna Reuters also notes that such a pledge is the equivalent to a binding promise of marriage and anticipates the imminent separation between the friends, for a separation tests

knighted shortly after swearing this vow (l. 58). This newly acquired social position shows that they have reached the age of reason and are able to make informed choices about their personal responsibilities. Second, it states that they loved each other as no children had ever done before. This love springs from neither a biological nor a familial connection: "Bitiux hem tuai, of blod and bon/ Trewer love nas never non" (ll. 139–40). This state of mutuality affirms that their elicited acts align with right reason. Being "war and wight" displays a conscious acceptance of those responsibilities connected to their "trouth plight" and the need to embrace those choices that cultivate the love within the other (l. 145). Indeed, the juxtaposition of opposites—"bi day and bi night,/ In wele and wo, in wrong and right"—underscores their willingness to face the numerous trials that challenge their bond (ll. 148–49). They must continually adapt to the circumstances particular to that trial. Since the will is contingent, for at that very moment of choosing, it could will the opposite, each friend must put into praxis an act that the will deems most appropriate for that situation. Whether the *affectio iustitiae* reigns supreme, moderates the *affectio commodi*, or permits the latter affection to pursue its own end, the will's self-determining properties choose freely and, in the process, individuate one friend from the other. The pledge, therefore, is not a stock feature that dramatizes a predetermined union, but a vital pact founded upon the will's liberty to balance personal happiness with the desire to seek out another's virtue for its own sake.

To claim that the friendship expressed between the titular heroes heeds classical guidelines or a knightly code of conduct undermines not only the complexity of their choices, but also what constitutes justness. While Aristotle maintains that a perfect friend is someone who acts in the best interest of the other, he also believes that each person ought to love himself most of all since the love given to a friend correlates to one's moral advancement.[44] The difference between Aristotle and Scotus centers upon love's object, and when applied to the text, validates Amiloun's decision to part from his wife and aid Amis. A classical view of *amicitia* struggles to explain why placing the friend before his wife does not devalue the marriage. From a Scotist perspective, however, Amiloun does not disrespect her because the decision is in accord with right reason. It falls within his powers

---

their commitment. See Reuters, *Friendship and Love in the Middle English Metrical Romances* (Frankfurt: Peter Lang, 1991), 53–56.

44 Aristotle, *Nicomachean Ethics* 9.8–9 (1168ba 18 – 1169b 2), trans. Terence Irwin (Indianapolis: Hackett Publishing, 1999), 147–49.

and seeks to better another's situation.[45] Unlike that of Amis, her integrity is neither threatened nor in demand of his immediate attention. Preserving his friend's well-being determines the action. By privileging Amis's dignity, Amiloun shows that choosing rightly can locate its meaning in another's worth without discounting other sources of love. He does not look upon a true friend as an image of himself as Aristotle claims, but upon the distinct value of Amis.[46] Such a view correspondingly indicates a belief in marriage as a sanctified union founded upon individuality and freedom of choice, which allows for separability and pursuit of virtue. Eliciting such an act of the will discloses a type of justice that supersedes marital convention.

The accusation leveled against Amis—lying with Belisaunt and being a traitor—suggests that he sought to denigrate her honor, but he had no such intention. His love is genuine as proven by his commitment to their relationship. Amiloun recognizes this goodness and defends his friend's honor because it satisfies his notion of what is right. His wife, however, does not consider this an acceptable reason. She becomes incensed that her husband elected to pursue such an action. The ensuing argument draws attention to the issue of what defines a righteous act. Notably, neither the Anglo-Norman nor the French romances feature this bedroom dialogue. Its inclusion in the Middle English text emphasizes the magnitude of Amiloun's choice and seeking virtue for its own sake. Moreover, it underlines that his volition is free in the sense of its being an act of self-determination elicited contingently and not deterministically. Amiloun first decries the steward's treachery and then vouches for Amis's worth:

> Y no dede it for non other thing
> Bot to save mi brother fro wo,
> and ich hope, yif ich hadde need,
> His owhen liif to lesse to mede,
> He wald help me also. (ll. 1496–1500)

Amis should not be subjected to misery and condemnation. The quality of his character is not deserving of such treatment. Indeed, his goodness causes Amiloun to believe that if he were similarly mistreated, Amis would readily come to his aid. This attraction to one's moral rectitude mirrors the tenets of the *affectio iustitiae* "because it inclines one to do justice to the objective goodness, the in-

---

45 Scotus writes, "Even as beauty of body is an harmonious blend of all that becomes a body so far as size, color, figure and so on are concerned so the goodness of a moral act is a combination of all that is becoming to it according to right reason" (*Ordinatio* II, d. 40, nn. 2–3 [XIII, 424–27]). **46** Aristotle, *Nicomachean Ethics* 8.11.68: "[t]he excellent person is related to his friend in the same way as he is related to himself, since a friend is another himself."

trinsic value of a thing, regardless of whether it happens to be a good for oneself or not."[47] Amiloun's decision to defend his friend's dignity is so complete that he does not grasp that his wife would not assent to this line of reasoning. His empathy thus fosters a kinship that engenders a heightened sense of self that prioritizes their fellowship.

When he went to fight the steward, Amiloun left Amis in his place. He knew that Amis would never take advantage of the situation. Indeed, Amis placed a sword between himself and Amiloun's wife at night to prevent any sexual trespass, which further attests to his integrity. When the wife learns of this substitution, however, she chastises her husband. Consequently, Amiloun's omission undermines the marital trust. He presumes that she would respect his decision and does not consider that her interests may lie elsewhere. While this oversight initially casts a critical light upon his choice, her reasons for being upset expose the dangers of letting social standards determine the will's acts. Her displeasure does not arise from having a stranger share her bed or having this knowledge kept from her, but from killing a supposedly righteous man: "With wrong and michel unright/ Thou slough ther a gentil knight" (ll. 1492–93). Calling this prurient malcontent "a gentil knight" shows that she cares little for assessing another's true nobility. Unlike her husband and Amis, she does not realize that the steward's actions spring from impure desires. Without considering what motivates him, she deems her husband's actions "ivel" (l. 1494). By relying upon social status to dictate her sense of right and wrong, she is unable to appreciate her husband's sense of justice. While Amiloun could have demonstrated more consideration for his wife's needs, his will vindicates its probity by accurately contrasting Amis's virtue with the steward's vice.

In addition, only this romance exposes the steward's degenerate nature. According to legend, the steward strives to undermine the closeness forged between the friends, but only *Amis and Amiloun* portrays him as an unseemly voyeur. When Amis and Belisaunt consummate their relationship, the steward peeps "in at an hole, was nought to wide" (l. 772). This perversion contrasts with the two friends' integrity. Subsequently, when the steward beseeches Amis to "swereous bothe brotherhed/ And plight we our trewthes to," Amis rebuffs him (ll. 362–63). Asserting his will to differentiate right from wrong parallels Scotus's view that to cherish another's goodness is the noblest act: "someone is first loved honestly, that is primarily because of himself or herself, and only secondarily because such a one returns our love."[48] Being true to another requires more

---

47 Wolter, "Native Freedom," 151; see Scotus, *Ordinatio* II, d. 6, q. 2.
48 Scotus, *Ordinatio* III, d. 27; Wolter, *On the Will*, 429.

than simply loving one's self rightly, it involves seeking out lovability. Rejecting the suspect friendship of a man controlled by salacious wants demonstrates a honed ability to recognize one's interior value.

For Amiloun and his wife, only by striking the proper balance between personal happiness and treasuring the other's virtue could their choices coincide. The wife, however, elects not to heed those inclinations aligned with the affection for justice. As a result, she becomes "wicked and schrewed" (l. 1561). When Amiloun contracts leprosy, she throws him out of the house. Her rejection "brac his hert withouten kniif" (l. 1562). He must now face the consequences of his decision to defend Amis. Diseased and unable to work, he begs throughout the countryside. The effects of the illness strip away his handsomeness, making him unrecognizable. He eventually comes to Amis's castle begging with the one remnant left from their shared childhood, a golden cup. Amiloun had commissioned the fashioning of two cups as a tribute to their friendship before parting from one another: "bothe thai were as liche, ywis/ As was Sir Amiloun and Sir Amis's" (ll. 250–51). Upon seeing the cup, Amis assumes that this leper murdered his friend and casts him into the mud. Not until he observes the scar on Amiloun's shoulder, borne from his duel with the steward, does he recognize his friend. This "grimly wounde" brings to light the fact that the friendship is not based upon material gain or social position, but those individual acts devoted to preserving the other's worth (l. 2144). The wound, an indivisible part of Amiloun's person, signifies the inimitability of both his choice and his person. Consumed with regret for treating his friend so harshly, Amis asks him, "this rewely ded foryif thou me" (l. 2144). His regret triggers the will's *affectio iustitiae* to such a degree that he elects to perform a sacrificial act that not only proves his belief in Amiloun's worth, but also defies all standards of decency.

In a dream, an angel informs Amis that bathing Amiloun in his children's blood will cure the leprosy.[49] The angel then reappears for three more nights to assure him that if Amis does as he instructs, "[h]is brother schuld ben as fair a knight/ As ever he was biforn" (ll. 2213–14). It also appears once in a dream to Amiloun. Susan Crane notes that the "quadruple repetition of the informing dream and its appearance to both Amiloun and Amis make its veracity

---

[49] Bathing in the blood of children to remedy this illness is not an uncommon occurrence in legend. See the legend of St. Silvester, Iacopo da Varazze in *Legenda aurea*, ed. Giovanni Paolo Maggioni, vol. 1 (Florence: Edizioni del Galluzzo, 1998), 110–11; *The Golden Legend*, trans. William Granger Ryan, vol. 1 (Princeton, NJ: Princeton University Press, 1993), 64–65. Also see, Geneviève Pichon, "La Lèpredans *Ami et Amile*," in *Ami et Amile: Une chanson de geste de l'amitié*, ed. Jean Dufournet (Paris: Champion, 1987), 51–66.

unquestionable."[50]Although the heavenly insistence to perform this act removes any doubt of its propriety, the sheer horror of this proposal precludes any thought of carrying it out. The dilemma confronting Amis and the ensuing choice marks the distinctiveness of both the tale and his character. The previous romances bypass the moral implications of the bloodletting. In the Anglo-Norman text, Amys, upon learning from a voice in a dream of this cure, states that whether "true or false, at least I want to test the voice, not ignore it on account of my children."[51] The disregard of their lives springs from a base curiosity rather than any consideration of their innocence. The French version also removes any ethical quandary by having the elder son voluntarily stretch forth his neck to ensure that the cut is a clean one. The Middle English text, however, stresses the difficulty of the decision-making process. Amis must determine which choice is the most just since both his children and Amiloun possess unquestioned virtue. Being confronted with two equally good inclinations, paternal and altruistic, his empathy stresses not only the will's rational potency, but also what distinguishes his notion of what determines a just act.

Amis's prayer proves that he believes in the children's innate goodness, for only the font of love can fully appreciate them: "To God of heven he made him mon/ And preyd with rewely chere" (ll. 2357–58). By acknowledging the maximal good, his will orients itself to the greatest object of love. The prayer, though solemn, reveals a heartfelt belief in the children's innocence. Since this morally rebarbative decision lies far beyond the bounds of human experience, what constitutes a volitional act becomes the central concern. The underlying issue, therefore, lies not in the drawing of blood, but in making a choice that prioritizes Amiloun's worth. This does not denigrate the value of the children, but highlights the free potency of the will to seek out the goodness in others in spite of the suffering involved. Saving Amiloun from destitution illustrates Amis's willingness to do whatever is necessary to honor his friend's worth, which validates Amiloun's earlier claim to his wife that Amis would sacrifice all for his welfare if placed in a similar situation. These sacrifices set them apart not only from one another, but from any other person in the text. The responsibility generated by the *affectio iustitiae* shows that seeking true goodness is the fullest expression of freedom, for it moves one beyond a personally charged impulse. Scotus's innovation focuses upon the complete liberty to select or neglect this rational prompt. Via the two affections, the will ceases being a mechanism for a single

---

50 Susan Crane, *Insular Romance: Politics, Faith, and Culture in Anglo-Norman and Middle English Literature* (Berkeley: University of California Press, 1986), 125.
51 Weiss, *Birth of Romance*, 186.

choice either for or against acceptance. It possesses the power either to embrace or reject its inclinations. The onus or apotheosis for both men, thus, centers upon their volition to cherish each other's value.

Just as Amiloun's affection for Amis prompts him to carry out an act that ultimately causes him great physical and emotional distress, Amis's disposition towards a selfless justice directs him to do the same. While the desire to preserve his own sense of contentment, the *affectio commodi*, may weigh heavily upon him, he freely pursues a higher goal. Although he "wepe with reweful chere," he overcomes his sadness by recounting those qualities which make Amiloun "so kinde and gode" (ll. 2292, 2296). The objective basis of this goodness refers to that aspect of Amiloun's person that can be loved. While the miraculous recovery of the children removes the anguish felt by their death, the reasons underpinning the decision to slay them never diminishes the import of either friend. The will-act provides Amis the opportunity to realize more profoundly than before the wellspring of Amiloun's goodness and how it betters their friendship.

The eponymous heroes' continual decisions to defy the expected course of action underscore the self-determining properties of the will. The complexity of these decisions cannot be glossed over by one-dimensional praise or censure of self-sacrifice. They align with the essential properties of a Scotistic will. Both exalt the primacy of the will's freedom and, in heeding the inclinations towards either personal happiness or justice, create space in which ethics takes place. The devotion each extends to the other surpasses an agreement to satisfy a social need or promote a knightly fellowship. It establishes a binding belief in the interior value of each person. When faced with overwhelming obstacles and authoritative counsel, neither Amis nor Amiloun respond in a predictable manner. The hyperbolic and marvelous mode of romance champions the distinct choices of each friend: Amiloun rejects the angel's warning and Amis sacrifices his children. These dramatic and traumatic acts highlight the unique character of each one. Their choices distinguish this romance from its predecessors and illuminate the will's nobility in privileging the profound goodness in another. Their individuality thus asserts the fundamental optimism about what it means to be human and the need to construct an empathic rapport to lead a fulfilled life.

The Sensory Power of Empathy in *The Second Nun's Tale*

Being the only saint's legend in the *Canterbury Tales* where the protagonist is an actual saint—Cecilia—*The Second Nun's Tale* portrays a religious fervor that surpasses mundane expectations of piety. Upon facing imminent martyrdom, Cecilia's faith prevents her from perspiring when placed in a boiling vat of water and then allows her to survive a battery of sword strokes. She lives for three more days all the while spurting blood from a partially severed head. Such graphic detail is the stuff of hagiographies that fascinate the uninitiated and create a temple of awe for the believer. Yet, despite its extraordinary ending, scholars have historically looked dismissively upon the *Tale*, stating that it is simply about "a saint's life 'Englished,' no more, no less."[52] Recent criticism, however, has praised its portrayal of feminine power in its stand against patriarchal authority[53] and refusal to accept an "increasingly secularized and impersonal Church."[54] While Cecilia's acts of faith have garnered a growing appreciation, the *Tale*'s status as a genuine "work of art" involves more than her extraordinary devotion.[55] It depends upon its striking depiction of how one can maximize one's capacity to know another by choosing to access that person's state of mind. The main characters initiate an empathetic act that puts into praxis their willingness to embrace the truth that Cecilia embodies. Her husband, the Roman statesman, Valerian, and his brother, Tiburce, forgo political loyalties and prioritize their fraternal bond by cultivating their mutual awareness of spiritual goodness.

Although drawn from an analogue found in the *Legenda aurea*, Chaucer's revision recasts the affection between Cecilia and Valerian.[56] In the words of Lynn Staley, the *Tale* presents a "radically new nature of this relationship" that refines Cecilia's abilities as a religious exemplar.[57] The process of proselytizing does not stem from didactic instruction, but from Cecilia attuning herself to her husband's mindset and abetting him to discover what makes their marriage so vital. By virtue of this emphasis upon personal choice, the *Tale*'s accessibility expands beyond Christian listeners to embrace those pilgrims on the trail

---

52 V. A. Kolve, "Chaucer's *Second Nun's Tale* and the Iconography of Saint Cecilia," in *New Perspectives in Chaucer Criticism*, ed. Donald H. Rose (Norman: University of Oklahoma Press, 1981), 139. Even Elizabeth Scala in her current book critiques the "flatness of its narrator and its hermetic independence from the rest of the storytelling" (*The Canterbury Tales: Handbook* [New York: Norton, 2020], 251).

53 Karen Arthur, "Equivocal Subjectivity in Chaucer's *Second Nun's Prologue* and *Tale*," *Chaucer Review* 32 (1998): 217–31.

54 Lynn Staley Johnson, "Chaucer's Tale of the Second Nun and the Strategies of Dissent," *Studies in Philology* 89 (1992): 314–33.

55 Carolyn P. Collette, "A Closer Look at Seinte Cecilia's Special Vision," *Chaucer Review* 10 (1976): 337, 347.

56 For an English translation of Saint Cecilia's story in the *Legenda aurea*, see Jacobus de Voragine, *The Golden Legend*, vol. 2, trans. William Granger Ryan (Princeton, NJ: Princeton University Press, 1993), 318–22.

57 Lynn Staley, "Chaucer and the Postures of Sanctity," in *The Powers of the Holy: Religion, Politics, and Gender in Late Medieval English Culture*, ed. David Aers and Lynn Staley (University Park: Pennsylvania State Press, 1996), 205.

to Canterbury who place personal matters before satisfying patriarchal expectation. As Paul Strohm points out, its inclusion is "adopted in furtherance of the particular kind of tale he has chosen to write rather than as the expression of any particular credo."[58] By privileging an interpersonal dynamic, it advocates the need to gain a more informed awareness of the other person. Elizabeth Robertson maintains that the driving force behind the characters' decisions "indicates that choice is itself a radical act of the will, unmediated and immediate."[59] The will's freedom, she asserts, finds its greatest elucidation in the voluntarism of John Duns Scotus. For him, the will distinguishes itself as a free cause from the intellect and, as such, empowers the individual to initiate an act designed to increase one's appreciation for another's worth, whether personal or spiritual. Being weighted with love for the good, its self-determination allows one to live a life of value. Thus, by striving to enhance their concern for one another, Cecilia and Valerian realize their potential in imitating God's highest expression of love.

The decision to gain a greater knowledge of another—whether spouse or brother—shows how an empathic act can fortify religious conviction. Even though the literary device of *deus ex machina* in the form of an angel's appearance provides empirical proof of Christianity's validity, the action ultimately rests upon the volition to gain a rich understanding of the experiences of the other and grasp each other's belief system. This pursuit involves more than an academic exchange or rigid acceptance of Christianity. It stems from a desire to connect in a meaningful way. Contextually, a healthy dynamic produces a heightened sensitivity to the other's interior worth and, in turn, the need to perfect oneself. Beginning with Cecilia imploring Valerian to appreciate what defines her state of being, the narrative emphasizes how her husband and brother-in-law consider what constitutes the other's drive and determine its compatibility with religious principles. Once grasping the profound connection that his wife shares with the divine, Valerian wants to mirror her virtue and also ensure that his brother acquires a similar level of knowing. This fluid interplay of thought and feeling prompts both men to conform their perspective not simply with Christian tenets, but the resolve underpinning Cecilia's faith. This alignment, however, does not result in losing one's identity, for doing so defeats

---

58 Paul Strohm, *Chaucer's Tale* (New York: Penguin Books, 2014), 81.

59 Elizabeth Robertson, "Apprehending the Divine and Choosing to Believe: Voluntarist Free Will in Chaucer's *Second Nun's Tale*," *Chaucer Review* 46 (2011): 112. The idea of Chaucer implementing Scholastic philosophy in his tales is not an isolated one. Lois Roney maintains that "Chaucer's concern is to bring these scholastic theories of psychology out into everyday life; that is to say, Chaucer takes these theories and makes them both readable and personal" (*Chaucer's Knight's Tale and Theories of Scholastic Psychology*, 39).

the individuating power of choice. Rather, it asserts each one's freedom to embrace this way of life and prize the other's inherent value. Thus, empathy does not center upon heeding religious orthodox practices as much as expressing a selfless interest in the other's well-being. This use of the will perfects not only one's awareness of self and others, but also the potential to access the divine's infinite love for humankind.

Affording the will the power to access, or at least emulate, God's capacity to love fully manifests the philosophical advances of this era. As aforementioned, Scotus prioritizes the will's facility to elicit or provoke an act of love. The will is not bound by the dictates of reason but guided by its two innate affections, the *affectio iustitiae* and the *affectio commodi*. Their interplay underlines the moral complexity of rational desire and establishes a harmony of goodness that empowers the individual with self-control.[60] The *affectio commodi* refers to those acts of self-interest and self-preservation that ensure our happiness. On the surface, this tendency may seem to compromise the ability to be virtuous and attentive to others, but is in fact essential to our well-being. No person, except a sainted human like Saint Cecilia, can or should live a life void of individual pleasure. Rather, the key issue lies in managing these desires so that they do not interfere with the more noble pursuits of this marriage. The *affectio iustitiae* exerts a controlling power, for it inclines the individual to love a thing primarily for what the other is or has in him or herself rather than what it can do for them.[61] In the context of the *Tale*, it directs Valerian and his brother to love God in Himself and not because He can grant them salvation and ecstatic joy.[62] Loving His goodness subverts any tendencies towards jealousy and ambition. By loving justly, they can care for others freely and wholly.[63] As such, Scotus's theory of the will explicates Valerian's insistence to heed his wife's words and decision to strengthen his fraternal understanding.

This process of knowing excludes impulsive responses to another's emotionally charged behavior. Such reactions offer only superficial insight. The mode of consciousness depicted here stems from a rational desire to gain a more informed perception of the other. It forgoes emotional contagion in favor of a mu-

---

60 The phrase "harmony of goodness" is drawn from Mary Beth Ingham's study of the same name. Mary Beth Ingham, *The Harmony of Goodness*, 2nd ed. (St. Bonaventure, NY: Franciscan Institute, 2012).

61 Allan B. Wolter, "Native Freedom," in *The Philosophical Theology of John Duns Scotus*, ed. Marilyn McCord Adams (Ithaca, NY: Cornell University Press, 1990), 151.

62 Scotus, *Ordinatio* III, d. 27, n. 15 (XV, 368).

63 Scotus writes, "Whoever loves perfectly, desires co-lovers for the beloved." See, *Ordinatio* III, d. 28, n. 2 (XV, 378); d. 37, n. 10 (XV, 844).

tual affection that fosters a cognitive assessment of the other's motivations and intentions. It prompts Valerian, Tiburce, and Cecilia to see how the joy generated by the other's religious experience promotes a heightened awareness of why that person perceives the event as significant both in itself and in relation to each of them. Whereas critics like Derek Pearsall believe that there is "little or no human feeling in the *Second Nun's Tale*, and no sense of pain or fear," I contend that the shared insight between Valerian and Tiburce fills them with a joy unaffected by worldly judgment and attuned to the sensual wonder existent in the supernal realm.[64] Their emotive experiences flow directly from their choice to believe in one another which leads them to appreciate what motivates Cecilia, namely embodying the kind of compassion imbued by the divine. Empathy thus conjoins the earthly with the empyrean.

From the beginning of the *Tale*, Valerian must moderate his impulses, for Cecilia informs him on their wedding night that she must remain a virgin because if "ye me touche or love in vileinye,/ He [an angel] right anon wol sleen you with the deede (ll. 156–57).[65] Such an ultimatum flies in the face of typical spousal interaction. Still, she patiently explains that if he respects her body, gets baptized, and expresses "clene love," then God will "shewe to you his joye and his brightnesse" (ll. 159, 161). This brightness will enable him to see the angel who zealously guards Cecilia. Despite this encouragement, Valerian, a pagan, is not pleased with the situation. Deep down, he believes that she is covering up an illicit affair. He threatens that if this supposed angel does not materialize, he "Right with this swerd than wol I slee you bothe" (l. 168). Suspicion and anger color the tenor of his speech. At this moment, the ineffable holds little intrigue. Although he agrees to her conditions, he does so simply to manage his emotions so that frustration does not blind him and cause him to do an unjust act. Given the stunning incredulity of her request, he needs a person of esteemed authority to assuage his concerns. Felicitously, he encounters one. He meets an old man clad in airy white clothes who reads from a book "with lettre of gold" that there is only "Oo Lord, oo faith, oo God withouten mo" (ll. 202, 207). Although the text does not explicitly assign a specific identity to this figure, the august ap-

---

64 Derek Pearsall, *The Canterbury Tales* (London: Routledge, 1985), 255. R. K. Root wonders about the "puzzling" lack of affective piety informing the *Tale* (*The Poetry of Chaucer* [Gloucester, MA: 1957], 277–80). Although Cecilia's austere expression of faith may not manifest itself through a graphic imitation of Christ's suffering, she demonstrates a heartfelt response to Tiburce's conversion: upon hearing him denounce idolatry, "she gan kisse his brest, that herde this,/ And was ful glad he coude trouthe espye" (ll. 290–91).

65 All passages from the tale are taken from *The Norton Chaucer*, ed. David Lawton (New York: W.W. Norton, 2020).

pearance commands Valerian's respect so much so that he responds with fear: "Valerian as deed fil doun for drede/ Whan he hym saugh" (ll. 204–5). This dread shakes him free from these previous worries and allows him to look at the man with open eyes. Whereas Cecilia's world of faith may initially, according to John Hill, exist on its own terms "as a book unopened to our experience and therefore untested on our imagination and intellect," this interaction enables Valerian to recognize the truth of her person.[66] He realizes that practical knowledge of the world does not gift one with the insight necessary to grasp the intrinsic dignity of another. He can now utilize this knowledge to appreciate her saintliness and determine how best to structure their relationship.

Valerian's emphasis upon interpersonal knowledge versus common sense leads him to accept both the old man's words without any debate and then his inexplicable disappearance: "Thanne vanished this olde man, he niste where" (l. 216). Despite absence of a reasonable explanation, he chooses to privilege the logic of love. By directing his will towards its highest end, he strikes the proper balance between Scotus's two moral affections and apprehends the affective and thinking process underlying Cecilia's chastity. Embracing the truth that she represents and that the old man imparts leads him to kneel before Pope Urban: "Pope Urban him cristenede right there" (l. 217). He can now return home confident that their marriage will be a fulfilling one. Indeed, when he finds her with an angel holding a crown of lilies and roses, he knows that their beliefs and feelings are in line with one another.

> This angel hadde of roses and of lilye
> Corones two, the whiche he bar in honde;
> And first to Cecilia, as I understonde,
> He yaf that oon, and after gan he take
> That oother to Valerian, hir make. (ll. 220–24)

As a manifestation of divine love, the flowers signify a conduit between the two realms as well as between Cecilia and Valerian. The sensory stimuli both affirm and heighten the affinity between them. It adds depth and purpose to their commitment which extends beyond that conventionally attributed to a marriage. They become aspirants of a virtuous ideal who seek to know each other's goodness as fully as possible. Poetically divinized, this ideal becomes realized by apprehending the diversity of the other's being and experiencing the joy drawn from the choices defining their relationship. By taking the crown of flowers

---

66 John Hill, *Chaucerian Belief: The Poetics of Reverence and Delight* (New Haven, CT: Yale University Press, 1991), 53.

from the angel, Valerian and Cecilia display an individuality which epitomizes a free will to lead a life interconnected with the other. Their *affectio iustitiae* reaches its fruition in seeking those goods worthy of love for themselves alone, not for self-preservation.[67] The sublimity of their shared insight highlights empathy's power to overcome social barriers, and sustaining its force underscores the central import of volition.

Valerian validates his worth by apprehending the mental and emotional states of his wife and then using this knowledge to fortify his devotion to her person. It transforms the abstract element of empathy into an actual one. Yet, on its own, empathy does not operate as a moral principle; it is a psychological experience. This experience and its potential altruism, however, can prove instrumental to moral action. It encourages a willingness to open oneself up to the other. The internal joy generated by this moment nurtures their underlying goodness. Though a tempered frustration and skepticism may initiate the action, striving to know what comprises Cecilia's belief system motivates Valerian to learn even more about her and advance their interpersonal awareness. The issue then is not whether or not empathy is a virtuous act, but how it fosters a positive rapport.[68] Martin Hoffman writes, "Empathy activates moral principles and, either directly or through these principles, influences moral judgment and reasoning."[69] Of course, gaining insight into another's state of mind does not guarantee that the observer will elect to use it in a constructive way.[70] The choice to do so thus establishes a conviction in the dignity of being human. Although each employs a distinct method of grasping the other's perspective, Valerian's and Cecilia's efforts demonstrate the freedom to pursue this course of action and produce a finely tuned intimacy.[71]

---

67 Scotus, *Ordinatio* II, d. 6, q. 2.

68 For a detailed account of how empathy lends itself to being a virtuous act, see Julinna C. Oxley, *The Moral Dimensions of Empathy* (New York: Palgrave, 2011). Although it cannot serve as a criterion of morally good action, she asserts that empathy plays a supporting role in making a moral decision (11). On a related note, Michael Slote argues that "empathy plays a crucial enabling role in the development of genuinely altruistic concern or caring for others" (*The Ethics of Care and Empathy* [New York: Routledge, 2007], 13); also see, Arne Johan Vetlesen, *Perception, Empathy, and Judgment* (University Park: Pennsylvania State University Press, 2000).

69 Hoffman, *Empathy and Moral Development*, 247.

70 Heather Battaly notes that just because one is motivated to attain truth, "they need not be motivated to attain truth because it is good . . . they may have ulterior ends that are epistemically bad" (300). See "Is Empathy a Virtue?," in *Empathy: Philosophical and Psychological Perspectives*, ed. Amy Coplan and Peter Goldie (Oxford: Oxford University Press, 2011).

71 For Descartes, the will, as subject of moral virtues, rejoices in its own movement which is determining the proper action to take. The passions "dispose the soul to will the things nature

Accepting the roses and lilies assures Valerian that his decision to dedicate himself to his wife has led to the highest good possible. He comes to "knowe the trouthe" (l. 238). Whereas Cecilia's request initially made it nearly impossible for him to relate to her, the flowers confirm that he has successfully matched her faith-inspired perceptions. He can now attend to those matters that capture his wife's interest, which in turn engenders an understanding that had been previously lacking. By defying the customs governing Roman society, he not only enriches his marriage, but also shows that the will's affection for justice guides right reason to maintain one's dignity.[72] Moreover, the sensual and supernal tangibility of the roses and lilies provides another means to access Cecilia's thoughts. They show that the physical can convey abstract truths. In other words, Valerian's mental powers can utilize this olfactory evidence to ascertain

---

tells us are useful and to persist in this volition" (*The Passions of the Soul*, trans. Stephen H. Voss [Indianapolis: Hackett Publishing, 1989], 51–52). The knowledge that informs this choice merely adds to the joy. By allowing passions in the will, Descartes, as Deborah Brown notes, adopts the Scotist view that emotions are not mere physiological processes ("The Rationality of Cartesian Passions," in *Emotions and Choice from Boethius to Descartes*, ed. Henrik Lagerlaund and Mikko Yrjönsuuri [Dordrecht: Kluwer Academic Publishers, 2002], 265–74). Neither relegates emotions to the secondary strata in the psychology of the mind. Both identify the will as the principle power leading to human perfection and locate emotions as playing an integral role in higher cognitive tasks about acting correctly.

A familiarity originating from similar natures or common experiences can increase their ardor and devotion. It directs the focus from one's self to the other. In his treatise, *The Passions of the Mind in General* (1604), Thomas Wright writes that "if thou wilt please thy master or friend, thou must apparel thyself in his affections . . . ; and as this means fostereth flattery if it be abused, so it nourisheth charity if it be well used" (*The Passions of the Mind in General*, 2nd ed. 1604, ed. W. W. Newbold [New York, 1986], 160). Selflessly matching another's expressions reveals a desire to know more about the other both emotionally and experientially, which implicitly accentuates each one's distinctiveness. While the affections displayed are determined by external stimuli, the felt emotion is drawn from within and extends towards the other person.

If a cultivated familiarity is not enough to establish or strengthen an intimate bond, then an even more pronounced commonality can be sought, namely a mimetic quality. Mirroring another's fervor creates a tendency to evoke the same kinds of emotions. Whether prompted by a beloved's or a lover's pleas, a strong emotive presence enlivens the other's feelings to such a degree that they begin to enact similar intonations and body language. Wright adds, "To imprint a passion in another, it is requisite it first be stamped in our hearts; for through our voices, eyes and gestures, the world will pierce and thoroughly perceive how we are affected" (212).

72 "[T]he affection for justice, which is the first checkrein on the affection for the beneficial, inasmuch as we need not actually seek that toward which the latter affection (*affctio commodi*) inclines us, nor must we seek it above all else—this affection for what is just, I say, is the liberty innate to the will" (Scotus, *Ordinatio* II, d. 6, q. 2, trans. Allan B. Wolter, *On the Will*, 298–99).

his wife's state of mind and affirm the divine's presence. Katherine Little addresses how the text asserts the integral need for an empirical reality:

> The description of the garlands, which have, of course, a symbolic meaning, emphasizes their "palpability," as the verbs of bearing, giving, and taking make clear. Indeed, Chaucer seems to have ensured that the garlands are understood as material by omitting the angel's phrase in the source, "et hoc vobis signum erit" [and this will be a sign to you].[73]

While the flowers' materiality ensures that Valerian has direct access to heavenly interaction, the angel's act of handing them to the couple is a distinctly human gesture, signifying the insistence that these two planes of knowing interlard with one another. In addition, the giving of flowers commonly expresses a mutual affection between the two people and their capacity to reciprocate this attentiveness. He thus comes to see that an awareness of self in relation to another depends on recognizing what is embodied and embedded in the world.

Although Valerian may not comprehend the full range of knowledge emanating from the angel's celestial source, the interaction extols the choice to seek a higher truth and relate to another more closely. No longer do his concerns center upon determining whether or not his wife is lying, but deepening his sensitivity to her inclinations and aspirations. Sherry Reames, however, believes that the emphasis on supernatural power is "at the expense of human understanding and choice," which causes "theological pessimism [about] the value of human nature and earthly experience."[74] While her study focuses upon the doctrinal teaching of the *Tale*'s proselytes, I maintain that conversion rests as much upon the will as heavenly intervention. Following Elizabeth Robertson's line of reasoning, I assert that the *Tale*'s dénouement revolves around "the radical and ineffable motions of the will that underlie not only the choice to believe but any choice."[75] Honoring his wife's plea and embracing what the crown of roses and lilies signifies shows that the will is designed to seek a good that is not dependent on public approval or other external force. In other words, the

---

73 Katherine Little, "Images, Texts, and Exegetics in Chaucer's *Second Nun's Tale*," *Journal of Medieval and Early Modern Studies* 36 (2006): 119.
74 Sherry L. Reames, "The Cecilia Legend as Chaucer Inherited and Retold It: The Disappearance of an Augustinian Ideal," *Speculum* 55 (1980): 39, 40. Her study rests upon Chaucer's revision of his source material as it pertains to the doctrinal teaching of the *Tale*'s converts. Her claim that reason's role becomes deemphasized does not actually subvert my claim. My study stresses that the human will rather than reason is the primary factor in proselytizing drama of Valerian and his brother, Tiburce.
75 Robertson, "Apprehending the Divine," 111.

will, as stated by Scotus, acts with, but is not determined by, knowledge.[76] By privileging her person above political duty, Valerian's selflessness displays his free will to devote himself to her.

That the garlands have been brought "fro Paradise" symbolizes an innate ability to pursue a moral life that transcends reason's purview, for the angel says no one will ever be able to see him unless he "be chast and hate vileinye" (ll. 227, 231). As such, Cecilia and Valerian's marital understanding now reflects the highest good in the most perfect manner, namely to align themselves as fully as possible with the divine. Experiencing first-hand this supernal moment creates an untenable bond with Cecilia's saintliness. Via this level of affective knowing, Valerian apprehends the value not only of cultivating spiritually imbued relationships, but also of helping others to realize the bounty of this good. Thus, when the angel grants him a wish, Valerian immediately replies that he has a brother whom he would also like to be baptized into this great truth:

> "I have a brother," quod Valerian tho,
> "That in this world I love no man so.
> I pray you that my brother may han grace
> To knowe the trouthe—as I do—in this place." (ll. 235–38)

Just as in his marriage, the choice to increase his affinity with a loved one drives him onward. Fulfillment does not stem from doctrinal teachings but from experiencing the joy central to sharing this faith with another. The prime mover is the will to realize their potential as fellow Christians. Scotus observes, "the will and the disposition of love concur in eliciting the act of love; here, the will is the first and principal cause with respect to its act, and love is the second and less principal cause."[77] Valerian's wish to connect with his brother shows that the will is constituted to love another selflessly. In this instance, conforming one's perspective with another prompts both to do what is just. Even though the stimulus for this pursuit differs, their result links them in a joint enterprise of love. Scotus observes that one can have a basic love of another in the sense that I will that he attain God in heaven without necessarily willing that he heed exactly what I do in regard to Christian teachings.[78] In other words, the empathy between them preserves each one's individuality, for their fraternal understanding may coincide in Christian belief, but the manner in which they arrive at and express

---

76 Scotus, *Questions on the Metaphysics* IX, q. 15, n. 7, p. 611; Wolter, *On the Will*, 158.

77 John Duns Scotus, *Lectura* I, d. 17, in *Duns Scotus on Divine Love*, ed. A. Vos et al. (Burlington, VT: Ashgate, 2003), 95.

78 Scotus, *Ordinatio* III, d. 28.

this affection distinguishes their person. It establishes a distinct reciprocity of care.

No sooner does Valerian state his wish than Tiburce comes into the room. The angel once again relies upon sensory sensation to initiate the proselytizing process. Neither words nor sight stimulate Tiburce's awareness of something greater than that which can be conceived. Fragrance sparks this epiphany.

> And whan that he the savour undernom,
> Which that the roses and the lilies caste,
> Withinne his herte he gan to wondre faste. (ll. 243–45)

Although he cannot see the flowers, the sweet smell emphasizes their reality. That it signifies love and purity describes the kind of character who can appreciate their meaning. He must be attuned both to the divine's presence in this world and actively seek His goodness in others. Only by recognizing the manifest connection between humanity and the divine can Tiburce hope to attain a full awareness of his true spiritual self. Consequently, the sensory response to these paradisiacal flowers causes him to look to his heart and ponder what he knows. The ensuing wonderment awakens him to the infinite power of divine love. Robertson considers its terminological import: "The *MED* definition of *wondren* as 'to be struck with awe or amazement' or 'to feel wonder' associates the verb with an experience of the affect rather than of the intellect. . . . Wondering is associated with a state of feeling that inspires desire; smelling the roses then activates the will rather than reason."[79] Their sensory impact, as it represents a condition of heaven, draws attention to Tiburce's decision to embrace the faith.[80] It adds momentum to the affection that he shares with his brother and parallels Valerian's response, particularly in regard to his concern for his brother's spiritual welfare.

The simultaneity of representing an empirical yet invisible entity, floral scent establishes the context for encountering, knowing, and living in relationship with the divine. Susan Harvey, in her masterful study of olfactory rhetoric in

---

[79] Robertson, "Apprehending the Divine," 116. Her study proceeds to recount the medieval treatises on the senses, which includes the writings of William of St. Thierry and Robert Grosseteste, who praises the senses, "recognizing that these were the channels, given by God, by which one could discover good and conduct oneself well" (117).

[80] Clifford Davidson explores how the fragrance of flowers is implied in the depictions of heaven as a garden, particularly in the Pentecost ceremony in which wafers and flowers were dropped on the congregation from the roof during the singing of the hymn *Veni Creator Spiritus*" (111). See Davidson, "Heaven's Fragrance," in *The Iconography of Heaven*, ed. Clifford Davidson (Kalamazoo, MI: Medieval Institute Publications, 1994).

early Christianity, notes that sensory experiences exuded theological implications for the Christian thinker who sought to use natural elements to illuminate biblical teachings.[81] Ambrose's imagery expounds upon Christ's good works and illustrates the tradition underpinning Chaucer's construction: "Christ is the flower of Mary, who sprouted forth from a virginal womb to spread the good odor of faith throughout the whole world, as he himself said: 'I am the flower of the field, and the lily of the valley.' (Song 2:1)."[82] Just as the lily of the valley's fragrance permeates the world, calling to mind the sweetness of God's love for humankind, it sparks both Valerian's and Tiburce's admiration for God's creative artistry and the beauty in the reality around them. Recognizing their interconnection as aspirants strengthens their bond as they perfect themselves by loving God, striving to become artists of human living. The garland's smell silently disperses throughout their surroundings and savoring their odor causes a transformative effect within Tiburce:

> The savour myghte in me no depper go,
> The sweete smel that in myn herte I fynde
> Hath chaunged me al in another kinde." (ll. 250–52)

The phrases "I fynde" and "change me" underline how this moment defines his person. This experience alters his very "kinde," signifying that much more is involved than simply prompting a cognitive response. His entire being—affective, intellective, and conative—responds to the flowers' power and, in doing so, shows that humanness plays an integral role in cultivating a spiritual connection. This inextricable tie between the physical and metaphysical affirms their capacity to realize another's motivation as well as the presence of a higher level of being. While some believe that the *Tale* extols metaphysical properties above physical ones, the continual reliance upon the senses and the happiness produced by the garland's "sweet smel" proves the import of each one's person

---

81 Susan Harvey, *Scenting Salvation: Ancient Christianity and the Olfactory Imagination* (Berkeley: University of California Press, 2006), 122. She examines how olfactory rhetoric plays an integral role for the early Christian thinker in articulating the connection between the two realms: "Invisible, silent, yet tangibly felt, smells were acutely effective in conveying divine presence or absence, demonic activity, or moral condition. Uncontainable, smells were transgressive in moving, crossing human and divine domains as intersecting paths of interaction" (7).

82 Ambrose, *The Holy Spirit* 1.8.95, in *Saint Ambrose, Theological and Dogmatic Works*, trans. Roy J. Deferrari (Washington, DC: Catholic University of America Press, 1963), 70.

and, implicitly, their freedom to choose.[83] Scotus, as opposed to his predecessors, avers that such feelings occur in the will.[84] Despite the prevailing view that emotions preclude direct choice of whether or not they can occur, Scotus explains that the *affectio iustitiae* and *affectio commodi* generate inclinations that produce emotions or passions. Although the will cannot control our passions, for it cannot cause one to stop being sad or happy just by willing it, it is directly affected by that action being willed. Hence, if that choice produces a specific emotive response, then the causal chain shows that this response operates through the will, even if only indirectly.[85] Being moved by the olfactory senses thus attests to Valerian's and Tiburce's freedom to accept the love underlying the angel's kindheartedness. They each decide that this interaction conveys a mystical significance in conjunction with the physical one that compels them "to consider the symbolic meaning imbued in each gesture or object."[86]

Savoring the flowers' fragrance marks the goodness comprising each brother's individual person as well as their fraternal bond, but its effect upon Tiburce's "hert" is distinct, for it affects his "kinde." This emphasis neither negates nor supersedes Valerian's efforts. Rather, it demonstrates that each person has their own relation with the divine. The mineness of this moment establishes

---

83 See Collette, "A Closer Look at Seinte Cecilia's Special Vision," 337–49. She avers that the saint's spiritual insight rather than fallible physical sight, empowers her to know that "mighty God is in his hevenes hye" (l. 508).

84 Aquinas holds that a passion involves not just the reception of a quality, but also the removal of the opposite quality; and since there must be material subject that persists through the loss of an accidental quality and the reception of another, passions can occur only in material subjects. They therefore can occur in the soul only accidentally, that is, insofar as it is joined to a body that is able to undergo material change (*ST* I–II, 22.1). "Since the will is a purely immaterial power: its acts do not necessarily involve a change in any bodily organ and so no material change is required for it to have an act of willing" (Ian Drummond, "John Duns Scotus on the Passions of the Will," in *Emotion and Cognitive Life in Medieval and Early Modern Philosophy*, ed. Martin Pickavé and Lisa Shapiro [Oxford: Oxford University Press, 2012], 55).

85 Scotus writes that "the will is not necessitated absolutely by the object; however, among those things that are shown to it, there can be a necessity of the consequence, as in 'if I am willing, I am willing.' And thus if there is a nolition of some object and that nilled object comes about, it seems to follow necessarily by a necessity of the consequence that sadness can come to be in the will" (*Ordinatio* III, d. 15, n. 49, V. 9, 500). As Drummond points out, "The will never loses its essential freedom to determine itself, but when it is in fact willing or nilling some object, it is not further determinable, and so at that moment it is not formally free" ("John Duns Scotus on the Passions of the Will," 66).

86 David Raybin, "Chaucer's Creation and Recreation of the *Lyf of Seynt Cecilia*," *Chaucer Review* 32 (1997): 197. Raybin makes this comment in relation to the reader's response to these mystical events. Despite this different perspective, his core argument applies equally well to characterize the character's response to these roses and lilies.

the uniqueness of this first-person experience. However, since Valerian wants his brother to know this truth, this moment enables him to become more attuned to Tiburce's present mindedness. Upon discussing their shared olfactory experience, Valerian points out to his "leve brother deere" that they can now "Bileve aright and knowen verray trouthe" (ll. 257, 259). This experience surpasses mere sentiment or inferential mindreading (l. 264). It allows access into each other's thoughts and feelings. They use this insight to put into praxis an altruism that looks beyond personal concerns. Exercising an other-centeredness does not diminish their faith, but increases its intensity so that it inspires each to pursue the same goal. As a result, Cecilia can "witnesse Tiburces and Valerians shrifte" (l. 277).

Upon establishing an affective mutuality, Valerian discusses how this understanding brings to light a higher truth, one which refines their bond. They are not simply brothers who care for each other's well-being, but realize the need to live a life in accord with Christian principles. This knowledge discloses a new reality that elevates their human connection to another dimension of being. No longer do social hierarchies of order structure their notion of right and wrong. Such perceptions are illusory when compared to appreciating each other's worth in light of a greater good.

> "In dremes," quod Valerian, "han we be
> Unto this time, brother myn, ywis,
> But now at erst in trouthe oure dwelling is" (ll. 262–64)

The collective pronoun "we" underlines an authentic fellow-feeling that has freed the other from transient customs and expectations and accepts their innate dignity. This realization supplants their ties to this world. Their concept of existence accordingly expands to consider the magnitude of God's eternal love. Eileen Jankowski writes, "heavenly 'tyme' is the only reality and truth one can strive to experience. Until this moment when both brothers recognize, accept, and act upon the truth that has been revealed to them, they have only been imagining life."[87] Time as a social construct fails to impede the understanding exchanged between them. The resultant knowledge flourishes through an empathy that produces a value-affirming and value-revealing event, and these events can be facilitated through either human or seraphic means. The ontological difference between a man and an angel as well as self and other, however, prevents a complete grasp of the other's being. The endeavor to perfect this knowing

---

[87] Eileen S. Jankowski, "Chaucer's 'Second Nun's Tale' and the Apocalyptic Imagination," *Chaucer Review* 36 (2001): 137.

thus continues perpetually. Still, its infiniteness does not deter either brother, for the text shows that silences, particularly when accentuated with the bestowal of flowers, indicate a shared understanding of not only what the flowers signify, but also what the empathizer knows about the other person. The space between them affirms an intellective and affective reciprocity. Silence or speech, movement or stillness, experiencing a similar event empowers each brother to appreciate the other as a person who has distinct desires and beliefs. The brothers' interplay produces a conscious awareness of love's movement as it explores the depth of the other's individuality and culminates in the absolute reality of God.

Savoring the fragrance and recognizing the limits of human constructs of reality discloses a shared understanding that does not seek to merge the two brothers' identities or impose one upon the other, but establishes their distinctiveness both as people and as God's beloveds. Their empathy employs a conscious approach to the other from a specifically defined position—compassion for the other brother's spiritual welfare—so that each enjoys a view which is inaccessible to the other. Despite its singular focus, however, the empathy does not envelope the other's perspective, for a first-person acquaintance of one's own mind can never be mirrored with precise exactitude. Rather, the brothers' efforts unveil an individuality that transcends bodily and behavioral expressions. Embracing this realization highlights their belief in their own and the other's quality of being. Cecilia validates this virtue when she greets Tiburce and "kisse his brest" (l. 290); she is "ful glad he coude trouthe espye" (l. 291). Her display of affection shows the integral role that humanness plays in cultivating a higher state of being. Her kiss signifies that Tiburce's desires now align with hers. She proudly declares, "This day I take thee for myn allye" (l. 292). Referring to him as an ally shows that she takes an active stance in accepting his independence to renounce idolatry and willingness to immerse himself in a Christian truth. No longer does the past control his future. He now enjoys an existence that is not determined upon social expectation. His will pursues a good that is not necessitated by any external force, but which is realized according to self-determination. His pursuit of a just life prompts him to assess the value of his sister-in-law's counsel. Only by giving oneself up to God's charity can he hope to attain a meaningful relation with another person.

The multidimensional elements of empathy serve as a keen hermeneutic in explicating the affective and cognitive affinity between these characters. It adds depth and purpose to their efforts to better their relationship. The joy felt by all three of them transcends a mere physical satisfaction; it attests to a profound understanding of each one's personal value. By rejecting the depersonalizing stereotype attributed to the emotions expressed, these characters assert an individuality which epitomizes free choice and desire to lead a life founded upon love or, at least, a belief in love's possibility. Whether described as a fraternal friendship or kinship via similar experiential knowledge, their bond springs from the conscious decision to express a genuine ardor in both the corporeal and the spiritual realm.

As attested to by the brothers' savoring the lily's fragrance and by Cecilia's kiss, bodily acts confirm the value of being human. Sensory responses and gestures allow the empathizer to coordinate his or her perspective with the other and increase the intelligibility of the other's feelings. These sensations, in the words of cognitive scientist Frédérique de Vignemont, provide an "affective valence" about the body and its immediate surroundings, which enable each one to ascertain the other's personal commitment.[88] Although an emotionally charged event or passion may incite this act, each one appreciates the other's personal and spiritual motivations. Expressive phenomena give Cecelia and the brothers the power to cultivate a shared conviction in Christian tenets. Maurice Merleau-Ponty explains how affections such as theirs never hide their meaning from one who actively strives to understand another:

> We must reject the prejudice which makes "inner realities" out of love, hate or anger, leaving them accessible to one single witness: the person who feels them. Anger, shame, hate and love are not psychic facts hidden at the bottom of another's consciousness: they are types of behavior or styles of conduct which are visible from the outside. They exist on this face or in those gestures, not hidden behind them.[89]

Whether or not Cecilia, Valerian, or Tiburce choose to conduct a detailed study or simply use common sense to discern the other's actions, physical gestures make the thoughts and beliefs transparent.

Whereas some critics negate the value of the body in the *Tale*, claiming that Cecilia "represents one extreme of medieval spirituality in her eagerness to shed her body and go to heaven," they fixate only upon one aspect of the story.[90] While her martyrdom supports this view, such a narrow focus negates the critical

---

88 De Vignemont, *Mind the Body*, 186.

89 Maurice Merleau-Ponty, *Le visible et l'invisible* (Paris: Tel Gallimard, 1964); *The Visible and the Invisible*, trans. A. Lingis (Evanston, IL: Northwestern University Press, 1968), 52–53.

90 C. David Benson, "Statues, Bodies, and Souls: St. Cecilia and Some Medieval Attitudes toward Ancient Rome," in *Medieval Women and Their Objects*, ed. Jenny Adams and Nancy Mason Bradbury (Ann Arbor: University of Michigan Press, 2016), 268. Benson continues to write, "Chaucer's 'Second Nun's Tale,' expresses little regard for the preservation of Cecilia's body, either before or after death" (279). While he presents this view to contrast it with the contemporary works of art portraying her, such as Carlo Maderno's *The Martyrdom of Saint Cecilia*, such a position glosses over the emotional value of Cecilia as a woman embracing her brother-in-law and rejoicing in her husband's care.

import of her efforts to know her husband and his brother on a more enlightened level. Refining this interpersonal knowledge necessarily involves a selflessness which mirrors the Christian principles of compassion. Moreover, it requires her to maximize her body's predesigned import, namely expressing its capacity for charity. Upon kissing Tiburce, she becomes a "blisful faire maide deere" (l. 293). Her bliss not only displays a keen affection for Tiburce's and Valerian's righteous beliefs, but also testifies to her joy at succeeding in strengthening this bond.[91] Being a "faire maide" shows that her happiness depends upon all of them rejoicing in the divine's goodness. Their motivation to embrace Christianity rewards them with love for each other, oneself, and God. Though the world offers moments of love and care, its finiteness inevitably succumbs to sadness and loss. Their attention, on the other hand, prioritizes the vertical gaze, utilizing the bounty of these human connections to supplement their religious aspirations. Empathy thus links them with an overpowering joy that stands in contradistinction to those bound to this world and its history.

Still, simply feeling similar emotions proffers no assurance that one will strive to promote a healthy rapport, much less a virtuous one. Consider the situation of someone suffering from a terminal disease. One may feel the pangs of sorrow, but refuse to immerse themself in that experience. Perhaps, the pain is too great because they have already lost someone close to them from that illness. According to Heather Battaly, an empathic person "need not aim at the apparent good."[92] Thus the choices of Valerian, Tiburce, and Cecilia to realize how and why their similar responses help create a meaningful bond. The bond's epistemic value enables them to recognize the value of the other for who he or she is rather than for what he or she can do for them. Exercising their affection for justice leads them to love God wholeheartedly, irrespective of the fact that he loves them in return or that his love causes supreme joy.[93] They respond positively to what the other experiences not simply because they believe in that person, but in their capacity to do what is right. Ulterior motives do not govern their choice. Empathy transforms their action from being a dispassionate, familial

---

91 Moments where emotions determine the action and resolution of complex moral dilemmas oppose traditional readings of the text that become mired in interpreting the tale as posing an "intellectual change." Rather, the issue lies in its being a human tale, comprising all facets of a person's powers. See James Dean, "Dismantling the Canterbury Book," *PMLA* 100 (1984): 749.
92 Battaly, "Is Empathy a Virtue?," 295. She maintains that empathy is neither a moral nor an intellectual virtue. It would be virtuous only if it is a voluntary ability rather than an automatic capacity.
93 Scotus maintains that the human will has the inherent ability to love God in this way. See *Ordinatio* III, d. 27, n. 15 (XV, 368).

duty to an intimate desire to better their awareness of self and other, which illustrates the veracity of Scotus's theory:

> To want an act to be perfect so that by means of it one may better love some object for its own sake, is something that stems from the affection for justice. And so the good could have wanted happiness so that by having it, they could more perfectly love the supreme good.[94]

To attain this happiness, they must cultivate that goodness in each other, for the reality of God's love lies in the spiritual integrity of that person.

In defense of this integrity, Valerian vows that he and Tiburce must forgo idolatry and confess their sins. His commitment to God displays the greatest expression of freedom because love can never be forced. This volition, which has already manifested itself in the decision to trust his wife and proselytize his brother, fosters an attentive familiarity whose intensity attests to more than a fundamental disposition to love. It underlies a consciousness of the other's capacity to produce this response. By itself, a disposition does not necessarily mean that one will put it into praxis. It requires the movement of the will to direct one towards this end.[95] Both the disposition and the will's movement, however, are essential in cultivating a heightened awareness of one another. When Tiburce asks Valerian where he should be baptized, Valerian replies that he should journey to Pope Urban and then offers to take him there. Their interplay shows how each exercises his free will to recognize the other's value as a vital, caring self. This charity allows each one to acquire an acute insight into the other's thoughts and cultivate a shared perspective. Tiburce appreciates his brother's effort; he "thinketh that it were a wonder dede" (l. 308). The decision to receive this sacrament focuses his love as he now becomes "Parfit in his lerninge, Goddes knight" (l. 353). Their fraternal charity achieves its highest fruition when directed towards divine goodness. It is a reflective act that demonstrates a willingness to ponder its expansiveness. Scotus encapsulates this idea when he writes, "If I love God perfectly, however, I want him to be loved by all who are capable of loving him in an appropriate way, and whose love is pleasing to

---

94 Scotus, *Ordinatio* II, d. 6, q. 2, n. 12 (XII, 356).

95 Scotus writes, "The will, however, is freely indeterminate, whereas love is negatively indeterminate (because it can be active or not active). Just like the will is first in causing, it must be determined first according to its causality. For the first cause must be determined to act prior to the second cause. Hence love does not determine the will to act in virtue of an activity which competes with the will, but the will determines itself in virtue of its freedom. . . . Nevertheless, the will is determined in itself structurally prior to the acting of love" (99). See Scotus, *Lectura* I, d. 17, in Vos et al., *Duns Scotus on Divine Love*.

him."[96] These empathetic expressions direct the brothers to share in experiences that elevate their appreciation of both their own person and God's creative bounty.

The motivation is not a monistic one, but a desire to grasp the other's well-being. This dual perspective both individuates and binds the brothers. The process is not one of abstraction, but is grounded upon an emotional reality that affirms a direct correspondence between them. The decisions extol their asymmetry. Neither becomes subsumed by affection to the point of forgoing a sense of self. Each exercises the requisite mental flexibility in modulating the proper balance between emotion and cognition to refine their perception of the other's spiritual state of being. Grasping another's point of view is, as Jean Decety writes, "an effortful and controlled process."[97] Empathy thus involves a direct perceptual relation with the other that both recognizes their subjectivity and remains true to one's emotional self.[98] Via these efforts, each learns as much as possible about the other's belief system, which enables them to construct a bond that can bridge the earthly with the empyrean.

Attaining this level of awareness enables Tiburce to see the angel as a real, living thing: "That every day he saugh in time and space/ The angel of God" (ll. 355–56). Here, the concept of time returns to the empirical world, a world which can reassure his faculties of knowing that what he sees exists within this dimension. It validates his expressions of charity, and the reciprocity with Valerian and Cecilia enables them to embolden each other's faith. Their rapport involves far more than "direct and theoretically unmediated acquaintance."[99] Being attuned to another's mental states—even those of a celestial being—illustrate the transcendent power of empathy. Whether receiving a bouquet of flowers or "every manere boone/ That he God axed, it was sped ful soone," Tiburce sees that

---

96 Scotus, *Ordinatio* III, d. 28. Translation in Vos et al., *Duns Scotus on Divine Love*, 53.

97 Jean Decety and P. L. Jackson, "The Functional Architecture of Human Empathy," *Behavioral and Cognitive Neuroscience Reviews* (2004), 84. They add, "Empathy . . . necessitates some level of emotion regulation to manage and optimize intersubjective transactions between self and other. Indeed, the emotional state generated by the perception of the other's state or situation needs regulation and control for the experience of empathy. Without such control, the mere activation of the shared representation, including the associated autonomic and somatic responses, would lead to emotional contagion or emotional distress" (87).

98 See Dermot Moran, "Intercorporeality and Intersubjectivity: A Phenomenological Exploration of Embodiment," in *Embodiment, Enaction, and Culture: Investigating the Constitution of the Shared World*, ed. Christoph Durt, Thomas Fuchs, and Christian Tewes (Cambridge, MA: MIT Press, 2017), 32.

99 See Pierre Jacob, "The Direct-Perception Model of Empathy: A Critique," *Review of Philosophy and Psychology* (2011): 538.

the angel's gifts are intended to fortify his faith in God and belief in Valerian (ll. 356–57). In this instance, striving to understand another's intentions and purposes engenders an awareness of self and the other that culminates in advancing his spiritual state. The love that binds him to Valerian also binds him to God. It is the optimal expression of empathy and by exercising the *affectio iustitiae*, both of them as well as Cecilia can refine their love most fully. What is true of one is also true of the other, namely that they can both see the angel.

The fullness of their affection for one another, however, does not remove the disquiet that Tiburce experiences when facing imminent martyrdom for seeking that which "is yhid in hevene prively" (l. 317). In spite of placing his faith in God, he cannot bury or repress his dread of being "ybrend in this world" (l. 318). His belief system does not dismiss what he feels as a human, nor should it. His humanness has been integral in solidifying his conviction in the divine's goodness and its presence in others. These bodily concerns merely distinguish his state of mind from his sister-in-law's. Whereas distress typically prompts others to sympathize in an attempt to help alleviate that person's fears, Cecilia's spiritual advancement elevates her above these matters. Her state of being flourishes on a plane beyond this world, which accounts for why she does not need a physical stimulus to comprehend Christianity's veritable presence. As stated in the Prologue, the etymological origin of her name as "hevenes lilye" underscores "her grete light/ Of sapience, and for hir thewes clere" (ll. 87, 100–101). Her focus rests upon the religious well-being of those around her. As such, her connection with Tiburce delves deeper than succumbing to an emotional reaction. Rather, she utilizes her knowledge of their shared faith by reminding him that "ther is bettre lif in other place,/ That never shal be lost, ne drede thee noght" (ll. 323–24). The promise of salvation assures him that whatever harm befalls him in this world, its pain is finite. In effect, she urges him to cultivate a more expansive awareness of what links all three of them.

The crux of her solace stems from their familial relation—"myn owene deere brother" (l. 321). Upon asserting her commitment to him as someone whom she cherishes, she establishes that her aid is not mere didacticism, but designed to strengthen their intimacy. It empowers her to draw closer to his interior worth. Cecilia proceeds to explain the Trinitarian theology behind the *Tale*'s soteriology and its surety that "other lif ther men may wone" (l. 332). Moreover, for a *Tale* constructed upon minimalist dialogue, her extended discourse, which consists of seventeen explicit lines of instruction and then a general reference to her being "ful bisily to preche" corroborates her dedication to ensure that Tiburce's intentions parallel hers (l. 342). While she epitomizes an unwavering avowal of Christian principles, which had long ago provided her direct access to an angel, her brother-in-law's conversion is fresh and still susceptible to earthly anxieties. She keenly assesses the context of the situation and adapts her perception of his state of mind accordingly. The marked difference between their willingness to accept the consequences of practicing their faith establishes the asymmetry between them. It proves that empathy does not spring from imitating mannerisms or facial gestures, but from the desire to participate in a shared experience and grasping its effect upon each other. An experience of this type produces an intense moment of love that is both personal and collective. Tiburce's decision and Cecilia's devotion inextricably bind them to one another and leads them to realize that when they love the other as he or she tends towards God, they love in the best possible way. As Scotus writes, "I say that everyone who loves out of love, loves himself in an ordering to the infinite good, because he loves that act or disposition by which he tends to that good; and it is in this way that this love is directed to someone else, for God is the main object of his act."[100]

Perfecting their self by exercising a positive empathy empowers each to love better than they could do on their own. Their affection exemplifies the kind of action that must be taken by any person who strives to better his or her life as well as those close to them. Being attuned to another's virtue reveals that what is true of another can also be true of oneself. In this tale, the efforts to form a meaningful bond generate a rectitude that becomes self-evident as each apprehends the other's value. Emboldened by the attentiveness of his "suster deere," Tiburce along with Valerian calmly accept the consequences of staying true to their religious beliefs (l. 333). Their decisions disclose the specific reasons why each embraces Christianity: an all-consuming piety coupled with personal fulfillment or marital happiness, respectively. The underlying drive to initiate an empathetic act distinguishes them from those outside the "family" because it leads them towards refining their person. For example, Almachius, a prefect, declaims that he "knew al hir entente," but does not use this knowledge to alter his perspective (l. 363). He stays fixed upon what society dictates instead of exerting the necessary energy to consider the validity of their position. As a result, he tries to force them to change their religious belief by demanding that they kneel before false gods like "the image of Jupiter" (l. 364). If he possessed a proper grasp of religious understanding, then he would not even presume that a believer would willingly abandon their faith. The text emphasizes that he has the option to act justly because another prefect, Maximus, is moved by the brothers' goodness. Upon hearing them preach, he begins "to trowe in God allone" (l. 378). Almachius, however, shuns this opportunity and

---

100 Scotus, *Ordinatio* III, d. 29, in Vos et al., *Duns Scotus on Divine Love*, 81.

elects instead to have them put to death. By rejecting the principles of empathy, he remains tied to what others tell him rather than find meaning in the goodness of others.

Their martyrdom testifies to a joint commitment to their faith and one another, for they set themselves down with humble heart and "losten bothe hir hevedes in the place" (l. 398). Their unswerving devotion mirrors Cecilia's "stedefast cheere" because they prioritize the preservation of their virtue above societal demands (l. 382). Upon dying, "hir soules wenten to the king of grace" (l. 399). The reciprocity between these characters extols not only the freedom to believe, but also the freedom to embrace another in a loving empathy. Whereas Robertson praises the voluntarist philosophy central to the *Tale*, claiming that the will is a "mysterious process that governs choice," I maintain that Scotus's dual affections explicate this process.[101] These affections account for why Valerian, Tiburce, and Cecilia elect to forge a beneficent affinity with one another. Their choice to pursue this end illustrates how these affections illuminate the epistemic value of constructing such a bond. By going against the reason governing Roman society to embrace a truth that defies empirical evidence, each one effectively privileges the will over the intellect. The means of putting it into praxis centers upon aligning their thoughts and feelings with one another. The resultant harmony fosters a greater appreciation of each one's virtue and their indebtedness to God's creative goodness.

---

101 Robertson, "Apprehending the Divine," 122.

Chapter 3 Empathy for an Aged Patriarch and a Young Lover:
A Phenomenological Inquiry into Shakespeare's Supporting Cast

Despite the closeness cultivated between Amis and Amiloun or Valerian and Ti-burce, the ruling power's interest in these pairs of "brothers" centers upon how well they follow prescribed courtly or religious practices. Their radical decisions, however, expose the failings of these practices to assess an individual's worth and, as such, undermine the value of free choice. By rebelling against prevailing custom, these men strive to privilege their friend's or family's perspective. This kind of commitment requires a deep-seated respect. If not, they would lose their identity and become lost in the other's consciousness.[1] For empathy to flourish, one must maintain one's individuality, for one's choices and ensuing actions vivify the dynamic linking the two people. It is not a passive response dictated by a misplaced notion of duty, but a volitional act that results in a profound interpersonal understanding.

The emphasis upon the will's freedom to produce such an individuating power carries over into early modern literature, particularly in its portrayal of dignity. From Spenser to Milton, the view of humankind was generally optimistic because its connection to the divine remained intact. The world was seen as the manifestation of an omnipotent God and from this perceived existence of order, an added emphasis was placed upon a person's ability to grasp its reality. In "Hymn of Heavenly Beauty," Edmund Spenser poeticizes the supernal achievements possible through this awareness. By moving from "th'easy view/ of this base world" up through the glistening stars and the angelic hosts to the "bright Sun of Glory," the Renaissance individual could use their gift of reason to moderate their sensuous appetites and to arrive ultimately at a higher truth of spiritual or conceptual matters (ll. 22, 139). This fervent belief in the sublime beauty of creation shapes their identity and allows them to stand more firmly on terra firma than their medieval predecessors who were directed to heed angelic council.

---

[1] Husserl believes that if a clear delineation does not exist between the two people, then the other loses their identity and becomes "a part of myself" (Edmund Husserl, *Cartesian Meditations: An Introduction to Phenomenology*, trans. D. Cairns [The Hague: Martinus Nijhoff, 1999], 159).

https://doi.org/10.1515/9781501515460-004

Writers like Sir Thomas Browne (1605 – 1682) exalt human faculties—will and reason—since they enable us to be "onely that amphibious piece between a corporeal and spiritual Essence, that middle form that links those two together, and makes good the Method of God and Nature."[2] The will is understood as capacity or action whereby a person is psychically attracted to an object that is apprehended as good or repelled when it is apprehended as evil. The will's movement involves a sort of affective approach to what is cognitively present to the conscious. Although the will is "the highest and most soveraigne virtue of desiring," it remains free to follow its own inclinations.[3] Ambition and selfishness can deter it from seeking a higher good which would perfect its use. When pursuing such a good, however, the will prompts the empathizer to work constructively with the other person to realize that their kinship operates on a more refined plane than simply feeling a congruent emotion. Humanist thinker, Battista Gelli (1498 – 1563) marvels at the will's far-ranging freedom. "What is prodigious," he says, is that "there is no object or force either terrestrial or celestial, that can command her [that is, the will] to will otherwise than she pleases."[4] Its initiative affirms the potency of one's individuality and lays the foundation for the literary characters of this period to assert their freedom of choice without being prompted by an authoritative charge or communal practice. Moreover, since empathy involves far more than reacting to another's emotionally charged situation, it springs from the unfettered willingness to determine how best to utilize a heightened awareness of the other's value.[5]

Despite the nobility accorded to the will, not all early modern thinkers share this view. Martin Luther constrains its power, citing its limitations as the basis of his religious belief. He avers that people do not exert any dominant control over

---

2 Sir Thomas Browne, *Religio Medici* (London: Printed for Andrew Crooke, 1642), 38 – 39.
3 Pierre de La Primaudaye, *The Second Part of the French Academie* (London: G. B[ishop], R[alph] N[ewbery], and R. B[arker], 1594), 205; Also see, John Davies, *Microcosmos: The Discovery of the Little World, with the Government Therof* (Oxford: Joseph Barnes for John Barnes, 1603). He writes, "And though shee [Will] waites on *Reason* to, and fro,/ Yet shee makes *Reason* waite her will to kno" (46). Ideally these two faculties work together, but the will retains "her" unchecked liberty.
4 Battista Gelli, *The Circe . . . Consisting of Ten Dialogues Giving a lively Representation of the Various Passions, and many Infelicities of Humane Life* (1549), trans. Thomas Brown (1702), 288.
5 Robert Burton's claim attests to the prevalence of this view in early modern thought, namely that "actions of the *Will* are *Velle* and *Nolle*, to well and nill: which two words comprehend all" (Burton, *The Anatomy of Melancholy. What it is, With all the kinds, causes, symptoms, prognostickes, and severall cures of it*. The Sixt. Edition, corrected and augmented by the Author [Oxford: Printed for Henry Cripps, 1651], 1.1.2.11, p. 30). His words indicate that its power lies in generating action and, in the context of this study, specifically interaction.

their will in regard to salvation or damnation. In effect, the individual is nothing more than a work horse.

> Man is like a horse. Does God leap into the saddle? The horse is obedient and accommodates itself to every movement of the rider and goes whither he wills it. . . . Then Satan leaps upon the back of the animal, which bends, goes and submits to the spurs and caprices of its new rider. . . .Therefore, necessity, not free will, is the controlling principle of our conduct.[6]

John Calvin also checks the will's freedom on moral grounds, but blames humanity's sinful nature as the cause. He does maintain that all people act "voluntarily, and not by compulsion,"[7] but adds that the faculty of willing is confined by being subject to the "bondage of sin."[8] While these bleak estimates of humanity's rational and moral capacities occupy a distinct place in early modern thought, they do not supplant the idea that fulfillment springs from choosing to lead a virtuous life, which consists of living according to nature, that is, rationally, following the pattern of God.[9]

Recognizing one's place within creation underlines the period's indebtedness to medieval thought.[10] Sir John Fortescue (ca. 1394–1479), Chief Justice of the King's Bench, posits that the universe follows a specific structural design: "In this order angel is set over angel, rank upon rank in the Kingdom of heaven;

---

6 Martin Luther, *De Servo Arbitrio*, 7:113, in *The Facts about Luther* by Patrick O'Hare (Rockford: TAN Books, 1987), 266–67.

7 John Calvin, *Institutes of the Christian Religion*, trans. Henry Beveridge, III.23.2, http://www.ccel.org/ccel/calvin/institutes.toc.html.

8 John Calvin, *Bondage and Liberation of the Will*, ed. A. N. S. Lane, trans. G. I. Davies (Ada, MI: Baker Academic, 2002), 70.

9 Thomas More writes, "For they [the Utopians] define virtue to be life ordered according to nature, and that we be hereunto ordained of God, and that he doth follow the course of nature, which, in desiring and refusing things is ruled by reason. Furthermore, that reason doth chiefly and principally kindle in men the love and veneration of the divine majesty" (Thomas More, *Utopia*, ed. David Harris Sacks (Boston: Bedford/ St. Martin's, 1999), 156.

10 For example, Bonaventure dedicates his entire *Collations* to delineating the hierarchy of creation: "These enlightenments consist in considering the Father, the Son, and the Holy Spirit as they are in Themselves, and they are three in number. Other enlightenments [consist in considering] them as related to each other, and they are six in number . . . And through this sixth vision, man is made to be formed into *a living being*, after which God finally reposes in the soul of the contemplative, ceasing to grant any new gift. And the soul itself, although suffering the state of pilgrimage, reposes in God" (Bonaventure, *Collations on the Six Days*, trans. José de Vinck [Paterson, NJ: St. Anthony Guild Press, 1970], 320 and 381).

man is set over man, beast over beast."[11] To remain true to our design, humans must employ their own abilities to determine how best to structure their relationships. No matter how beneficial the intercession of angels may be to abet human interaction, it upsets this great chain of being. We must look within, recognize its bounty, and see that it serves as a microcosm for the entire universe.[12] One hundred years later, Sir Walter Raleigh (ca. 1554–1618) notes, exercising the will in a positive way reflects our divine origins.[13] When properly directed, it allows us to break free from the shackles of social expectation and realize our empathetic potential.[14] Our humanness expresses itself through the freedom to acquire and then utilize a heightened awareness of others to refine their rapport. It marks an interstice between human and divine, fostering a kindred understanding and respect for each other.

An affective understanding of another's state of mind completes our creative purpose. It brings to light the value that lies within all of us. Even when bemoaning his dysfunctional family situation, Hamlet still looks optimistically at the quality of humanity's greatness:

> What a piece of work is a man—
> how noble in reason; how infinite in faculties, in form

---

11 John Fortescue, *The Works of Sir John Fortescue, Knight, Chief Justice of England and Lord Chancellor to King Henry the Sixth*, vol. 1, ed. Lord Clermont (London, 1869), 322.

12 According to French courtier and poet, Guillaume de Salluste Du Bartas (1544–1590), humans reflect the varied compositions of nature:

> For in man's self is Fire, Aire, Earth, and Sea,
> Man's (in a word) the World's Epitome,
> Or little Map, which here my Muse doth trie
> By the grand Patterne to exemplifie. (Guillaume de Salluste Du Bartas, *Deuine Weekes & Workes translated and dedicated to the Kings most excellent Maiestie by Joshua Sylvester* [London: Humfrey Lounes, 1611], 205)

13 A human is "internally endued with a divine understanding, by which he might contemplate and serve his Creatour, after whose image he was formed, and endued with the powers and faculties of reason and other abilities, that thereby also he might govern and rule the world, and all other God's creatures therein" (Sir Walter Raleigh, *The History of the World*, bk. 1.2.5, ed. C. A. Patrides [London: Macmillan, 1971], 126). Raleigh's position reflects the medieval view that we are inextricably linked to the divine in image and person. Hugh of St. Victor (1096–1141) writes, "The spirit was created for God's sake; the body of the spirit's sake, and the world for the body's sake, so that the spirit might be subject to God, the body to the spirit, and the world to the body" (Hugo de S. Victore in *Patrologia Latina*, ed. Jacques-Paul Migne, vol. 175, col. 13).

14 Sir Walter Raleigh notes that the will's propensity to desire that good which leads us to seek God and heaven "is the one point by which we are men, and do excel all other creatures living upon the earth" ("Treatise of the Soul," in *The Works*, vol. 8 [Oxford: The University Press, 1829], 586–87).

> and moving; how express and admirable in action; how
> like an angel in apprehension; how like a god; the
> beauty of the world; the paragon of animals. (2.2.269–73)

Human ascendancy stems from using God-given abilities to govern both oneself and other earthly creatures. Marked by thought and will, consciousness empowers us to act with critical acumen. As a result, we can distinguish and integrate the three dimensions of physical existence: the self, other, and the world. Their interconnectedness reveals that meaning flourishes most fully when recognizing the vitality of a healthy relationship, which validates our privileged position. Via this knowledge, we possess the means to appreciate another's value and their contribution to the experience.

Yet, just as heavenly matters ultimately lie beyond our purview so too does a full awareness of the empathized. Within the other lies an essence that extends far deeper than what gestures and words convey. These bounds, however, neither diminish nor nullify the merit of one's efforts. Rather, they attest to each person's facility to persevere in perfecting this capacity to know the other. It creates a space where one can express one's individuality and shared understanding of the other.[15] To appreciate the process of gaining this realization and what it means to be human, this chapter examines two Shakespearean plays that extol the unwavering commitment of two characters who expend their cognitive energies to forge a bond with someone who either has little regard for them or relatively little knowledge of who they are. This allegiance attests to a conviction in another's dignity that supersedes all other concerns, showing that personal fulfillment is not determined by material success or social acclaim. As dramatic models of how an individual invests his or her person into forming such a bond, *The Tragedy of King Lear* and *The Tempest* place the spotlight upon two empathizers who are not dissuaded by social or political constraints. The Fool and Miranda, respectively, actively contribute to an experience that increases their awareness of both themselves and the other.

Before examining their attempts to construct a substantive bond with those closest to them, I must first lay a foundation of the philosophy used to explicate

---

15 Kathryn Schwartz aptly characterizes this freedom as "livable space" where the individual seeks not simply to break free from "the drives of dominance and opposition, but respond to a more foundational imperative of coexistence" (Schwarz, *What You Will: Gender, Contract, and Shakespearean Social Space* [Philadelphia: University of Pennsylvania Press, 2011], 3). Although her principal concern rests upon gender issues, we can consider its implications for characters who refigure prescribed roles to form connections with people outside of their social circle.

their empathetic process and paint in broad strokes its applicability. Their interactions rely upon the power of experience to reveal a reality that occurs immediately and noninferentially. This reality enables them to grasp both the other's
mental state and their individuality. As Husserl states, "All the difficulty disap-
pears if empathy counts as the mode of presentation of foreign consciousness."[16]
The other's foreignness springs from the potent asymmetry of their personalities.
Ascertaining how it reveals the other's intentions and desires generates a more
informed sense of self. The concerted focus on the experiential life of another
makes clear that a phenomenological hermeneutic underlies this chapter's critical focus, specifically the theories of Husserl and Stein. Where the former proffers a comprehensive theory of what constitutes empathy, the latter draws from
her dissertation and integrates its ideas in her succeeding research, exploring
how it forms "an exemplary basis for the consideration of the essence" of that
moment and what it reveals about the other's distinctiveness.[17] Both make it a
point to stress that no matter how attuned one is to another, one cannot grasp
the other's experience in its original presence.[18] Every person has a unique perception of what constitutes that moment. This intrinsic uniqueness proves that
an empathic concern depends upon the vital contribution of the observer's insight. If the observer chooses to immerse themself wholly in the other's situation
and its well of emotion, then they would look upon the other simply as an extension of themself; the observer's individuality would be forsaken.[19] Believing that
empathy simply revolves around replicating another's feelings annuls the individual and intellectual nature of this act.

The exchanges between the Fool and Lear as well as between Miranda and
Ferdinand thrive off the inherent differences between them. Understanding what
determines this radical otherness creates a means to appreciate the other's con-

---

16 Edmund Husserl, *Zur Phänomenologie der Intersubjektivität*, 1:20.

17 Stein, *On the Problem of Empathy*, 4. In *Philosophy of Psychology and the Humanities*, Stein
discusses how "our glance rests in the natural attitude with everything that's in it, is a correlate
of our consciousness. . . . To every object and to every class of objects there correspond certain
adapted coherences of consciousness." The intensity of these experiences produces a stronger
experience than the content seems to warrant (Edith Stein, *Philosophy of Psychology and the Humanities*, trans. Mary Catherine Baseheart and Marianne Sawicki [Washington, DC: ICS Publications, 2000], 7).

18 Husserl, *Zur Phänomenologie der Intersubjektivität*, 1:347 and 440.

19 Husserl avers that if we had the same access to the other's consciousness, then the other
would cease being an other and become a part of myself. See Husserl, *Cartesian Meditations*,
159. For a study of the inextricable relation between self-awareness and otherness, see Dan Zahavi, *Self-Awareness and Alterity: A Phenomenological Investigation* (Evanston, IL: Northwestern
University Press, 1999).

dition. As the empathizer strives to access what these interchanges say about that person, he or she relies upon the surety of self-knowledge and how his or her consciousness is affected by the other's perspective. In other words, one's person becomes most fully realized when it becomes present to itself in relation to the other. Dan Zahavi states, "the self is not something that stands opposed to the stream of consciousness, but is, rather, immersed in conscious life; it is an integral part of its structure."[20] Self-awareness establishes the first-personal character of experience and produces "a quality of mineness."[21] Its distinctiveness reveals the experience as one's own and, in turn, distinguishes it from anyone else's. Engaging another in this manner shows how each person contributes to the significance of the moment and produces an individuality socialized in a community of consciousness.[22]

For both the Fool and Miranda, they elect to engage their respective other as a singular being whose gestures and emotions are expressive of their state of mind.[23] They do not impose their will upon those interactions, but perceive them as distinct experiences, imparting objective knowledge about the other person's state of mind.[24] The ensuing awareness of self and other may ultimately reveal an elusive inaccessibility, but the increased involvement with the other's psychological life draws both parties closer to an awareness of their interconnection. As Husserl writes, "The origin of personality lies in empathy and in the social acts which are rooted in the latter. To acquire a personality it is not enough that the subject becomes aware of itself as the center of its acts: personality is rather constituted only when the subject establishes social relations with others."[25] Empathy sustains a mindful continuity with others. Through the lived ex-

---

20 Dan Zahavi, *Subjectivity and Selfhood* (Cambridge, MA: MIT Press, 2008), 125.

21 Shaun Gallagher and Dan Zahavi, *The Phenomenological Mind* (New York: Routledge, 2012), 226. "The mineness or for-me-ness in question is not a quality like yellow, salty, or spongy. It doesn't refer to a specific content of experience, to a specific *what*, but to the unique mode of givenness or *how* of experience" (226). It belongs specifically to that person and underlies their singularity.

22 Husserl believes that the self becomes fully realized only when personalized intersubjectively. See Edmund Husserl, *Ideen zu einer reinen Phänomenologie und phäanomenologischen Philosophie* bk. 2, *Phänomenologische Untersuchungen Zur Konstitution*, ed. M Biemel (The Hague: Martinus Nijhoff, 1952), 265.

23 Stein believes that a reliance on one's own experiential life to inform this interaction only affects the extent or degree of fulfillment. It is not necessary to acquire an awareness of the other's person or influence the presentation of the experience (Stein, *On the Problem of Empathy*, 128–29).

24 Edmund Husserl, *Erst Philosophie (1923/24)*, vol. 2, *Theorie der phänomenologischen Reduktion*, ed. R. Boehm, Husserliana 8 (The Hague: Martinus Nijhoff, 1959), 176.

25 Husserl, *Zur Phänomenologie der Intersubjektivität*, 1:175.

perienced, the empathizer comes to realize their capability to better the existence of the other as well as themself. The empathizer's very being thrives in the world of consciousness, defying any notion of being self-enclosed or self-sufficient.

Whether it is the Fool's witty repartee with Lear or Miranda's playful dialogue with Ferdinand, these interactions depict an affection that springs from neither the fraternal bond nor angelic intrusion indicative of their medieval predecessors. Rather, out of their own volition, they strive to construct a connection where none had existed before. For example, although the Fool and Lear work together in the court, neither has ventured into the other's realm of being—either professionally or personally. The imminent unemployment caused by Lear's abdication in conjunction with an unflagging loyalty account in part for why the Fool elects to stay by the King's side, but the kind of support that he extends restructures the parameters of their relationship. He exercises a concerted attentiveness about Lear's well-being in an attempt to reconcile the King's past misguided actions with reality. His selfless use of his knowledge about Lear discloses a genuine affection. Both the Fool and Miranda initiate actions to construct experiences that enable them to draw nearer to the other's person. In many ways, their efforts dramatize a compassionate evolution of Scotus's *affectio iustitiae*. A deep-seated belief in another's goodness creates a bond designed to flourish outside an established social caste system or the discerning eye of patriarchal authority. Their varying levels of success in achieving this end illustrate the difficulties in striking such a rapport yet the attempt itself champions the inherent link between humans.

When trying to connect with Lear and Ferdinand, the Fool and Miranda, respectively, quickly realize that cultivating empathy involves far more than expressing a general concern for the other's situation. It is a conscious mode of knowing that recognizes how the two perspectives differ. These differences establish that each one is a minded individual who can respond freely to the other's actions. However, the empathized in these two plays is initially out of touch with the everyday world, which diminishes the quality of knowledge exchanged. In Lear's case, he cannot accept the reality of his situation: "Does any here know me? Why, this is not Lear" (1.4.217).[26] This internal turmoil places the onus on the Fool to discern the King's true state of being. For Miranda, she may not have to face such serious identity issues in regard to Ferdinand, but his infatuation is so extreme that he tosses reason aside. He proclaims that she must be a "goddess/

26 Because Foakes's edition identifies clearly if the words, phrases, and lines are from the Quarto or Folio, all passages are taken from *King Lear*, ed. R. A. Foakes, Arden Shakespeare edition (London: Bloomsbury, 1997).

On whom these airs attend" (1.2.505). Despite these obstacles, both the Fool and Miranda persevere and eventually develop a connection that allows their respective other to recognize the value of this interpersonal connection. These experiences intertwine the two parties and create something that did not exist before. The other becomes the center of reference. Still, this focus does not sacrifice individuality, for asymmetry lies at the core of their bond. The fundamental difference between what the Fool and Miranda perceive and what Lear and Ferdinand experience reveals an otherness distinct to the empathizer, thus proving that this particular type of connectedness is more a question of appreciating the differences between them. The goal is not to become like that person but to respond to a more fundamental human need, namely embracing the other's singular dignity.

While prior history or context may help make the other's life accessible, the complexity of each person prevents this life from being wholly transparent. Since an unexpressed interiority is ever-present, Husserl and Stein maintain that empathy works along a continuum. Stein believes that empathy expands its awareness by drawing from the affective elements of the interaction.[27] These feelings gain meaning through a cognitive assessment of their import and how they are expressed through gestures: "For I not only feel how feeling is poured into expression and 'unloaded' in it, but at the same time I have this expression given in bodily perception."[28] Attuning oneself to how these expressions are imbued with feelings generates a more comprehensive understanding of the experience. For the Fool and Miranda, it evolves into a heightened grasp of the other's personality, adding depth to the emotions communicated by Lear and Ferdinand. This continually evolving awareness produces an experience comprising both views.

With this foundation of empathy, I will first investigate the discourse between the Fool and Lear and then that of Miranda and Ferdinand to show how their interplay draws them closer to one another. Despite not being able to penetrate fully the core meaning of the other's self, their persistent and engaging discourses proves that "the phenomenon of foreign psychic life is indubitably there."[29] Pursuing this course of action hones this specialized form of knowing and creates a space of interpersonal awareness that involves the whole person; it is not something that reaches fruition by an impulsive reaction. Whether close or distant, the empathy expressed by these characters gives life to some-

---

27 Stein, *On the Problem of Empathy*, 25 – 29.
28 Stein, *On the Problem of Empathy*, 53.
29 Stein, *On the Problem of Empathy*, 5.

thing that does not exist, namely a substantive bond that pierces the veil of the other's self.

The Wise Fool

In her historical study of courtly fools, Enid Welsford notes that the wise fool serves an archetypal purpose by speaking the truth, but shrouding it in seeming folly or madness.[30] This type of folly receives its greatest praise in Erasmus's work where he observes that "the sort of fools which princes of former times introduced into their courts were there for the express purpose of exposing and thereby correcting certain minor faults through their frank speech which offended no one."[31] Being candid without offending is a skill that few possess, yet custom breeds this type of fool. Custom alone, however, cannot guarantee that the words spoken will not cross the line—as blurred as it may be—and insult the court's sensibilities. The requisite traits for such a fool include a sharp intelligence and an intimate understanding of political machinations. In *Twelfth Night*, Viola observes that the wisdom of Feste's comments rise above the nonsense of a common clown: "This fellow is wise enough to play the fool,/ And to do that well, craves a kind of wit" (3.1.53–54).[32] He adeptly judges the personalities of the people and knows when to talk and when not to.

Simply being "wise," however, does not make such a fool empathic. He must elect to use his intellect to cultivate a connection that appreciates the other person's individuality and improves the lives of both people. Indeed, the Fool in *King Lear* makes a series of decisions that separate him from the conventional wise fool so that his incisive comments serve more than expose folly. The Fool's insight urges the King to look within and realize that his needs are no different than any family man: the want of a daughter's love and the realization that professional success (or failure) has little, if any, bearing upon one's affection for one's children. He voluntarily follows the King when he leaves the court and strives to help him recognize the error in dividing the kingdom between Goneril and Regan and then disowning Cordelia. The Fool's concern shows that he is not a one-dimensional character relegated to the same faceless position as the attendants and servants. Rather, he plays an active role in helping Lear regain

---

30 Enid Welsford, *The Fool: His Social and Literary History* (New York: Faber & Faber, 1968).

31 Erasmus, *Praise of Folly* and *Letter to Maarten Van Dorp 1515*, trans. Betty Radice (London: Penguin, 1993), 141.

32 William Shakespeare, *Twelfth Night: The Arden Shakespeare*, ed. Keir Elam (London: Bloomsbury, 2008).

his integrity and cultivate a strong sense of self. Such an interchange affirms the authenticity of his commitment, which discloses a value that transcends courtly or historical classifications. By generating its own type of originality, the transforming power of his compassion parallels the empathic process. Stein points out that empathy is a unique expression different from conventional emotions, such as joy or sorrow. Being in a class by itself, a *sui generis*, it is not felt as one's own feeling or recollected as a past experience, but exists in the here and now, given by the other.[33] His interaction with Lear distinguishes him not simply from other fools, but from anyone who claims to be a confidant.

Paradoxically, the absence of a name reflects the uniqueness of his character. His dialogue with Lear thus surpasses the standard commentary of a wise fool. Stephen Booth declares that the Fool "breaks out of every category in which he might be fixed."[34] Unlike Feste, Touchstone, and Lavatch, he strives to know another's state of mind in order to establish a mutually attentive relationship. This requires both a persistence and willingness to try different rhetorical tactics, ranging from cutting witticisms to gentle affection. Though his efforts ultimately fall short of this goal, his efforts bring to light the differences between them and thus illuminate the force of his person. He is, as Marvin Rosenberg notes, "not merely a 'dramatic device,' a 'poetic distraction,' but a fully developed character."[35] As a result, a close examination of his actions and speech, no matter how seemingly nonsensical or sardonic, reveals concern for the King's well-being and desire to promote communication between them.

His individuality has already endeared him to Lear, fostering a relation that extends beyond customary politeness. Even before the Fool sets foot on stage, the audience has learned that Lear struck one of Goneril's gentlemen for mistreating the Fool (1.3.1–2). And then, when he learns that the Fool is overcome with melancholy because of Cordelia's banishment, Lear directs his knights to call him hither. Yet, when he arrives, instead of being grateful, the Fool mocks Lear for assuming a position of authority. He has just observed Lear reward Kent, disguised as a lowly servant, for physically removing Goneril's steward, Oswald. He deadpans, "Let me hire him too, here's my coxcomb" (1.4.93–94). That Lear acts like a man with power and position reveals a limited self-awareness. He

---

33 Stein writes, "Thus empathy is a kind of act of perceiving *sui generis*. [It] is the experience of foreign consciousness in general, irrespective of the kind of experiencing subject or of the subject whose consciousness is experienced" (*On the Problem of Empathy*, 11).
34 Stephen Booth, *King Lear, Macbeth, Indefinition and Tragedy* (New Haven, CT: Yale University Press, 1983), 39.
35 Marvin Rosenberg, *The Masks of King Lear* (Berkeley: University of California Press, 1972), 107.

has neither. Despite this repression of reality, he harbors a genuine affection for the Fool: "Poor fool and knave, I have one part in my heart/ That's sorry yet for thee" (1.4.191; 3.2.72–73). Though admirable to express such concern, Lear's emotional state suffers from much greater tribulation. Since both are perceived as wise and foolish, this juxtaposition of opposites underscores the dynamic interplay in their relationship as it resists presumptive conclusions. It simultaneously connects and delineates them, for as Husserl states, the two are seen "as being alike and as belonging together, while still being separate and different."[36] Whether referring to the Fool's derisive critique or the King's misplaced concern, both men must strike a delicate balance between what one knows about himself and what he knows about the other—no matter how limited that knowledge may be.

Lear uses the information he has learned about the Fool to express concern for his well-being, and the Fool uses it to show how attuned he is to Lear's situation. Both demonstrate an invested interest in the other's life As Zahavi writes, "At one end of the scale, empathy is understood as a basic sensitivity to the mindedness of others. It can also, however, provide us with a direct acquaintance and grasp of the more specific character of the other's psychological life."[37] A concerted attentiveness to another's thoughts and needs produces an experience that transcends socially imposed boundaries. Still, the unpredictable nature of their discourse suspends the expectations of how their relationship will progress, but its attentiveness to the other's intellectual, emotional, or personal well-being lays the foundation for each to realize his capacity to see in others a truth that revolutionizes the value of experience.

Recognizing that Lear is caught between the crown and the coxcomb, the Fool relies on his biting wit to explain what constitutes a wise act. He does not offer complex, abstract theories of what defines virtue or attempt to grade them in degrees of moral importance. Rather, he grounds his lessons in common sense and presents them in a childlike rhyme.

Have more than thou showest,
Speak less than thou knowest,
Lend less than thou owest,
Ride more than thou goest,
Learn more than thou trowest. (1.4.116–20)

---

36 Edmund Husserl, *Erfahrung und Urteil*, ed. L. Landgrebe (Hamburg: Felix Meiner, 1985 [1939]), 225.
37 Zahavi, *Self & Other*, 169.

This worldly wisdom is much more manageable to process than the reasons why his daughters, Goneril and Regan, treat him with such disdain. It simply involves not bragging about material possessions, not extending excessive financial assistance, and not lording one's knowledge over others. The only challenge posed by these aphorisms is not their content, but if the singsong cadence annoys Lear. Preoccupied with other matters, he retorts, "nothing can be made out of nothing" (1.4.130). His reply effectively repeats what he told Cordelia when she refused to quantify her love for him, proving that he has not yet grasped the fault of failing to consider her point of view.[38] His dismissal of the Fool's rhyme discloses a lingering selfishness that limits their relationship's potential. In order to lessen the distance between him and the Fool as well as anyone else who wishes to help him regain his dignity, he must accept that another's view may differ and even oppose one's own. Only by putting this truth into practice can he approach the kind of wisdom that will distinguish his person.

Although the Fool's words appear sarcastic, the interchange possesses the power to reveal each other's singular worth and, in turn, traverse the constraints of a rigid caste system. As Husserl maintains, the experience is "co-intended and dependent upon each one's presence," for its interiority constitutes the essence of selfhood.[39] To reach this understanding, however, they must overcome a history of hierarchical separation. Evidence of this discrimination manifests itself in the terms of endearment exchanged between them. Neither one has any qualms about calling the other "sirrah," a term normally used by those in authority to address inferiors or boys.[40] For example, after being subjected to the Fool's acerbic wit, the King threatens the Fool, "Take heed, sirrah, the whip" (1.4.108). Unaffected, the Fool offers to instruct Lear further on how best to conduct oneself and states pointedly, "Sirrah, I'll teach thee a speech" (1.4.112). Their bantering also includes the King repeatedly calling him "boy" (1.4.105, 130, 141), and the Fool replying with similar pejorative terminology, "nuncle" (1.4.104, 115, 129, 148, 173, 170, 177, 205). R. A. Foakes notes that the term "nuncle" is a variant of "uncle," contracted from "mine uncle," but the initial "n" could be associated

---

38 When he asks Cordelia to voice how much she loves him, she tells him that she has nothing to say, for her love for him lies beyond words. Unwilling to accept this truth, he states defiantly, "How, nothing will come of nothing. Speak again" (1.1.190).

39 Husserl, *Zur Phänomenologie der Intersubjektivität*, 1:27; Husserl, *Einleitung in die philosophie Vorlesungen* (1922/23), ed. B. Goossens, Husserliana 35 (Dordrecht: Kluwer Academic Publishers, 2002), 107.

40 The *OED* defines "sirrah" as a term of address used to men or boys, expressing contempt, reprimand, or assumption of authority on the part of the speaker; sometimes employed less seriously in addressing children.

with "n" in "nothing" and "never."⁴¹ This emphasis upon nothing, which is a dominant theme throughout the play, and the context indicate a negative meaning. The Fool ridicules Lear's dysfunction as a father—for example, "I have used it [singing his songs], nuncle, e'er since thou mad'st thy/ daughters thy mothers; for when thou gav'st them the/ rod and putt'st down thine own breeches" (1.4.163–65). The folly of allowing such an unnatural order to supplant Lear's monarchial reign indicates a glaring flaw in his logic. The pointed tenor of these words markedly differs from the playful exchange about conducting oneself in the world. The disrespect and even derisive way that they address each other facially works against fostering a positive rapport.

Their interactions, however, provide the opportunity to recognize something of value about each other. The Fool's language is not meant to insult the King as much as satisfy his professional function to mirror the court's foolishness. The late twelfth-century English satirist and poet, Nigellus Wireker, dedicates an entire work on man's struggle to utilize the knowledge conveyed by a fool:

> The title of this book is *Speculum stultorum* [*Mirror of Fools*]. It has been given this name in order that foolish men may observe as in a mirror the foolishness of others and may then correct their own folly, and that they may learn to censure in themselves those things which they find reprehensible in others. But even as a mirror reflects only the outward appearance and the form of those who look into it, but never holds the memory of a past image, so is it with fools. Seldom, and then only with difficulty, are they drawn away from their folly no matter how much they may have been taught by the foolishness of others.⁴²

His harsh speech draws attention to Lear's unkindness towards others, particularly Cordelia. Whether insulting his daughters, such as calling Goneril "a thankless child," or threatening to hit the Fool, Lear struggles to accept his vulnerability as a man and a father (1.4.281). His focus remains fixed on privilege and entitlement, which precludes him from restructuring his frame of thinking. As such, the Fool must employ harsh, even cruel, rhetoric in hopes of sparking the King to reflect upon his past actions and present state. No matter how closely he mirrors him, however, he can only capture one dimension of the man, for it "never holds the memory of a past image." To see the viable aspects of their relationship, Lear must insert himself into the conversation and consider the subtext of the Fool's speech. Whether barbed comment or witty observation, the

---

41 Foakes, *King Lear*, 197.
42 Nigellus Wireker, *The Book of Daun Burnel the Ass: Nigellus Wireker's "Speculum stultorum,"* trans. Graydon W. Regenos (Whitefish, MT: Literary Licensing, 2011), 23.

Fool's divers rhetorical approaches interlace with one another, cementing an uneasy yet indelible bond.

As opposed to the theocratic universe of the medieval world where one strives to maintain the proper correspondence between higher and lower forms of reality and thus to glory in God's infinite wisdom as revealed in so orderly a universe, the interplay between these two men strives to cultivate the wisdom culled from their particular experiences. It has the means to foster an understanding separate from that imposed by authoritative institutions, whether political or religious. Empathy empowers the individual to apprehend what that moment reveals about the other person rather than let external factors influence one's perception. Yet, adopting the other's point of view, as stated in the *Mirror of Fools*, is a herculean task, but the Fool's marginal success does not diminish his importance. His efforts to have Lear accept this moment for what it is—a chance to embrace the companionship of one who appreciates his situation—enhances their shared history. It underlines the fact that they are inextricably tied to one another and illustrates the veracity of Husserl's statement about two people aspiring towards an empathetic act: they display "phenomenologically a unity of similarity and thus are always constituted precisely as a pair."[43] They come face-to-face with an otherness of a completely new kind.[44] In effect, it is a dialogue where their verbal exchange provides the means not only to assess the other's state of mind, but also to consider one's role in this experience. Reality thus incorporates a multiplicity of perspectives that hold the potential to produce a valued understanding.

To make this transition, the Fool continues offering his insights on the workings of the world. He asks Lear if he would like to hear what separates a bitter from a sweet fool. The King urges him to explain the difference: "No, lad, teach me" (1.4.136).

> That lord that counseled thee to give away thy land,
> Come place him here by me; do thou for him stand.
> The sweet and bitter fool will presently appear,
> The one in motley here, the other found out there. (1.4.137–40)

---

43 Edmund Husserl, *Cartesianische Meditationen und Pariser Vorträge*, ed. S. Strasser, Husserliana 1 (The Hague: Martinus Nijhoff, 1950), 142.
44 Edmund Husserl, *Zur Phänomenologie der Intersubjektivität*, 3:442.

Found only in the Quarto, this clever play on words identifies Lear as the bitter fool for, in the order given, the sweet one wears the motley.[45] The inversion of expectation is designed to provoke Lear to use his mind in a critically perceptive manner: to comprehend the harm that he actually inflicted upon himself by basing a political decision on whether or not his daughters could verbalize how much they admired him as their father. Since love eludes any definitive explanation, his folly is self-evident. The desperation to hold onto his past self prevents him from living in the present and causes him to lash out at the Fool: "Dost thou call me fool, boy?" (1.4.141).[46] Although his defensiveness illustrates that he is not yet ready to conduct the kind of introspection necessary to acknowledge the consequences of his misguided judgments, his reply affirms the validity of those maxims found in the contemporary work on human knowledge, *Nosce Teipsum*:

> Yet if *Affliction* once her warres begin,
> And threat the feebler *Sense* with sword and fire;
> The *Minde* contracts her selfe and shrinketh in,
> And to her selfe she gladly doth retire.[47]

The stress of becoming dependent upon Goneril's and Regan's care as well as exiling Cordelia, for he shall never see "that face of hers again," has upset his equanimity (1.1.266). Living under this duress both constrains his intellectual vision and compromises his freedom of will, for the will is most free when we are in a secure, stable relationship. Modern science explains how emotional surety

---

45 These lines account for Hornback's view that the Quarto depicts a character who "is a funnier, wiser, and more bitter artificial fool" than the one portrayed in the Folio, "a sweet, natural Fool" (Robert Hornback, *The English Clown Tradition from the Middle Ages to Shakespeare* [Rochester, NY: D. S. Brewer, 2009], 153). His position contrasts with Harry Levin who argues in the conflated *Riverside Shakespeare* edition, "the nameless Fool in *King Lear* is a natural, a half-witted mascot, a simpleton inspired with the intuitive wisdom of nature" (Harry Levin, "General Introduction," in William Shakespeare, *The Tragedy of King Lear*, ed. Harry Levin in *The Riverside Shakespeare*, ed. G. Blakemore Evans [Boston: Houghton Mifflin, 1974; rpt. 1997], 21).
46 One way for him to see his folly "presently appear" would be to stare into a looking-glass. Though no stage direction explicitly mentions such a device, Allan Shickman believes that a mirror makes dramatic sense, for it "is at once comic and painful when the King is led (as a child might be) to peer curiously into the glass, realizing after a brief but crucial moment that the joke is on him" (Allan R. Shickman, "The Fool's Mirror in 'King Lear,'" *English Literary Renaissance* 21 [1991]: 80). It makes manifest Lear's difficulty processing this information. Yet if he can alter his perspective, it would redefine the nomenclature of him being a fool, encouraging him to go with those who see him for who he truly is.
47 John Davies, *Nosce Teipsum*, www.luminarium.org/renlit/humane2.htm.

generates higher brain functioning.[48] As Sally Severino explains, "in a physiological body-state of security, our desire is freest for us to love and, consequently, our will is freest for us to choose rightly."[49] Familial stress does not permit him to view himself in an honest light. The Fool's wisdom lies in discerning how the words, how this moment, reveal something important about his person and, implicitly, his connection to the Fool. Until he accepts that awareness of self correlates to his openness to others, Lear's mind will "shrinketh in" and foment bitterness.[50]

When the Fool's words strike too close to his vulnerabilities, the King threatens physical repercussions. Upon hearing that he "mad'st thy daughters thy mothers," he exclaims, "we'll have you whipped" (1.4.163, 172). Overwhelmed by familial distress, he struggles to maintain lucidity, which prompts the Fool to make fun of his flawed reasoning and impotence as former ruler:

> I marvel what kin thou and thy daughters are. They'll have me whipped for speaking true, thou'll have me whipped for lying, and sometimes I am whipped for holding my peace. I had rather be any kind o'thing than a fool, and yet I would not be thee, nuncle. Thou hast pared thy wit o'both sides and left nothing i'the middle. (1.4.173–79)

Instead of being offended or scared, he points out how the King does not pay attention to what this moment offers. He does not appreciate that the Fool initiates this commentary not so much because duty dictates it, but rather because he wants Lear to move past his negative thoughts and promote mental health. By adopting another's perspective, he could discover and ponder those possibilities that he has been reluctant to consider. It is, as Sarah Borden writes, where "I become real to myself."[51] Empathy, therefore, is not some casual or passive response to another's actions or emotional reactions. Rather, it demands a keen awareness of what that moment says about oneself in relation to that person. The King is a "fool," but this is not necessarily an insult. Although it derides his sagacity, it also provides an identity wholly separate from his previous one which is actively suffocating his willingness to look at others and himself honestly. As personified by the Fool himself, this name grants him the power to

---

48 Bruce Perry and Maia Szalavitz, *Born for Love: Why Empathy Is Essential—and Endangered* (New York: HarperCollins, 2010).
49 Sally K. Severino, *Behold Our Moral Body: Psychiatry, Duns Scotus and Neuroscience* (London: Versita, 2013), 77.
50 Husserl believes that one becomes aware of the self specifically as a human person only when cultivating such intersubjective relationships. See *Zur Phänomenologie der Intersubjektivität*, 2:175; also see, Zahavi, *Self-Awareness and Alterity*, 157.
51 Sarah Borden, *Edith Stein* (London: Continuum, 2003), 29.

speak the truth without fear of repercussion. Pushing Lear to the point of exasperation coupled with giving him a new title has the potential to foster a new horizon of understanding, namely one that views the Fool as a kindred believer in his worth.

While Lear's distress may prevent him from grasping the import of the Fool's speech, attaining such an awareness does not have to be intellectually based. It can draw from their established familiarity with one another and the affection that it produces. In fact, cognitive scientists have proven that positive empathy thrives when expressed towards someone who is close to the observer.[52] Even before the Fool appears on stage, Lear laments how he misses him, "But where's my fool? I have not seen him this two days" (1.4.69–70). Being cognizant of how much time has passed since they were together discloses an attentiveness to the Fool and emotional need for his presence.

Similarly, the Fool's choice to stay with him illustrates a bond that surpasses that of a casual acquaintance. His concerted interest in the King's person reflects the natural ability to perceive and be sensitive to another's emotional state. The motivation to care for his well-being attests to an empathetic act designed to facilitate cooperation between them. Yet, to realize this end, both must embrace the totality of their interchange. It is more than a feeling or thought; it is the experience itself. The Fool's song shows how such a moment involves each of them. As a listener, Lear becomes an active participant who is directly impacted by the music. Akin to language, it creates a system of meaning that belongs to itself. Explicating its evocative power lies between thought and phenomenon. When the Fool revisits his standard theme of the King's folly, the lyrical harmony emphasizes the care underlying the words.[53]

> Then they for sudden joy did weep
>   And I for sorrow sung,
> That such a king should play bo-peep,
>   And go the fools among. (1.4.167–69)

The sadness that he feels when the King divested his land lies beyond the professional duties of a court fool. His keen identification of what Lear lost as king,

---

52 Yuki Motomura et al., "Interaction Between Valence of Empathy and Familiarity: Is It Difficult to Empathize with the Positive Events of a Stranger?," *Journal of Physiological Anthropology* 34 (2015): 1–9.

53 Of course, the play's director determines if the song follows an upbeat or gloomy melody. The point being made here is that music universally incites an emotional response, which necessarily involves Lear in the experience.

father, and man shows that he has invested thought and reason to ascertain most fully the situation affecting the King. This sensitivity attests to a basic ability to discriminate between his own needs versus those of the King. The song's ability to stimulate a synesthetic sensation—aural, sadness, and a variety of other feelings—meld into one experience, and the Fool's openness to how Lear responds to this moment highlights his selflessness. Stephen Davies observes, "the music is not the emotional object of the listener's response—the response is *to* the music without being *about* it—because moved listeners do not believe of the music that it satisfies the formal object of sadness."[54] Although the song incites Lear to threaten the Fool with being whipped, the fact that he identifies the Fool as the locus of his problems shows that he also identifies the Fool as an integral figure in his insular world. The song thus achieves its goal of creating an event that involves both of them.

Within this melodious moment, Lear has the chance to fashion a mutually informing relation that complies with Stein's view of empathy as the basic cognitive source for our comprehension of others.

> [T]he experience is no longer an object for me, but has pulled myself into it. I am now no longer turned towards the experience, but instead I am turned towards the object of the experience. I am at the subject of the original experience, at the subject's place, and only after having fulfilled a clarification of the experience does it appear to me as an object again.[55]

The experience itself affords Lear the opportunity to assess and even reciprocate an affect akin to the Fool's concern. This expanding perception fosters a heightened awareness of what both people value above all else. If Lear could maximize the interpersonal knowledge contained within this experience, the Fool's empathy would liberate him from the servitude of political order and enable him to live a life of purpose. Both his and the Fool's contributions to this moment disclose that a greater potential of being exists.[56] Hence, the Fool's efforts, whether successful or not, are properly directed, affirming his positivity in Lear's life.

When Goneril appears, she derails the flow of their dialogue. Lear promptly forgets about the Fool and asks, "How now, daughter? What makes that frontlet on?/ Methinks you are too much of late i'the frown" (1.4.180–81). Despite having denounced her steward as a "whoreson dog" a hundred lines earlier, he displays

---

54 Davies, "Infectious Music," 136–37.
55 Stein, *On the Problem of Empathy*, 18.
56 Husserl states that although we don't have the same type of experience as the other person, the fact that there is more to it than what we are grasping is significant (Husserl, *Zur Phänomenologie der Intersubjektivität*, 3:631).

no such imperiousness here (1.4.78). He acts with a reserved solicitousness, demonstrating a rational ability to prioritize people in his life. Still, the Fool sees the inherent danger in trying to foster a relationship with a daughter of her ilk. He employs absolute terminology to censure this perceived recklessness: "I am a fool, thou art nothing" (1.4.184–85). Despite its harshness, it privileges their connection, which Lear has consistently mentioned since his arrival at Goneril's palace: "Where's my knave, my fool?/ Go you and call my fool hither" (1.4.42–43), "Where's my fool? Ho, I think the world's asleep" (1.4.46), "Go you; call hither my fool" (1.4.75). The Fool strives to keep Lear attuned to the honesty that he proffers. He poses no threat of traitorous self-interest that Goneril represents.

By lessening Lear's status from a "fool" to nothingness, he highlights the stagnant use of his mind. If Lear's focus stays fixed upon himself, then he will never move past his delusions of regal grandeur. He will remain Lear "an O without a figure" (1.4.183). By giving away all he has in the "name and all th' addition to a King" (1.1.137), the "O" symbolizes an empty map of state and the mirror of this condition.[57] Placing so much belief in the power of property divests Lear's world of meaning, emptying his person.[58] Misguided notions of power and privilege have stripped him of a viable identity. The Fool then states, "I am better than thou art now" (1.4.184). He draws from his knowledge of court hierarchy to point out further Lear's loss of political importance. In order to rectify this misperception, Lear needs to stay immersed in his discourse with the Fool because it requires him to recognize what constitutes his reality. Only by recognizing his personal skills and those supportive of him can he regain his dignity. Husserl explains how expressing one's individuality fosters an ability to cultivate a healthy sense of self: "What is most originally mine is my life, my 'consciousness,' my 'I do and suffer,' whose being consist in being originally pre-given to me . . . in being experientially and intuitively accessible as itself."[59] Abandoning his conversation with the Fool effectively undermines his chance to look outside himself and realize that the self is present to itself most fully when it is engaged

---

57 The symbolism of being an "O with a figure" can be "understood as a direct reference to medieval cartography: medieval maps of the world were drawn in the form of an 'O' containing a 'T.' The circular world was neatly divided into sections by the three continents that made up the 'T': Europe, Asia, and Africa" (Dan Brayton, "Angling in the Lake of Darkness: Possession, Dispossession, and the Politics of Discovery in *King Lear*," *English Literary History* 70 [2003]: 425).
58 If Lear looks at the bestowal of property as a form of binding others to him, then "good governance" must spring from mutual agreements where both parties exercise control over the matter (Brian Sheerin, "Making Use of Nothing: The Sovereignties of *King Lear*," *Studies in Philology* 110 [2013]: 789–811).
59 Edmund Husserl, *Zur Phänomenologie der Intersubjektivität*, 3:429.

in a productive exchange. From Husserl's perspective, it would be "a decisive mistake to interpret the present notion of a core, or minimal, self . . . as some kind of self-enclosed and self-sufficient interior."[60] By continuing to be embedded in this familial dysfunction, Lear relives the same moment over and over again. He remains a pawn controlled by his daughter's words of approval.

Taking advantage of his self-imposed folly, Goneril releases an invective that excoriates the integrity of those subjects who still respect him.

> Not only, sir, this your all-licensed fool,
> But other of your insolent retinue
> Do hourly carp and quarrel, breaking forth
> In rank and not to be endured riots. (1.4.191–94)

She undercuts the Fool's sincerity by stating that the veracity of his words is merely a function of his professional duty. Being "all-licensed" secures him from any punishment for speaking the truth and thus implies that his claims of Lear being a fool merely serve to hurt Lear further. She does not want to consider that anyone other than family would want to care for her father or that her father would need such support. Her attack against those knights who still follow the King reveals the extent of her disinterest in her father's well-being. Nothing he represents has any bearing upon her amoral compass. Her destructive nature affects the King's state of mind, causing it to question his own sanity. He states with a desolate sadness, "Who is that can tell me who I am?" (1.4.221). Asking such a question reaffirms the salience of the Fool urging Lear to restructure his perspective of the world, which would grant him an identity separate from his monarchial and paternal role. His experiences with Goneril do not afford him the chance to express his originality, but rather defy the very principles of human interaction by separating him from the communal world, a world in which he plays a vital role. As a result, he stays mired in the false illusions of being a forgotten king, and the relation between the self as an experiential dimension and the person as a distinct individual fails to be realized.

The growing distance between the Fool's insight and Lear's self-awareness illustrates a reversal of the King-Fool configuration, but whereas R. A. Zimbardo avers that it functions as a pattern underlining their changing social or political clout, this study asserts that it highlights their distinctiveness.[61] A valued connection can only occur when both parties possess an originality that invites

---

60 Zahavi, *Subjectivity and Selfhood*, 126.
61 R. A. Zimbardo, "The King and the Fool: *King Lear* as Self-Deconstructing Text," *Criticism* 32 (1999): 1–29.

the other to consider and embrace these differences. Otherwise, the compassion expressed would be either superficial or designed to serve a purpose other than an interpersonal one. Moreover, the polysemy of "fool" in the play denotes not simply a diminished social status, but also the power to speak the truth and readily adapt to another's perspective. Existence, whether or not Lear wants to accept it, is fluid. He must cognize that a self's meaning draws from the interactions with others and accept its diversity of knowledge. While the King may struggle with exercising the kind of selflessness necessary to attain this goal, his insistence to engage the Fool indicates a willingness to lay the proper foundation to cultivate a healthy bond (which he ultimately achieves in his relationship with Cordelia).

The continual movement from king to fool and vice versa describes a relationship that operates apart from the expectations of courtly demands. In the context of this rapport, neither the Fool's nor Lear's actions are bound by the prescribed taxonomy of being either wise or foolish, but oscillate between the two as they strive to express care and appreciate the other's perspective. This interplay prevents the Fool's efforts from being "an act of displacement that enacts the usurpation of the sovereign by the clown."[62] This chapter's gravamen is predicated on the idea that the Fool must adapt to whatever changes the situation dictates and use his knowledge to help Lear from slipping too deeply into a state of disbelief. He seeks neither power nor acknowledgment. From being a court fool to a companion to Lear as he roams from one sister's domicile to another, he consistently strives to understand and apprise the King of those factors affecting the King's state of mind and instill a sense of dignity that betters Lear's person. The interlacing of these experiences underpins a concerted attentiveness to the Fool's beliefs and needs, whether they are intellectual, emotional, or personal, and depicts the kind of affection that he exemplifies.

When Goneril urges Lear to put away "These dispositions, which of late transport you/ From what you rightly are" (1.4.213–14). The severity of his disquietude upset her so much that even she concedes that he once possessed a rational capacity, which does little to calm him. The uncertainty caused by her disregard for those people important to him diminishes his sense of self.

> Does any here know me? Why, this is not Lear.
> Does Lear walk thus, speak thus? Where are his eyes?

---

62 Richard Wilson, *Free Will: Art and Power on Shakespeare's Stage* (Manchester: Manchester University Press, 2013), 262. Wilson downplays the source of Lear's "anger and self-hate, in the negative dialectic of *King Lear*" in favor of examining "the defilement that held a mirror up not only to the grime of 'The Wisest Fool', but the filth of the fool himself" (262).

> Either his notion weakness, or his discerning are
> Lethargied. (1.4.217–20)

Since Goneril refuses to treat him with kindly respect, his identity as a father falls to the wayside. Coupled with his banishment of Cordelia, he is rapidly losing any testament to his paternal role. With no kingdom to rule and no daughters expressing their devotion, he declares that he is not "Lear." He may perform the actions of a man, but they are indifferent to those interior qualities that define his very being. They are merely motions, absent of any moral quality. He may feel love for Goneril, but her disinterest in his situation eliminates any avenue to express it. Unable to communicate his thoughts and feelings in any meaningful way, his humanness becomes compromised. These words do not signify a loss of ratiocinative skills as much as a perceptive observation about the need to form a valued relationship. Indeed, Philip Schwyzer avers that *King Lear* cannot only be about "denials, undoings, and evacuations," since "only a Dadaist would construct an aesthetic object solely on the basis of refusals."[63] The rhetorical import of his questions illustrates that he knows clearly what comprises his wants and beliefs.

Without attempting to understand either the Fool or himself, Lear cannot fulfill his creative design. By aligning one's thoughts with another, one gains not only a more informed insight of the other person, but also a self-awareness of one's ability to express compassion. Alastair MacIntyre writes: "Empathetic awareness allows us to understand others in the same way. . . . And just as in the case of certain others we find ourselves, after we have become aware through iterated empathy of how they view us."[64] Whereas Goneril's words serve only to frustrate Lear's ability to express himself both socially and personally, the Fool's speeches and songs, though facially upsetting, encourage the King to cognize a self-worth that thrives beyond political position and familial duty. The King does not have to let Goneril's cruelty control his view of himself. He can, if he grasps the Fool's wisdom, move past his mistakes and find solace in a compatible relationship. The art of empathy extols the individual's volition to attune oneself to another regardless of how debilitating or imposing the obstacles encountered may be. The particularity of these challenges facing Lear and his own melanchol-

---

63 Philip Schwyzer, "The Jacobean Union Controversy and *King Lear*," in *The Accession of James I: Historical and Cultural Consequences*, ed. Glenn Burgess, Rowland Wymer, and Jason Lawrence (Basingstoke: Palgrave Macmillan, 2006), 44.
64 Alastair MacIntyre, *Edith Stein: A Philosophical Prologue 1913–1922* (Lanham, MD: Rowman & Littlefield, 2006), 86.

ic view shows that empathy has its own kind of originality.[65] The Fool, as opposed to Goneril, appreciates Lear's situation, strives to fortify Lear's integrity, and forges a valued bond.

Although Goneril does not insult her father directly, she derides his folly in maintaining a retinue by saying that such men "besort your age" and demands their immediate expulsion from her palace (1.4.242). Upset with her insensitivity, Lear replies that he will leave and retaliates by calling her a "degenerate bastard" (1.4.245). Such an outrageous affront reveals the dire need for a discernible identity. Accusing her of illegitimacy and sexual perversion goes against the very grain of what it means to be a father. Filling a child's life with stable, secure love is the prime agenda of a conscientious parent. To violate these paternal precepts defies logic. Yet, despite a fading certitude in himself, Lear is still rational. His words, therefore, are not intended as factual statements, but designed to provoke an emotive response. He wants to hear her cry out in angst that a father should never say something so reprehensible. Such a drastic attempt to calm his ego shows how his past mistakes have distanced him from a mature, healthy connection. From this point onward, their discussion devolves into an exchange of insults and threats. It ends when he announces that he will seek the support of Regan. He submits that this daughter will be "kind and comfortable" and "flay thy wolvish visage" upon hearing of Goneril's disrespect (1.4.298, 300). Believing that a difference exists between the same two sisters who pledged such absolute love for him when he was divesting his kingdom—"I am alone felicitate/ In your dear highness' love"—shows that folly still reigns. He has become, as the Fool aptly says, "Lear's shadow" (1.4.222).

Being under such duress consumes Lear. Upon exiting Goneril's palace, he and the Fool engage in a disjointed repartee that takes on a different tenor than before. Although the Fool continues to taunt with personal gibes and seemingly nonsensical riddles, the King does not immerse himself in the conversation and deliver emotionally charged replies. Instead of threatening to whip the Fool, he uses a monosyllabic vocabulary that discloses the psychological strain caused by Goneril. When the Fool asks if he can answer the riddle, Lear succinctly states, "No." And, when the Fool explains "why one's nose stands I'the middle on's face," the King's response has nothing to do with the riddle (1.5.19). Rather, it betrays his deepest thoughts. He utters, "I did her wrong" (1.5.24). Given Goneril's spite, it is more likely that Cordelia is the object of his compunction. Yet, the significant feature of this utterance lies in the fact that he grasps how his actions directly impact a relationship and an acceptance of his responsibility to act

---

65 Husserl, *Zur Phänomenologie der Intersubjektivität*, 1:225.

thoughtfully. Despite being shrouded in a despondent rumination, the utterance signifies a conscious act that requires being attuned to another's state of mind and motivations. Even though he cannot express this burgeoning understanding to his daughter, it shows that empathy is not a uni-dimensional endeavor. Whether springing from sadness or joy, this mode of consciousness elevates his awareness to assess objectively his role in debilitating their bond and offers him the chance to act on this knowledge. But shame overwhelms him and he redirects the conversation to something concrete and non-human, namely his horses: "Be my horses ready?" (1.5.31). As human experience continually shows, expressing an empathetic understanding requires a confidence in oneself, a belief in the other, and a conviction to put its tenets into praxis; it is not for the weak of heart.

Though recognizing Lear's anguish, the Fool still chooses to mock his physical vulnerability: the senility of an aging man. This harshness proves analogous to breaking a crooked leg in order that it heals straight, for just as pain can heal bodily injury, insult, when properly employed, can ignite perspicacity.

> Fool If thou wert my fool, nuncle, I'd have thee beaten for being old before thy time.
>
> Lear How's that?
>
> Fool Thou shouldst not have been old till thou hadst been wise.
>
> Lear O let me not be mad, not mad, sweet heaven! I would not be mad.
> Keep me in temper, I would not be mad.[66] (1.5.38 – 45)

Since he just demonstrated an epiphany about his role in sending Cordelia away, Lear's plea to not "be mad" does not signify a defective reasoning capacity as much as how his earlier decisions have led to this present situation.[67] It indicates a need for someone positive in his life, a shared understanding that could help him see past his wrongs. Yet, shame and pride prevent him from conceiving a reality other than the one consuming his present thoughts. The Fool's barbs, therefore, serve a vital function in helping expose the hubris holding him back and redirect his thoughts. His empathy subverts the hierarchical differences imposed by political practice and deconstructs the predetermined classification

---

66 The second "not mad" is in the Folio edition, and the statement, "I would not be mad" is in the Quarto. Whether separated or joined, these phrases contribute to the speech's main emphasis: Lear's fear of losing his reason.

67 Hoeniger believes that Lear suffers from hypochondriac melancholy caused by the clash of two passions, anger and grief, since the play's beginning. See F. D. Hoeniger, *Medicine and Shakespeare in the English Renaissance* (Newark: University of Delaware Press, 1992).

of wise man and fool. It urges the King to recast the use of his cognitive and emotive faculties, break free from his preoccupation with his daughter's mistreatment and embrace another's perspective.[68] To recognize that his capacity for empathy lies outside Goneril's dominion, Lear sees that the Fool is not an adversary, but offers him the succor that he so desperately seeks.

Even though Kent had earlier voiced his concern about the King's state of mind, this is the first time that Lear explicitly worries about being mad. Kent had made this observation when the King exiled Cordelia: "When Lear is mad. What wouldst thou do, old man?" (1.1.147). In the play, discerning selflessly the words of someone who both emanates love and is loved determines mental stability. This leitmotif affirms the Fool's decision to privilege empathy above other concerns. Even when couched in pointed taunts, his speech strives to awaken the King to a reality that he can accept and, in turn, resuscitate his dignity if he puts into praxis the kind of knowing necessary to cultivate a mutual understanding. Noticeably, both Kent's and the Fool's critiques indicate a link between madness and old age. By doing so, they shift the blame from a mental failing to a physical one that affects every person sooner or later. It does not denigrate his person, but encourages him to be more conscientious towards another person's expressions—verbal or physical. Such optimism is affirmed when Lear struggles against madness and implores "sweet heaven" to confirm this belief. Although an idiomatic phrase, it shows that the bitterness that he harbors against Goneril has not infected his hope that something better exists for him.

To claim that he should not "have been old till thou hadst been wise" may seem unduly harsh, but "wisdom" denotes neither an accumulation of knowledge nor a savvy use of political power. Rather, it signifies an emotional intelligence that draws a meaningful connection with others so that one can refine one's inner value. Moreover, the Fool is certainly no fool, exercising a distinct initiative in aiding a man abandoned by those daughters physically closest to him. His commitment to Lear stands apart from conventional wisdom. The paradoxical rhetoric strips away the certainty of logic, supplanting it with the transforming power of compassion.[69] Indeed, the passion in protecting one's or an-

---

68 Edmund Husserl, *Cartesian Meditations: An Introduction to Phenomenology,* trans. Dorian Cairns (The Hague: Martinus Nijhoff, 1960), 139.

69 The Preacher in Ecclesiastes relies extensively upon this rhetorical motif, recounting the "heart of the wise" or "of fools" (7:6). His paradoxes of wisdom and folly depict the challenge of forgoing earthly ways to embrace transcendent ones: "And I gave mine heart to know wisdom and knowledge, madness and foolishness: I knew also that this is a vexation of the spirit" (1:17). He also writes, "For the wise man's eyes are in his head, but the fool walks in darkness: yet I know also that the same condition falls to them all" (2:14).

other's sense of self characterizes their dynamic and accounts for their manipulation of these two terms. The give-and-take of their gibes and even Lear's preoccupied utterances dramatize a heartfelt desire to attain a greater interpersonal or self-awareness. The intense compounding of thought and feeling precludes their discourse from ever devolving into a stagnant monism. William Hazlitt addresses its intensity when examining their rapport in "On Wit and Humour" (1819):

> Lear and the Fool . . . the sublimest instance I know of passion and wit united, or of imagination unfolding the most tremendous sufferings, and of burlesque on passion playing with it, aiding and relieving its intensity by the most pointed, but familiar and indifferent illustrations of the same thing in different objects, and on a meaner scale.[70]

The union of passion and wit subverts the polarity of "wisdom" and "folly" and brings to light how their verbal repartee, though barbed, underlines a deep-seated affection. The Fool's words may operate "on a meaner scale," but Lear's familial difficulties prevent such observations from being wholly inappropriate. The wit, in the words of W. P. Albrecht, "lies in the tension between the pertinence of the Fool's comments and the impertinence of his language. The Fool's remarks both 'relieve' and 'aid' the intensity of passions."[71] These emotions, however, do not revolve around pity or maudlin impulses. Rather, the barbed wit brings to light the anxious hope that Lear's experiences, whether familiar or not, can affirm his value as both a King and a man. He simply has to combat a counterproductive solipsism and open himself to the Fool's concern.

Before he can attempt to participate in a constructive relationship, Lear must endure another meeting with his daughters. It does not go well. He first visits Regan, who tells him what he has already heard, namely that his retinue is superfluous and should be let go. Then, as if to throw salt in his wounds, she tells him to return to Goneril and say that "you have wronged her" (2.2.341). Clearly, she has no intent to pick up a knife and flay her sister's "wolvish visage" (1.4.298). The prospect of going before Goneril once again subdues his pride and, in a radical change of behavior, he gets down on his knees, begging that she will "vouchsafe me raiment, bed and food" (2.2.345). Although physical frailties force him to adjust to his surroundings, his emotional self struggles to be so amenable. When Goneril arrives and Regan tells him that he does not need even

---

70 William Hazlitt, *The Complete Works of William Hazlitt*, vol. 6, ed. P. P. Howe (London, 1933), 24.

71 A. P. Albrecht, "Hazlitt, Passion, and *King Lear*," *Studies in English Literature, 1500–1900* 18 (1978): 620.

one attendant, he loses composure. He calls them "unnatural hags" and swears that he will exact vengeance upon them (2.2.467). This outburst displays not only a heated defiance against their control over him, but also regret for granting them this power. Although he no longer has access to his former political resources, he draws strength from his person and refuses to give them the satisfaction of seeing him cry: "You think I'll weep,/ No, I'll not weep" (2.2.471–72). His strength of character shows that he is not a passive figure who deserves to be pitied, but acknowledged as someone worthy of their respect.

Still, emotional volatility plagues his thought process. He voices once again a fear of madness, but this time, his worry does not stem from trying to solve one of the Fool's perplexing riddles, but from trying to find someone to believe in him: "O fool, I shall go mad" (2.2.475). His cry to the Fool reveals a growing awareness of his dependence on others, a realization that was nonexistent when he exiled Cordelia. The alienation imposed by Regan and Goneril throws into relief the advantage of coordinating one's perception with someone who genuinely cares for that person. It fulfills the essence of one's nature. Within the context of the overarching argument, this kind of awareness engenders a higher order of empathy that stresses one's interdependence on another.[72] As Kris McDaniel explains, it is "through the higher-order empathetic act that I come to recognize myself as a physical object imbued with psychological states. Not only must I have empathy but there must also be other people who have empathy in order for me to have this kind of self-knowledge."[73] While the Fool represents a person capable of extending this kind of knowing, he along with Lear and his daughters exit the stage after these disheartening words are spoken. Thus, Lear misses an opportunity to form a more thoughtful bond with the Fool and better his self-understanding.

Without attaining any peace of mind, his inner turmoil begins to overwhelm his reasoning capacities. He stands out in a thunderstorm, exposed to its wind and rain, and challenges the lightning-streaked night skies to "[s]inge my white head" (3.1.6). To some critics, this bluster symbolizes Lear's unbridled anger, functioning as a type of pathetic fallacy, but, I submit, that it qualifies him to identify with its destructive nature and provides the opportunity to

---

72 Husserl believes that when both parties are aware that they are being experienced and understood by the other, they enter into a higher interpersonal unity, a "we." See Husserl, *Zur Phänomenologie der Intersubjektivität*, 3:472.
73 McDaniel, "Edith Stein," 218.

rage with someone—or, more properly, something—that defines itself by this elemental expression.[74]

> Blow winds and crack your cheeks! Rage, blow!
> You cataracts and hurricanes, spout
> 'Till you have drenched our steeples, drowned the cocks!
> You sulphurous and thought-executing fires,
> Vaunt-couriers of oak-cleaving thunderbolts,
> Singe my white head! (3.2.1–6)

Lear's words are more than sound and fury. The force of his words and energy pulsating through his speech underscores his familiarity of facing nature's brutal force.[75] Since he has had such difficulty communicating with Goneril and Regan, anthropomorphizing the storm so that it can respond to his commands illustrates the yearning to feel part of a moment where he plays a commanding role. He breaks free from the self-involved thoughts about his past mistakes and does not attempt to compare the storm's wrath to his own. Rather, the detail in describing its various features illustrates an attentiveness to what constitutes its distinct power. It drenches church steeples, drowns farms animals, and splits centuries-old oak trees. All of creation, whether natural or manmade, is subject to its might. Its omnipotence validates Lear's own power in daring it to strike him. While some downplay his ability to control the storm as "imaginary" or a sign of delusion that he is unable to stem the tide of his eventual madness, this challenge establishes his identity as a man who possesses the strength, both inner and outer, to vie with such an indomitable force.[76] In his mind, it

---

74 Interpreting the storm as metaphoric for Lear's conflicted state of mind has received much scholarly attention throughout the years. William Elton believes that demystifying the storm correlates to Lear's own process of forlorn realization and acceptance (*King Lear and the Gods* [San Marino, CA: The Huntington Library, 1966]). See E. Catherine Dunn, "The Storm in King Lear," *Shakespeare Quarterly* 3 (1952): 329–33; Josephine Waters Bennett, "The Storm Within: The Madness of Lear," *Shakespeare Quarterly* 13 (1962): 137–55; Arthur Kirsch, "The Emotional Landscape of King Lear," *Shakespeare Quarterly* 39 (1988): 154–70.
75 Janet Adelman interprets this speech as authorizing Goneril with the power of the weather: "No longer under the aegis of a male thunderer, the very wetness of the storm threatens to undo civilization, and manhood itself, spouting rain until it has 'drench'd the steeples, drown'd the cocks', its power an extension into the cosmos of Goneril's power to shake Lear's manhood" (Adelman, *Suffocating Mothers: Fantasies of Maternal Origin in Shakespeare's Plays, Hamlet to The Tempest* [New York: Routledge, 1991], 110). While the misogyny in Lear's speech is undeniable, his claim that "all germens spill at once" references man's contribution to reproduction complicates the view that the storm represents a female counterpoint (3.2.8).
76 Gwilym Jones, *Shakespeare's Storms* (Manchester: Manchester University Press, 2015), 76.

shows that he is neither weakened by age nor a person who can be pushed around by others. Even though provoking a non-human entity puts into question his wisdom, it demonstrates a powerful drive to be heard by others. It is a drive impelling him to the most intense activity: the acting and the being acted upon.

As indicated by his tone and declamation that the winds should "Rage, blow" and "all-shaking thunder,/ Strike flat the thick rotundity o'the world," Lear does not want to imagine or infer the torments it can produce. He wants to feel its force and counter it with his own vitality. By doing so, he can prove his mettle, but the Fool, who faithfully stands beside him, points out that this night "pities neither/ wise men nor fools" (3.2.12–13). For the first time in the play, "wisdom" and "folly" are not pitted against one another. These two social character traits fall into one category inclusive of both the King and the Fool, namely fear. Yet, although the storm threatens each one's well-being, the King has little interest in working cooperatively or astutely with another. Rather, his interest lies in proving to himself that his life still has merit. If not as a father, then he can establish his worth as a physically robust man. The Fool may express compassion, but the King stays fixed upon his own wants. Despite the Fool's compassion, the King's self-involved actions create an aesthetic of contradictory motives. These contradictions, however, do not deter the Fool, for they engender a continued alertness to the substantive differences between him and the King. A dramatic portrayal of these differences captures the dynamic and dialectical intertwinement between self and other. Indeed, a phenomenological account of empathy, according to Matthew Ratcliffe, revolves around appreciating the differences more than stressing the similarities.[77]

While the Fool's words put into play an understanding that can promote a mutual understanding, Lear remains fixated upon his own affairs and continues taunting the storm: "Rumble thy bellyful! Spit fire, spout rain!" (3.2.14). His realm of knowing is constituted in feeling. Experiencing the danger around and above him, his defiance gives him a purpose in establishing his position. He states that his anger is not directed at "you elements," but rather his children (3.2.16). He explicitly tells the storm, "You owe me no subscription" (3.2.18). Whereas his dealings with Goneril and Regan prove enervating, those with the storm enkindle a desire to clear his mind. Paradoxically, it humanizes him.

Instead of continuing to shout at the darkening skies, he looks inward and confesses a belief that undermines the strength of character that he has just revealed. He describes himself as a "poor, infirm, weak and despised old man" (3.2.20). The harshness of his words echoes the words of his ungrateful daughters

---

77 Ratcliffe, *Experiences of Depression*, 26–35.

and, as such, indicates a struggle to resuscitate the feelings of dignity that has been derided. The harm inflicted by the daughters' invective has indelibly colored the perception of himself. When telling the storm that "I stand your slave," he displays a submissive mentality which prevents him from realizing that others, like the Fool, recognize his worth and want him to enter into a world where he can act as an equal (3.2.19).[78] Believing that the only conclusion is to let the storm and "two pernicious daughters" battle him underlines the need to befriend someone (3.2.22). To decry that their disregard for a head so "old and white as this. O ho! 'tis foul" illustrates a sad realization of his vulnerability in this world (3.2.24).

To compound this awakening further, the Fool's cajoling ceases to possess the same kind of attentiveness to Lear's person as before. His riddling no longer seeks to goad the King into taking responsibility for his mistakes, but simply mocks the decision to stay in the storm. He delivers a sexually loaded allusion that compares the folly of not having a shelter to those men who allow carnal desires to determine their choices:

> The codpiece that will house
> Before the head has any
> The head and he shall louse:
> So beggars marry many. (3.2.27–30)

A codpiece, the appendage at the front of breeches, both hides male sex organs and emphasizes their presence. Referencing this piece of apparel shows that the subject matter has taken on a much different tone than before. The lines contend that a man who fornicates before he has a home for his head will end up unhappy, a beggar whose only company is promiscuous women. Such a comment neither appreciates nor adapts to Lear's self-realization. He has just admitted his frailties and even accepted defeat at the hands of his daughters and the storm. A lust-ridden diatribe is out of place. The Fool may not be as old as Lear, but he is equally vulnerable to nature's elemental forces. The exposure to the wind and cold rain has no doubt taken its toll on the Fool as well. The wisdom of his words merely rise to the level of a court fool, whose purport centers upon entertaining the court, and every audience responds readily to jest in-

---

78 Husserl believes that when both parties are aware that they are being experienced and understood by the other, they enter into a higher interpersonal unity, a "we." Although this is the Fool's goal, the King cannot see this possibility. See Husserl, *Zur Phänomenologie der Intersubjektivität*, 3:472.

terlaced with sexual references. The weather and his endangered health have biased his view of the situation as a whole.

Indeed, when Kent walks onto the heath and asks, "Who's there?," the Fool replies with his cherished dialectic of opposites: "Marry, here's grace and a codpiece—that's a wise man and a fool" (3.2.39, 40–41). Even though he has just called Lear a codpiece, he is the one who has chosen to follow an old man into a downpour. It is uncertain who is "grace" and who is "a codpiece," much less "a wise man" and "a fool." Despite this uncertainty, the counterpointing of wisdom and folly illustrates the inextricable tie between the two men and their capacity for mutual understanding. That this understanding has yet to be fully realized, however, underscores the difficulty of constructing an empathic rapport when one party elects to ignore the value of the other person. Lear must accept his mistakes in order to appreciate what the Fool offers. Otherwise, as Augustine writes, there can be no movement from one state to another:

> From this it appears that there must be some intermediate state through which a transition is made from wisdom to folly, a state to which it is impossible to ascribe either wisdom or folly. This intermediate state cannot be understood in this life by men, except through contraries. Thus, no mortal may become wise unless he passes from foolishness to wisdom.[79]

If he wishes to fashion a legacy that will preserve his dignity, then the King must conduct an honest self-reflection and affirm the value of his experiences with the Fool. Since he fails to achieve this state of knowing, the distance between the King's potentiality and actuality widens. As a result, it becomes more unlikely that the Fool's empathy, in the words of Husserl, will transcend itself and become confronted with an otherness of a completely new kind.[80]

Although his capacity to consider another's views begins to weaken, Lear is not wholly oblivious to his surroundings and the danger they present. He worries about the Fool's health and expresses his concern by drawing a likeness between them, "Come on, my boy. How dost my boy? Art cold?/ I am cold myself" (3.2.68–69). Admitting that he too is cold discloses a sensitivity and deep-seated affection towards the Fool that recalls his earlier self. He admits candidly that he prizes his companionship: "Poor fool and knave, I have one part in my heart/ That's sorry yet for thee" (3.2.72–73). While his words cause the Fool to recast his approach, they do not possess the profundity of knowing necessary to construct a mode of consciousness compatible with the Fool's insight. Still, his attempt to establish some common ground causes the Fool to alter his strategy. He

---

79 Augustine, *On Free Choice of the Will*, bk. 3 (Indianapolis: Hackett Publishing, 1991).
80 Husserl, *Zur Phänomenologie der Intersubjektivität*, 1:8–9.

forgoes acerbic witticisms and employs a playful song that gently urges Lear to "make content with his fortunes fit" (3.2.76).[81] Recognizing that the physical and psychological tribulations have severely limited Lear's ability to forge a truly interactive bond, the Fool merely directs the King to rest his mind by not dwelling upon misfortune. The willingness to change his rhetorical tactic demonstrates that the Fool is not a stock character, a run-of-the-mill fool, but one who is astutely aware of what constitutes an empathetic rapport.

As much promise as this exchange may suggest, the sanctity of their bond becomes diluted by the increasing participation of other characters. Kent and Gloucester become more direct in telling Lear what he should do so that he no longer appears as a vagabond king, and Edgar's ramblings become more pronounced, further confounding Lear. When the Fool and Lear do speak to one another, the subject matter deals either with cryptic questions, such as "whether a madman be a gentleman or a yeoman" or, as presented in the Quarto, a mock trial of Goneril. Neither topic strengthens their interpersonal rapport. In fact, the final lines of the Fool in both versions have no bearing upon their relationship. In the trial, the Fool states that he took Goneril "for a joint-stool," a sarcastic excuse for overlooking someone (3.6.51).[82] And, in the Folio, he replies to Lear's illogical announcement that "we'll go to supper i'the morning" (3.6.81–82) with the neatly fitting retort "And I'll go to bed at noon" (3.6. 82). He says nothing more, and Lear is left on his own to resuscitate his dignity. When the King reappears later in the play, the crown of wild flowers adorning his head makes clear that the Fool's efforts have failed to yield a positive outcome.

Despite these anti-climactic sentiments, one statement exists in both the Quarto and Folio that stays true to the theme underpinning their relationship. Just before his final scene, the Fool states, "This cold night will turn us all to fools and madmen" (3.4.76). The implication is clear: a wise man will seek shelter. This consistent counterpointing of "wisdom" and "folly" collapses the integ-

---

81 In the Folio, an extended speech delivered by the Fool follows. Lear has left the stage and the speech functions as a soliloquy, but one whose meaning remains a bit elusive. As such, it does not address or build off the rapport that he had just previously established with Lear. Instead, it looks at the entirety of the Kingdom's situation, decrying society's moral decay before concluding that people with good sense will ultimately prevail. This critique of social abuses contributes to the characterization of the Folio Fool as a bitter satirist, yet it also accentuates that his gentleness becomes most apparent when he interacts with Lear. During these exchanges, the traits of compassion and care come to the fore.
82 Foakes explains in his commentary that a joint-stool "was one properly fitted together by a joiner rather than by rough carpentry" (Foakes, *King Lear*, 290).

rity of these two terms. As a result, the basis for understanding and fulfillment cannot be determined by the social construct of language. The linguistic meaning generated by the interplay between "wisdom" and "folly" lies in the combined affective and intellective choice to empathize with one another. Its meaning cannot be characterized in rigid, exclusionary terms; the paradoxical construct of wise folly signifies that each term enhances the meaning of the other term.[83] Just like the two men, these two terms ultimately depend upon each other for meaning. The supplemental relation between this wisdom and folly characterizes the relationship between the two men. By subverting the traditional, hierarchical notions classifying opposites, the empathy expressed between them invites a broader, more liberal dimension of understanding to define them. The subversive element of this juxtaposition inheres in the idea that no fixed or bounded meaning exists for either term or either man. In spite of the absence of a terminal denotation, empathy brings to light the constructive capabilities of this paradox and allows for the traditional definitions of the two terms yet recognizes them as co-existing, underscoring the affectionate knowing exchanged between Lear and the Fool.

Empathy's Tempest

Unlike Goneril and Regan, Miranda is attentive to her father and respectful of his learning and authority. Despite these virtuous tendencies, however, she receives little acclaim in Shakespeare criticism beyond that of being a pawn to her father's political machinations or a victim to Caliban's primal urges. The objectification of her body often defines her purport. When addressing the father-daughter dynamic, Lori Leininger observes: "Prospero needs Miranda as sexual bait, and then needs to protect her from the threat which is inescapable given his hierarchical world—slavery being the ultimate extension of the concept of hierarchy."[84] He does fix his gaze on exacting vengeance upon those who usurped his power and cast him onto the sea in a "rotten carcass of a butt, not rigged"

---

83 The term "supplement" refers both to "that which supplements something already complete in itself, and that which supplies what is missing from something incomplete in an important aspect" (Derek Attridge, "Puttenham's Perplexity: Nature, Art, and the Supplement in Renaissance Poetic Theory," *Literary Theory/ Renaissance Texts*, ed. Patricia Parker and David Quint [Baltimore: Johns Hopkins University Press, 1986], 260).
84 Lori Jerrell Leininger, "The Miranda Trap: Sexism and Racism in Shakespeare's Tempest," in *The Woman's Part: Feminist Criticism of Shakespeare*, ed. Carolyn Ruth Swift Lenz, Gayle Greene, and Carol Thomas Neely (Urbana: University of Illinois Press, 1980), 289.

(1.2.146).[85] But, his revenge never comes to fruition because the love that he holds for Miranda has shaped his perception of others. Her affectionate understanding awakens him to a truth that supersedes mundane matters.[86] It frees her from the constraints imposed by the expectations assigned to her as a woman or daughter. Striving to foster a substantive bond with those who either ask nothing of her or wish to know her more fully underlines an unassuming selflessness. Her empathy inspires those with whom she engages directly to reciprocate the kindness expressed, engendering a greater awareness of their own humanness and hers.

For a woman whose world consists only of her father and Caliban, she seeks out situations where she can meet new people in order to expand her interpersonal knowledge and lay the foundation for a relationship to exist. For example, after Ferdinand becomes stranded on the island and their paths cross one another, she wants to know him better, but her father assigns him the task of moving logs. Dismayed, she tells him to forgo her father's commands and offers to finish the work because "my good will is to it,/ And yours it is against (3.1.30 – 31). Recognizing his disinterest in carrying out this labor shows both her attentiveness and her willingness to lessen his burden. By going against her father, she is free to express the affection that she feels within. It is only in the process of interacting that she establishes her individuality and Ferdinand's singular importance. Keeping mind that Bakhtin's definition of sympathy proves synonymous with empathy, Miranda's action displays "an enriching character of sympathetic understanding" that transposes another's experience to an entirely different axiological plane, into a new category of valuation and affirmation.[87] Her insight into Ferdinand's state of mind serves a greater purpose than mere kindness. It redefines Ferdinand from some non-descript laborer to someone with whom Mir-

---

85 All quotations are taken from *The Tempest: The Arden Shakespeare*, ed. Virginia Mason Vaughan and Alden T. Vaughan (London: Bloomsbury, 1999).

86 While critics assert that his civic responsibility to the state ultimately accounts for the forgiveness that he extends to the King of Naples and his brother, this consideration for their welfare reflects the lessons of empathy revealed by his daughter's care towards him and others. Elliot Visconsi examines the social and psychological ramifications of English constitutional law and how they account for why Prospero cannot let go of his responsibilities to the state. The "persistence of the indelible affective bonds of obligation between sovereign and subject" ultimately enable him to realize the limited value of punishing his brother (Visconsi, "*Vinculum Fidei: The Tempest* and the Law of Allegiance," *Law and Literature* 20 [2008]: 1). For other studies that examine the political subtext, see Simon Palfrey, *Late Shakespeare: A New World of Words* (New York: Oxford University Press, 1998); Constance Jordan, *Shakespeare's Monarchies: Ruler and Subject in the Romances* (Ithaca, NY: Cornell University Press, 1997).

87 Bakhtin, "Author and Hero in Aesthetic Activity," 102.

anda can fashion a cherished bond. He becomes the center of orientation. Attuning her thoughts with his illustrates how the volitional motive does not move her from the outside, but from within her own consciousness. That she takes the time to discern Ferdinand's viewpoint requires a certain maturity and selflessness, highlighting the essentially social character of empathy.[88] Jessica Slights lauds her initiative, noting that "interactions with both her father and her husband [function] as the defiant actions of a self-fashioning woman rather than the programmatic reactions of a dehumanized cipher."[89] These "defiant actions" affirm her independence in communicating a heartfelt belief in another's interior value.

At the beginning of the play, however, Miranda does not display such a discerning eye in assessing the moral quality of another person. Instead of drawing from past experiences to confirm the veracity of the heightened emotions pulsating through her body, she relies upon a shoreline observation to judge the moral worth of mariners trapped on a sinking ship. The titular tempest has caused them to cry out in fear, leading one to exclaim "I would give a thousand furlongs of sea for an acre of barren ground" (1.1.65 – 66). Hearing these cries, she is overcome with grief and laments, "O, I have suffered/ With those that I saw suffer" (1.2.5 – 6). Since she has never even met them, her proclamation is excessive and melodramatic. Its intensity may attest to what she feels in that moment, but the lack of knowledge limits her understanding. She cannot rely on experience either to determine the appropriate amount of sentiment or distinguish men of virtue from those of vice. She may intellectually grasp that a difference exists, but since she does not have the means to know them personally, she cannot ascertain their motivations and belief system with any substantive accuracy. Even if this "suffering" is felt only by her, however, it attests to a genuine desire to extend support and experience vicariously what it feels like to face imminent peril.[90] Ultimately though, it reveals a longing to connect with someone new.

---

88 Diana Brydon compares Miranda's situation to the demands of a Canadian immigrant. Prospero's daughter is "attempting to create a neo-Europe in an invaded land, torn between Old World fathers and suitors while unable to ignore the just grievances of those her culture is displacing" (Brydon, "Sister Letters: Miranda's *Tempest* in Canada," in *Cross-Cultural Performances: Differences in Women's Re-visions of Shakespeare*, ed. Marianne Novy [Urbana: University of Illinois Press, 1993], 166).

89 Jessica Slights, "Rape and Romanticization of Shakespeare's Miranda," *Studies in English Literature 1500 – 1900* 41 (2001): 371. Slights contends that "past and present readings of *The Tempest* alike have misread the play by emphasizing the nature of Prospero's relationship with the island of his exile without considering the alternative models of selfhood, moral agency, and community life posited by the magician's daughter" (359).

90 Her empathy, according to Marjorie Garber, makes her "the ideal spectator of tragedy and catharsis" (*Shakespeare after All* [New York: Pantheon, 2004], 857). Also see, James Morrison,

Mirroring the sailors' emotional condition does not produce first-hand knowledge of their person. Stein stresses that such a connection requires far more than a transference of emotions: "It should be sufficiently clear that the theory of imitation cannot serve as a genetic explanation of empathy."[91] It involves entering into the minded life of others and asks one to make a deliberate decision to assess the others and how that experience affects them. Miranda has no background knowledge of their character. She may be conscious of the danger that they face, but without a face-to-face encounter, cannot determine how their intentions and wants differ from her own.[92] Still, the desire to foster an intimate link is both laudable and a basic tenet of empathy. This tenet empowers one to appreciate the full dimension of the other's person because through it the empathizer has an interpersonal experience that interlards body, psyche, and spirit: "The individual lives, feels, and acts as a member of the community, and insofar as he does that, the community lives, feels and acts in him and through him."[93] The mariners' ignorance of Miranda may prevent her from realizing such an awareness, but striving to forge such a link shows that her efforts function more than an emotive response. They operate as "a kind of act of perceiving *sui generis*" and, as such, mark the beginning stages of empathy.[94] They present a distinct view of what determines meaning in her world. Striving to access another's perspective proves that she is neither a secondary character nor a submissive daughter. Her independence manifests itself in actions that lay the foundation for her to enter into a valued relationship.

Indicative of an early modern optimism in another's dignity, Miranda characterizes the ship as a "brave vessel" that "had no doubt some noble creature in her" (1.2.6 – 7).[95] Despite the obvious naïveté of such a statement, the psychic attraction to people whom she apprehends as good highlights her yearning to connect with people of merit. That she views these men as noble shows that her interest is not an impulsive reaction to the direness of their situation. Rather, it demonstrates a mindfulness of the innate goodness accorded to all humans.

Shipwrecked: Disaster and Transformation in Homer, Shakespeare, Defoe, and the Modern World (Ann Arbor: University of Michigan Press, 2014), 47.

91 Stein, *On the Problem of Empathy*, 24.

92 Edmund Husserl, *Phänomenologische Psychologie: Vorlesungen Sommersemester 1925*, ed. W. Biemel, Husserliana 9 (The Hague: Martinus Nijhoff, 1962), 321.

93 Edith Stein, *Philosophy of Psychology and the Humanities*, 139.

94 Stein, *On the Problem of Empathy*, 11.

95 Her action exhibits a Renaissance optimism in humankind's dignity and calls to mind Pico della Mirandola's position that we have the freedom to choose our own destiny. See Pico della Mirandello, *Oration on the Dignity of Man* (Indianapolis: Hackett Publishing, 1998), 5 – 6.

Even though her sentiment may not produce a shared understanding, it exhibits a sincere effort to make this experience epistemically significant. Being part of this moment makes her more attuned to human vulnerability and, as such, affirms her belief in the value of life. As a whole, it holds the potential to increase her appreciation of others as well as herself.

Yet, the distance separating them—both physically and personally—precludes her from developing an empathetic kind of knowing. Instead, her actions bring to light how emotion functions more as an experience than as an expression. Hearing the sailors plight moves her with such force that "the cry did knock/ Against my very heart!" (1.2.8–9). The pounding of her heart underscores her immersion into the drama surrounding the sailors' plight. The resultant knowledge helps shape her understanding of those who undergo great tribulations and how fear throws into relief the primal desire to live and life's ultimate fragility. Emphasizing its impact upon her "very heart" shows that this self-awareness fundamentally differs from her perception of the sailors. This involves her whole being, which continually expands and evolves. The sailors, on the other hand, are perceived as objects whose existence is defined by this harrowing moment. Bakhtin examines the line of demarcation between observer and observed: "For me, the other is gathered and fitted as a whole into his outward image. My own consciousness, on the other hand, I experience as encompassing the world, as embracing it, rather than as fitted into it."[96] Miranda's speech reveals a subjective inner self that determines how these feelings define her person and their applicability to the situation. Cognizant of the one-sided nature of her response, she notes that if she had the power to save these men, she would have "sunk the sea within the earth" (1.2.12).[97] Although hyperbole once again characterizes her position, the core meaning is both relevant and commendable. If possible, she would be willing to make the necessary effort to aid them. Her commitment to them shows that an empathetic pursuit can serve a beneficial purpose. While some philosophers maintain that kindness or offering support is not necessary, her initiative both here and later in the play illustrates that a virtuous use of the intellect can foster empathy.[98] Wanting to safeguard another's well-being

---

96 Bakhtin, "Author and Hero in Aesthetic Activity," 45.

97 Tom McAlindor examines the compassionate side of Miranda as she pleads with Prospero on behalf of the sailors in "The Discourse of Prayer in *The Tempest*," *Studies in English Literature* 41 (2001): 340.

98 Peter Goldie does not believe that empathy has any bearing upon allaying one's suffering or sympathizing with his or her condition. See Goldie, *The Emotions*, 215. Coplan states directly that empathy "does not in and of itself involve . . . an impulse [to help the other]" ("Empathic Engagement with Narrative Fictions," 146).

fulfills the criteria of a righteous act and, in Martin Hoffman's estimation, is essential in developing and expressing a healthy empathy.[99] Of course, this does not mean that it always culminates in a virtuous act because the ensuing choices may prove applicable only to that person and not to the other.[100] Miranda's motivations, however, are selfless and spring from a genuine desire to forge a link with these mariners.

This concern for another's well-being attests to an embedded altruism that stems from a conscientious use of the intellect as well as an affectionate upbringing that nurtured these tendencies of care and consideration.[101] While a wide expanse of water effectively prevents any verbal exchange with the mariners, her father stands right beside her. Attentive to her worries, he assures her that "There's no harm done" to them (1.2.13). He wants to alleviate her distress and make sure that this suffering does not cloud her mind. Moved by her awareness of the world and yearning to participate in its offerings—no matter how upsetting or different from her own life—he realizes that it is time to share their past family history. This knowledge will empower her to complete the maturation process so that when she does meet someone of value, she can act with the surety that an informed self-awareness provides. He first impresses upon her how much he has devoted his life to her and how little she knows of her past:

> I have done nothing but in care of thee,
> Of thee, my dear one, thee my daughter, who
> Art ignorant of what out art. (1.2.16–18)

Although the impetus of Prospero's tempest is to set in motion the action necessary to resolve past political conflicts and regain his title as the rightful Duke of Milan, it neither defines him as a person nor as a father. He has dedicated the last twelve years to raising his "dear one." Being confined to an insular existence, however, has severely diminished her need to learn about the past. Indeed, when hearing him speak about her past, she replies that this topic "[d]

---

99 Hoffman, *Empathy and Moral Development*; R. J. R. Blair takes this position further when he asserts that empathy is in fact necessary for moral development. See R. J. R. Blair, "A Cognitive Developmental Approach to Morality: Investigating the Psychopath," *Cognition* 57 (1995): 1–29.
100 Consider the paradigm of the friend who grasps the other's condition with such intensity that he elects to express this understanding via an act that violates legal, cultural, or religious precepts. For a rigorous examination of how empathy does not qualify as a virtue, see Battaly, "Is Empathy a Virtue?," 277–301.
101 Hiewon Shin asserts that "Miranda's compassion was most likely inculcated by Prospero's paternal instruction, since she has no women around her, and no mother" ("Single Parenting, Homeschooling: Prospero, Caliban, Miranda," *Studies in English Literature* 48 [2008]: 384–85).

id never meddle with my thoughts" (1.2.22). Yet, with the imminent prospect of stranded sailors coming to the island, she needs to be fully aware of who she is and realize that she holds a place of distinction in society.

The ensuing dialogue provides the kind of direct, thoughtful interaction that was so lacking in her unilateral reaction to the sailors' plight. In fact, Prospero urges her to "ope thine ear/ Obey and be attentive" (1.2.37–38). Carefully listening to his wisdom fosters the harmony between them. In fact, A. D. Smith observes that the root of empathy is a basic attunement to the responsiveness of the other, for he responds to her and her actions in a way that is unique to their relationship.[102] While the subject matter of Prospero's counsel facially relates their past in Italy, its purport is to make her more discriminating in her assessment of other people. Despite her conviction that the sailors are noble creatures, the complexity of one's moral state cannot be ascertained simply by reacting to their emotional state of being. It requires a thoughtful consideration of their intents and wants as well as a solid grasp of oneself. He proceeds to relate how his brother, "whom next thyself/ Of all the world I loved," betrayed him and overtook his duchy (1.2.68–69). To ensure that she grasps the difficulty of truly knowing another, he asks if she grasps how this perfidy impacted her person: "Thy false uncle—/ Dost thou attend me?" (1.2.78–79). As noted by Virginia Vaughan, his insistence for her to pay attention here and later in lines 87 and 106 does not imply that she is inattentive; it more likely indicates his increasing agitation as he recalls his brother's treachery.[103] Realizing that even being a blood relation and loved offers no guarantee of faithfulness underscores the importance of understanding as fully as possible the other's motivations. This requires that she exercises her burgeoning independence by engaging those whom she truly holds "noble" with a keen insight into their wants and beliefs.

The end result ideally fosters a connection where both people apprehend the other's thoughts. For Husserl, this coincidence of attentiveness produces higher-order empathy, which helps expose any inclinations towards deception.[104] Whereas a basic level of empathy simply apprehends the other as a body capable of sensing and experiencing the surrounding world, a high level strives to understand what the other's expressions signify, specifically their intentions and purpose.[105] Miranda pursues this end when she asks about her father's line of reasoning for creating the tempest: "For still 'tis beating in my mind, your reason/

---

102 A. D. Smith, *Routledge Philosophy Guidebook to Husserl and the Cartesian Meditations* (London: Routledge, 2003), 243.
103 Vaughan, *The Tempest*, 176.
104 Husserl, *Zur Phänomenologie der Intersubjektivität*, 2:315.
105 Husserl, *Zur Phänomenologie der Intersubjektivität*, 1:435–36.

For raising this sea-storm?" (1.2.176–77). Wanting to know his state of mind indicates both a genuine concern for the welfare of others and an effort to gain a deeper understanding of what drives him. He explains that this storm has brought those responsible for his exile to the island where he will now have the opportunity to remedy his fortune. While he uses his authoritative, magical power to satisfy his notion of justice, she seeks interpersonal experiences to lead a fulfilled and just life. Her inquiry displays a willingness to consider another's perspective as well as a mature understanding of consequences. It is not the submissive act of a young girl dependent upon her father for guidance. Independent thinking underpins the originality of this exchange and the immanence of the self and other.

The first opportunity to exercise this self-awareness and forge a meaningful rapport with someone capable of reciprocating her concern occurs when she meets Ferdinand. He had been on the sinking ship along with his father, the King of Naples, and her devious uncle, Antonio. In fact, he is the first man whom she has ever met close to her own age, thus inciting her immediate attraction. She exclaims that he is "a thing divine, for nothing natural/ I ever saw so noble" (1.2.418–19).[106] Though still subject to hyperbole, her speech simply reflects the dizzying excitement of romantic attraction rather than the desperate longing to feel a connection with someone other than her father. This interaction stimulates the maturation process and illustrates how another person, another body, can impact her reality. She is no longer a jejune girl bemoaning the fate of unknown mariners, but a woman immersed in an experience that redefines her interests. Ernest Cassirer writes, "Life cannot apprehend itself by remaining absolutely within itself. It must give itself form; for it is precisely by this 'otherness' of form that it gains its 'visibility,' if not its reality."[107] Ferdinand's nobility alters her perception of the world and her role in it. She can put into praxis her skill in assessing what this experience reveals about his intentions and decide for herself how best to reciprocate his interest.

Since neither one has met a romantic counterpart who has filled them with such intrigue—for her, he is the first "That e'er I sighed for"—each one's focus

---

106 This praise both expresses a wondrous affection and reflects the contemporary view of the body's inextricable link to the divine. Sixteenth-century political theorist, Thomas Starkey, states that when examining the constitution of man, "we schal nothing dowte of hys excellent dygnyte, but plainly affyrme, that he hath in him a sparkful of Dyvynyte, and ys surely of a celestial and dyuyne nature" (*England in the Reign of King Henry the Eighth, A Dialogue between Cardinal Pole and Thomas Lupset*, ed. J. M. Cowper, *EETS*, vol. 12, pt. 2 [1871], 12).

107 Ernest Cassirer, *The Philosophy of Symbolic Forms*, vol. 3, trans. R. Manheim (New Haven, CT: Yale University Press, 1957), 39.

lies intently upon the other (1.2.447). Consequently, the spark between them affects not only her speech, but also his. He describes her as a deity: "Most sure the goddess/ On whom these airs attend!" (1.2.423). Being heir to the throne, he has been immersed in the thick of societal affairs throughout his life so his use of hyperbole cannot be readily dismissed as naïveté or even an impulsive, hormonal teenage reaction. Equating her with a figure of great beauty that arouses adoration shows that he appreciates her aesthetic inner and bodily value in its distinctiveness. Seeing herself from his perception reveals a facet of her person that, without this experience, she would not perceive in the same manner.[108] This mode of consciousness increases the means to apprehend the extent of our possibilities; it engenders self-knowledge. This budding romance, replete with awkward pauses and questions far too inquisitive, reflects an honest interest in each other's well-being.

When Ferdinand inquires about her sexual state, she assures him that she is "certainly a maid" (1.2.428). Whether grounded in chastity, benevolence, or honesty, her virtue and his desire to embrace it ensure that their relationship will be founded upon something far more substantial than sensory appeal. What their bodies represent is polyvalent, depicted as conscious, conceptual, and emotive. Although she is not biologically different from any other woman, Ferdinand's attention distinguishes her and, in turn, shows that an intrinsic relation exists between them.[109] Husserl notes the dual nature of the body: "My body is given to me as an interiority, a volitional structure, and as a dimension of sensing, but it is also given as a visually and tactually appearing exteriority."[110] Affected by the totality of her person, Ferdinand draws a surety from this knowing and relates how his father perished in the shipwreck. She replies with compassion, "Alack, for mercy!" (1.2.438). Expressing a mutual awareness and appreciation for each other's value lays the foundation for the general cognitive and emotive preconditions necessary to produce an empathetic experience.

While some aver that Prospero's magic underpins the characters' metamorphosis and accounts for why "the scale is vertical and the agency transcendent," Miranda's maturation thrives on the human plane and draws its insight from her

---

108 Stein, *On the Problem of Empathy*, 88.
109 Bermúdez considers the experienced spatiality of the body is part of what marks out the experience of one's body as a unique physical object. See José Luis Bermúdez, "Ownership and the Space of the Body," in *The Subject's Matter: Self-Consciousness and the Body*, ed. Frédérique de Vignemont and Adrian J. T. Alsmith (Cambridge, MA: MIT Press, 2017), 117–44.
110 Zahavi, *Subjectivity and Selfhood*, 156.

interpersonal experiences.[111] Instead of critically assessing her growth as the result of a "manipulable, artful process," emphasizing her participation in relationships where she actively considers the other's well-being underscores her individuality and skill in apprehending another's intents and purpose.[112] She knows in her heart and mind that he too is a good person. When her father accuses Ferdinand of being a spy, she readily defends him, pronouncing with surety that "nothing ill can dwell in such a temple" (1.2.459). Her heightened awareness of the virtue evident in his person assures her of his qualitative worth. Hence, when he draws his sword to protest Prospero's threat of imprisonment, she readily defends his character. She pleads with her father to not make "too rash a trial of him, for/ He's gentle and not fearful" (1.2.467–68). Even though their time together has been relatively short, it has empowered her with a keen insight into what drives him and empowers her to assume a role reversal with her father. She determines what constitutes authoritative knowledge and Prospero is the one expected to heed this wisdom. The certitude drawn from their interaction elevates their bond above those around them and demonstrates a bold confidence in the goodness of being human.

Miranda's independence manifests itself most fully when she urges Ferdinand to forgo the labor assigned by her father. As aforementioned, Prospero has ordered him to stack up thousands of logs for no clear purpose other than to keep him busy. Her singular devotion, however, transforms the father-daughter dynamic. The experiential knowledge that she shares with Ferdinand enables her to appreciate him for his own sake. While a simple act of kindness implies only a general relation to the good for its own sake, empathy prompts her to direct her affections specifically to his service. It communicates his goodness and allows her to respond in kind. Similarly, Ferdinand finds solace in thoughts of her beauty as he carries out this mean task. It would "be as heavy to me as odious, but/ The mistress which I serve quickens what's dead" (3.1.4–6). While this work prevents him from doing anything other than draw comfort from these feel-

---

111 Greene observes that most of Shakespeare's plays rely upon a "lateral resourcefulness" and "horizontal maneuvering and adaptations" by characters, yet "only in the last play, *The Tempest*, does Shakespeare remove from the human sphere the responsibility for metamorphosis and assign it to magic, to the supernatural . . . almost uniquely in Shakespeare, the scale is vertical and the agency transcendent" ("The Flexibility of the Self in Renaissance Literature," in *The Disciplines of Criticism: Essays in Literary Theory, Interpretation, and History*, ed. Peter Demetz, Thomas Greene, and Lowry Nelson [New Haven, CT: Yale University Press, 1968], 263).
112 Stephen Greenblatt, *Renaissance Self-Fashioning: From More to Shakespeare* (Chicago: University of Chicago Press, 1980), 2.

ings, she is not burdened by external demands. Free to exercise her mind, she determines what would best remedy the situation:

> Alas now, pray you,
> Work not so hard. I would the lightning had
> Burnt up those logs that you are enjoined to pile!
> Pray set it down and rest you. (3.1.15 – 18)

Just as when she wished for the power to sink "the sea within the earth" to save the sailors, she wishes for nature to intercede and allay Ferdinand's burden (1.2.11). The focus on miracles or manipulating nature to care for the empathized underscores the effect that her father's magic has had on her world. With a parent who relied upon "art to enchant," she must discover what comprises her own, natural talents (Ep. 14). They do not include charms and commanding spirits, but rather honing the inner drive to grasp another's state of mind and protect their well-being. Husserl discusses how the individual's sense of self takes form through their social connections:

> The origin of personality is found in empathy and in the further social acts that grow out of it. For personality, it is not enough that the subject becomes aware of itself as the center of its acts; rather, personality is constituted only as the subject enters into social relations with others.[113]

The desire to become part of a world that radically differs from her upbringing attests to Miranda's desire to learn through the lived experiences of another, restructure her perspective, and hone her interpersonal skills. The demand to put down the logs and rest adds momentum to her ever-evolving character as a woman capable of loving concern. This volition establishes the distinctiveness of her personality and, in turn, the underlying difference between her and Ferdinand.

As opposed to the sailors on the sinking ship, she can see him as an individual whose life can be bettered by her affection. In Husserl's words, empathy allows her to apprehend him originally; for what she sees is neither a sign nor an analogue, but rather his actual person.[114] This reality makes him present to her in a way that is immediate and enables her to realize her potential as a person capable of profound compassion. She assumes a position of authority and coun-

---

113 Husserl, *Zur Phänomenologie der Intersubjektivität*, 2:175.
114 Husserl claims that a difference necessarily exists since the observer can never experience the other's life in the exact same manner. For the observer, it is shown; for the other, it is lived through. See Husserl, *Zur Phänomenologie der Intersubjektivität*, 2:385; 3:506.

ters the established system of social order on the island: "Pray give me that;/ I'll carry it to the pile" (3.1.23–24). By taking this action, she puts into motion the process of becoming her own person. Ferdinand recognizes this and expresses his similar capacity to care by declaring, "No, precious creature,/ I had rather crack my sinews, break my back/ Than you should such dishonour undergo" (3.1.25–27).[115] That she not "dishonour" herself illustrates a firm belief in her goodness. His impassioned plea does not spring from some general, socially contrived notion that a woman should not perform physically intensive labor, but a conviction in her independent worth. Mutual respect underpins the originality of this exchange and identity is drawn from their distinct responses and grasping the other's perspective.[116]

She assures him that since her motivation springs from good will, performing manual labor does not demean her dignity. In fact, it would show that she can carry out a task as well as he can: "It would become me/ As well as it does you" (3.1.27–28). Selflessness transforms a work of drudgery into an act that draws them closer to one another. She recognizes his disinterest in this work, but his expressivity is imbued with psychological meaning.[117] It calls forth her skill in discerning why his will is against this work. Her insight attests to her liberty in fostering a healthy, compatible relationship. Her agency, as stated by Slights, "should not be dismissed as the inevitable consequence of Prospero's political ambitions. Miranda's choices are admittedly few, but she is presented as an imaginative and headstrong young woman who shows no signs of acquiescing unthinkingly to her father's wishes."[118] She may worry that "my father's precepts/ I therein do forget," but makes no attempt to walk away from her "patient log-man" (3.1.57–58, 67). She actively subverts these precepts which, given her insular existence, limit her social experiences. She wants to cultivate a knowing that takes into account his needs and desires. In return, his commitment expands beyond all limit of what else is in the world, causing him to state that he does "love, prize, honour you" (3.1.71–73). The emotional transference conveyed through their acts does not forsake the identity of either one, but valorizes their love, elevating it to a status of noble dimensions.

---

115 Husserl, *Zur Phänomenologie der Intersubjektivität*, 2:288.

116 Husserl stresses that a person apprehends their identity by drawing from their own lived body and from the other's perspective of their person. See Husserl, *Zur Phänomenologie der Intersubjektivität*, 2:420.

117 Edmund Husserl, *Ideen zu einer reinen Phänomenologie und phänomenologischen Philosphie*, bk. 2, *Phänomenologische Untersuchungen zur Konstitution*, ed. M. Biemel, Husserliana 4 (The Hague: Martinus Nijhoff, 1952), 235–44.

118 Slights, "Rape and Romanticization of Shakespeare's Miranda," 367.

Miranda My husband, then?

Ferdinand Ay, with a heart as willing/
         As bondage e'er of freedom. Here's my hand.

Miranda And mine, with my heart in't. And now farewell. (3.1.87–90)

This interpersonal belief flows from an empathetic bond, which grasps another's consciousness and uses this distinct mode of knowing, as Husserl famously points out, "transcends itself."[119] This transcendence empowers both Miranda and Ferdinand to appreciate each other's desires and act on them. Neither one's efforts are unilateral. Rather, they culminate in synchronous harmony, which integrates the perspectives of each into a dynamic experience that does not gloss over the intricacies within their reality. Prospero's art may have brought them together, but it does not dictate how each chooses to structure their response.

Their relationship advances from an understanding founded upon an affectionate attentiveness towards the other's well-being to apprehending the compatibility of the other's defining essence. Her empathy engenders a directedness that binds her to Ferdinand. Their shared understanding of each other results in a proposal of marriage. Where love precedes knowledge, empathy informs her action. She freely gives him her heart. She does this because the highest good is no longer simply grasping the value of his person, but an act, for the value of love is itself. Empathy's movement may draw upon the knowledge exchanged between them, but putting it into praxis is the only way its expression can be conceived. Its dynamic nature involves their whole person, which transforms the conventional notions of freedom. It disregards physical, political, or social liberties, which preoccupy Prospero's thought, to a volition centered upon his singular value. As such, Miranda's expression of concern for Ferdinand's well-being calls to mind Husserl's notion of transcendence.[120] Zahavi explicates Husserl's repeated insistence that "empathy allows us to encounter true transcendence, and that our consciousness in empathy transcends itself and is confronted with, as he puts it, otherness of a completely new kind."[121] This new kind of knowing enables this couple to appreciate each other's goodness. The result is a love that enriches their world and vivifies their consciousness with a profound affection that supersedes mundane matters. Neither one's efforts are unilateral. Rather, they culminate in synchronous harmony, which integrates each one's

---

119 Husserl, *Zur Phänomenologie der Intersubjektivität*, 2:8–9.
120 Husserl, *Zur Phänomenologie der Intersubjektivität*, 2:8–9.
121 Zahavi, *Self & Other*, 134.

perspective into a dynamic experience that thrives off the interaction of their individual wholeness. Prospero's art may have brought them together, but it does not dictate how each chooses to structure their response.

This freedom of choice comes to the fore when they meet again to play chess. For a young woman who has had virtually no prior interaction with men her age, she has quickly adapted to the age-old game of teasing one's beloved as a way of expressing and receiving affection.

> Miranda Sweet lord, you play me false.
>
> Ferdinand No, my dearest love,
>   I would not for the world.
>
> Miranda Yes, for a score of kingdoms you should wrangle,
>   And I would call it fair play. (5.1.172–74)

Although no threat of deceit actually exists, it affords Miranda the opportunity to hear Ferdinand speak of his faithfulness to her. His protestations of innocence assure her of his affection. In turn, she states that she would never stand in his way if he chose to "wrangle." She is not condoning bad acts but merely emphasizing the extent of her love. Although playful in tone and purpose, this tête-à-tête also underscores their individuality. Each one's response reveals a heartfelt devotion. Miranda's surety in his personality stems from their interaction and her ability to discern her state of mind. What matters then is not striving to gain more knowledge but acting upon what she has already acquired. This movement brings into existence values that are bound to sensory responses. Empathy refines their co-experience into a potent force that instills a heartfelt confidence in his goodness, paradoxically displayed by the lighthearted teasing of his supposed cheating. She becomes dependent upon him to generate this intimate understanding. In his phenomenological explication of self-value, Bakhtin writes, "I myself cannot be the author of my own value, just as I cannot lift myself by my own hair."[122] Through discussions with her father and previous experiences on the island, Miranda enters into this dialogue as a uniquely defined self, but realizes through her understanding of Ferdinand and his perception of her that she is capable of a profound loving empathy. It affirms and bestows value on the other as a fully developed individual.

The seeds of this burgeoning awareness find their root in Prospero's attentive care to her maturation. He respects her concern for the well-being of others and fosters this understanding by disclosing the unknown details of her own history

---

122 Bakhtin, "Author and Hero in Aesthetic Activity," 55.

so that she can better grasp the potential complexity of her future interactions. Prospero's reflectiveness also indicates an awareness that he too needs others to reciprocate this kind of conscientiousness to confirm his value as a person. The decision to forgive the King of Naples and his usurping brother attests to a virtue akin to Miranda's. He reasons that the "rarer action is/ In virtue than vengeance" (5.1.27–28). Although the moral character of some of these men does not merit his kindness, he wants to embrace the kind of knowing that elevates him above this world's worries. When the King of Naples expresses regret for exiling him, Prospero readily replies, "Let us not burden our remembrances with/ A heaviness that's gone" (5.1.198–99). The desire not to gain political power, but interpersonal stability allows him to immerse himself in the present moment and engage in a dialogue that will strengthen their rapport. Indeed, he invites them to his "poor cell" where he will relate "the story of my life" (5.1.302, 305). Exchanging this knowledge allows what were once foes to become friends who can assess his motivations and state of being.[123]

His growth as a person is indebted to his daughter's conviction to express compassion and privilege empathy as a means to communicate. She represents the evolution of the self by immersing herself in experiences that enable her to explore and access another's perspective. She actively explores the full dimensionality of the other person. Via her example, Prospero no longer views the world as a place that he must control and elects to forgo a solipsistic belief that retribution best serves his interests. This shift in thought fosters an appreciation of another's singular value and recasts what constitutes a valued relationship. Its core expands beyond the affective to consider the intentions, wants, and beliefs of another. Cultivating this consciousness instantiates empathy as an understanding culled from close, interpersonal experience. The culmination of this interpersonal expression is his desire "to see the nuptial/ Of these our dear-beloved solemnized" (5.1.309–10). Meaning in this world centers upon witnessing love's fulfillment founded upon his daughter's grasp and appreciation of Ferdinand's goodness. This concerted focus possesses an epistemic value that reveals the authenticity of her devotion and confirms the intrinsic value of sharing in constructive experiences that produce an expanding dynamic of inclusivity. Her commitment thus valorizes the intrinsic value of being human, its uniqueness, and need to enrich its intimacy.

---

123 Husserl believes that when both parties are aware that they are being experienced and understood by the other, they enter into a higher interpersonal unity, a "we" (Husserl, *Zur Phäno-menologie der Intersubjektivität*, 3:472).

Chapter 4 Projecting an Empathy that Transgresses This World's Bounds in Seventeenth-Century Metaphysical Poetry

The transition from medieval to early modern depictions of empathy evolves from an emphasis upon preserving fellowship and familial ties to heightening the passions of lovers who strive to attain a transcendent bond. Whether these romantic aspirations flourish in this realm or the next, John Donne and Richard Crashaw carefully structure the narrative of their love poetry upon protagonists who simulate the emotional and mental states of their beloved. This process of duplication reveals vital truths about the other's state of mind. The resultant insight allows these protagonists to transgress the boundaries separating not only the mundane from the ethereal, but also life from death. It enriches their interpersonal knowledge to such a degree that no obstacle can weaken or threaten the bond with their beloved. While late twentieth-century findings in neuroscience provide an empirical basis to explain the physiological inclination to mirror another's gestures and condition, the concurrent developments in simulation theory most fully inform the empathic interplay between Donne's and Crashaw's lovers.

Spearheaded by Alvin Goldman's writings, this theory attributes specific states to another person via the act of copying his or her behavior. A necessary condition for this "mindreading process" is that "the state ascribed to the target is ascribed as a result of the attributor's instantiating, undergoing, or experiencing, that very state."[1] Envisioning or re-enacting these states, whether bodily, cognitive, or emotive, enables the observer to ascertain that person's state of mind. As a result, it reveals what makes the other distinct and worthy of such an unwavering commitment.[2] While imitating another's distress or joy conveys a general acknowledgment of that person's condition, the observer strengthens the rapport if he or she uses this imitation to infer complex mental states, such as intentions and expectations. This inference sheds light on the psychological etiology underpinning that person's behavior. Simulation theory thus pres-

---

1 Goldman states that a necessary condition for mindreading "is that the state ascribed to the target is ascribed as a result of the attributor's instantiating, undergoing, or experiencing, that very state" (Alvin I. Goldman and Chandra Sekhar Sripada, "Simulationist Models of Face-Based Emotion Recognition," *Cognition* 94 [2005]: 208).
2 Goldman, *Simulating Minds*, 19.

https://doi.org/10.1515/9781501515460-005

ents a framework of how a mind thinks about other minds. It is, in the words of Goldman, "an extended form of empathy" that allows one to consider the world from the other's perspective, input those specific mental states, and then put oneself in that person's shoes.[3] Mirroring another's behavior is not simply a biological reaction to an external stimulus, but an epistemological resource that unlocks profound realizations about that person's thought process. Hence, a semblance of another's behavior brings to light that emotional and cognitive faculties naturally align and can strengthen the intimacy.

For Donne's protagonists, matching the beloved's behavior ensures that their connection transcends corporeal constraints. Elaine Scarry comments upon the unique emphasis upon the body in Donne's poetry, noting that it "insists on the obligation to touch the human body, whether acutely alive or newly dead, with generosity and fierce decency."[4] While being "newly dead" may eliminate the possibility of bodily reciprocity, it does not prevent the speaker in "Nocturnal upon St. Lucy's Day" from envisioning how this state of existence affects his deceased lover. Immersing himself in the winter solstice's long, cold night and all that its darkness represents, he imagines what it is like to be in this otherworldly realm. Replicating the emotive states of emptiness and desolation paradoxically reinforces their link. Whether it is physical, emotional, or intellectual, the protagonists' simulation highlights the desire to connect with his beloved in her present state—no matter the circumstances surrounding its reality.

Traversing the fleshly bonds of a sensory reality to sustain the ineffable bonds of love ascends to even greater heights in the eyes of Crashaw's lachrymose protagonist, Mary Magdalene. Imitation allows her to move past the reaches of death and situate herself within the supernal. In "The Weeper," overflowing tears represent a refined attunement to Christ's humanness that allows her to follow Him "where'er he strays" (l. 109). As Richard Rambuss notes, "Mary's still streaming tears alchemically mix with Jesus's flowing blood, then glitteringly harden into gemstones, into the previous currency of rubies and pearls—love gifts for them to exchange."[5] The intermixture of tears and blood resonates with a compassion akin to the divine's. When the tears transmogrify into jewels, their preciousness underlines not only the success of his mimesis, but also the surety generated by this kind of knowing. Structuring an honest reflection upon the humility underpinning virtuous affection illustrates how human

---

3 Goldman, *Simulating Minds*, 4.
4 Elaine Scarry, "Donne: 'But Yet the Body Is His Booke,'" in *Literature and the Body: Essays On Populations and Persons*, ed. Elaine Scarry (Baltimore: Johns Hopkins University Press, 1988), 70.
5 Richard Rambuss, ed., *The English Poems of Richard Crashaw* (Minneapolis: University of Minnesota Press, 2013), xli.

senses, when properly directed, empower her to bridge two realms. The two poets' emphasis upon matching another's behavior thus affirms a transhistorical link between early modern poetry and twenty-first century philosophy of the mind.

As a literary heuristic, simulation theory explains the protagonists' desire to synchronize their minds and bodies with their beloved. Yet, before examining how it enriches their rapport and enkindles passion, a brief review of its indebtedness to physiology's natural inclinations sheds light on the reasons underpinning its philosophical origins. As early as the eighteenth century, Adam Smith (1723–1790) discussed how a person's movements can trigger a similar response in the observer: "When we see a stroke aimed, and just ready to fall upon the leg or arm of another person, we naturally shrink and draw back our own leg or our own arm."[6] This focus on the automaticity of bodily reaction anticipates the late twentieth-century discovery of mirror neurons. These neuroscientific findings show that the neurons in the brain fire when the subject watches another's movements and then cause the observer to mimic that person's actions pre-re-flexively.[7] While these neural pathways may enable one to copy another's behavior, this physiological reaction generates only a facial or, as Goldman states, a "low-level" simulation.[8] He and Vittorio Gallese point out that mirror neurons in themselves do not "constitute a full-scale realization of the simulation heuristic."[9] Still, this pre-reflexive act establishes a basic link that provides direct knowledge about the other's immediate condition.[10] It creates an avenue to assess the other's state of mind, free from bias, and look upon that person as he or she is.

The goal of placing oneself in another's "mental shoes" is to achieve symmetry between one and another's state of being.[11] Cultivating a properly aligned in-

---

6 Smith, *The Theory of Moral Sentiments* (1759/1976), 10.

7 Vittorio Gallese explains, "Although we do not overtly reproduce the observed action, nevertheless our motor system becomes active *as if* we were executing that very same action that we are observing" (Gallese, Keyes, and Rizzolatti, "A Unifying View of the Basis of Social Cognition," 397).

8 Goldman, *Simulating Minds*, 113–25.

9 Vittorio Gallese and Alvin Goldman, "Mirror Neurons and the Simulation Theory of Mindreading," *Trends in Cognitive Sciences* 24 (1998): 498.

10 Jean Decety writes, "It is highly plausible that part of the mirror neuron circuitry contributes to the lower level processing involved in mimicry. However, the functional impact of top-down, controlled processes on the mirror neuron system remains to be demonstrated" (Decety, "Action Representation and its Role in Social Interaction," in *Handbook of Imagination and Mental Simulation*, ed. Keith Markman et al., [New York: Psychology Press, 2015], 12).

11 Gallese and Goldman, "Mirror Neurons and the Simulation Theory of Mindreading," 497.

tellective and emotive correspondence depends upon appreciating the integral role that the body plays. According to cognitive scientist Frédérique de Vignemont, it is the "the common 'currency' between oneself and others."[12] She maintains that to respect bodily congruency, imitation, and vicarious bodily sensations, the individual must exploit interpersonal body representations to establish a frame of reference that is given by the body map. This bodily map, though similar in composition, possesses distinctive features. Mirroring another's behavior does not result in or signify an exact copy of that person. Rather, it establishes a similarity that both links and distinguishes the two parties. The observer must then be aware of their own biases so as not to impose them in the simulation. To avoid an egocentric bias, the observer must re-center their vision to gauge the other's condition objectively. As Robert Gordon states, the observer must prioritize the other so that there is "no question of comparing [the other] to myself."[13] The subtle differences inherent in any copy reveal insights particular to that person. This specialized knowledge supersedes the kind generated by bodily reaction. It discloses the reason's underpinning the other's decisions and actions.

Even from its centuries-old origins, this theory stresses the importance of a strong sense of self and maintaining this individuality when observing the other's actions. It brings to light each one's distinctiveness:

> [When] we place ourselves in the other's situation, we conceive ourselves enduring all the same torments, enter, as it were, into his body, and become in some measure the same person with him and thence form some idea of the sensations and even feel something which, though weaker in degree, is not altogether unlike them.[14]

By imagining oneself "enduring all the same torments," the observer becomes attuned to the emotional impact of the event affecting the other person. Although matching its degree of intensity with absolute precision may be unattainable, its similarity enables the observer to discern the other's state of mind. It engenders an understanding that exists only between them, attesting to the observer's potential to adapt to a wide variety of situations. The observer is neither deterred by physical obstacles nor blinded by passion in inferring the other's mental states.

---

12 De Vignemont, *Mind the Body*, 131.

13 Robert Gordon, "Simulation without Introspection or Inference from Me to You," in *Mental Simulation*, ed. T. Stone and Martin Davies (Oxford: Blackwell, 1995), 56.

14 Smith, *The Theory of Moral Sentiments* (1759/1976), 261.

Modern studies in cognitive science also maintain that imitation fosters empathy. Rick Van Baaren notes, "The mechanism of imitation, the direct mapping of observed behavior onto our own behavioral representations, constitutes a rudimentary form of empathy because, in essence, imitation means that interaction partners have at least some of the same constructs or behavioral representations activated in the brain."[15] These constructs disclose a similarity between the two people that lays the foundation for higher forms of mimesis. Whether it is imitating the passion in the voice or the bodily gestures, the observer's mind "immediately passes from these effects to their causes, and forms."[16] This cognitive process converts these imitations into a higher understanding of the reasons underpinning the other's actions. It engenders a mode of consciousness that promotes an attentiveness, which draws the two people closer together. The choice not only to mirror the other person's acts, but also to utilize the knowledge conveyed through this imitation displays a conscientious interest in the other person. Indeed, recent studies show that empathic individuals tend to imitate other people more than less caring individuals.[17] Simulation and its higher forms of knowing fulfill the observer's desire to forge a thoughtful awareness of the other person's condition and valorizes the link between their two persons.

In the select love lyrics of Donne and Crashaw, the protagonist invests all of his or her energy in executing this task as completely as possible. The simulation transforms the body from a stimulus-driven machine into a temple of higher awareness. The empathizer actively exercises a devout belief in the other's value; this realization supersedes an autonomic reaction. As a signifier of the beloved's distinctiveness, the body acquires an epistemic significance that enlightens the protagonist of the factors affecting the beloved's well-being. Through this imitation, the protagonist learns how best to align the ever-deepening desire. Ideally, it is a selfless expression that prioritizes the other's condition.[18] It may initially spring from a pre-reflexive reaction to the beloved's movements, but this imitation sparks a consideration of his or her goodness, intensifying the un-

---

15 Rick Van Baaren et al., "Being Imitated: Consequences of Nonconsciously Showing Empathy," in *The Social Neuroscience of Empathy*, ed. Jean Decety and William Ickes (Cambridge, MA: MIT Press, 2009), 31–42.
16 David Hume, *A Treatise of Human Nature* (1739), ed. L. A. Selby-Bigge (New York: Oxford University Press, 1958), 576.
17 Tanya L. Chartrand and John A. Bargh, "The Chameleon Effect: The Perception-Behavior Link to Social Interaction," *Journal of Personality and Social Psychology* 76 (1999): 893–910.
18 Martin Hoffman's definition stresses this very point: empathy is an affective response more appropriate to another's situation than one's own (*Empathy and Moral Development*, 15–25).

derstanding between them. The observer gains a profound realization of what constitutes the essence of their empathy, namely an intimate grasp of the beloved's person.

Even when the body is absent or undergoing a transcendent metamorphosis, the protagonist relies upon memory, imagination, and even faith to initiate the simultaneous encoding of sensory input in order to activate similar behavioral expressions. This mirroring generates an emotional transference that allows the protagonist to respond with greater sensitivity towards the other's situation than they would otherwise be able. The various ways of replicating and then interpreting these actions may at times complicate the efforts, but the process of mirroring ultimately accentuates the force of the protagonist's cognitive powers to fashion a dynamic knowing.[19] Attaining emotional and intellectual synchrony requires a selflessness that, in spite of shared feelings, thrives off the differences between them. If the protagonist were to lose sight of what makes the beloved distinctive, then any attempt at semblance would be flawed. As stated earlier, it must be unbiased and maintaining this objectivity shows that it is neither an involuntary reaction nor a passive endeavor. While an emotionally charged event may trigger one to copy another's behavior, a decision is necessary to determine how to apprehend the intentions and reasons underlying these actions. Ascertaining their purport discloses the empathizer's commitment not just to the other, but to the relationship itself. The cause does not have to stem from a previously established closeness, but can arise from that very moment and the knowledge it conveys. Familiarity may increase the readiness to act, but the controlling factor centers upon the observer's ability to manage his or her feelings and desire to strengthen the bond. Hence, the choice to respond constructively initiates the act.

While the body serves as a vital epistemological source, the insistence to copy the other's behavior does not stem so much from a desire to fulfill a corporeal need as much as to access the others' state of mind. Blaine Greteman observes that "physical bodies are at the core of Donne's most striking poetic moments, representing a range of human emotions and experiences."[20] These moments, however, do not terminate in sexual intimacy, but become heightened

---

19 Peter Carruthers claims that a first-person account of mental states does not rely solely upon knowledge of one's own states and inclinations, but also on the recognition of a multitude of perceptual events. See Peter Carruthers, *The Opacity of Mind: The Cognitive Science of Self-Knowledge* (Oxford: Oxford University Press, 2011).

20 Blaine Greteman, "All This Seed Pearl": John Donne and Bodily Presence," *College Literature* 37 (2010): 27.

by what the simulated acts reveal about the beloved. They inform and elevate the empathic embrace. When scholars like Richard Sugg and Ramie Targoff conduct detailed analyses of Donne's anatomical precision as a means to characterize a passionate or spiritual self, they lay the foundation to appreciate the protagonist's effort to mirror the beloved's acts.[21] The mimesis is not mere romantic hyperbole, but a striking visual that emphasizes the effort exerted to align oneself with the other's thoughts and feelings. As bodily knowledge fashions the couple's emergent identity, intellective and emotive imitation highlights the sanctity of their affection. Whether describing their connection as "like souls" or as two pointed branches of a compass, semblance depicts an undying devotion that remains unfettered by physical constraints ("Ecstasy," l. 62).

In Donne's *Songs and Sonnets*, specifically "The Ecstasy," "A Valediction Forbidding Mourning," and "A Nocturnal upon St. Lucy's Day, Being the Shortest Day," the protagonists rely upon imitation to construct a conduit that enables them to grasp what constitutes their beloved's subjectivity. Acquiring this knowledge both establishes their connection and adds momentum to the shared affection. As noted by Shaun Gallagher, this process of duplication ensures that "one's own body is already in communication with the other's body at perceptual levels sufficient for intersubjective interaction."[22] When their bodies are separated by immense distances, the protagonist simply draws from past knowledge of the other's behavior to ensure that the surety of their bond can continue to thrive. Gordon avers that once a personal transformation has been accomplished, "there is no remaining task of mentally transferring a state from one person to another."[23] As evidenced by the disconsolate speaker in "A Nocturnal upon St. Lucy's Day," he remains painfully aware of what separates his existence from his beloved's reality. In response, he finds comfort in the shadows of night and crafts an emotive simulacrum that mirrors her deceased state and sustains his love. Despite its verisimilitude, it cannot transport him into another realm. His feet stay firmly fixed on this terrain.

His passion in effecting this replication maintains a clear awareness of what his beloved's body once conveyed and what it presently conveys. The very difference between life and death epitomizes a bold line of demarcation between self and other. A concerted study of this lyric poem illustrates how the protagonist's insistence to mirror a condition void of the sensory delights of this world vivifies

---

21 Richard Sugg, *Murder after Death: Literature and Anatomy in Early Modern England* (Ithaca, NY: Cornell University Press, 2007); Ramie Targoff, *John Donne, Body and Soul* (Chicago: University of Chicago Press, 2008).

22 Shaun Gallagher, *How the Body Shapes the Mind* (Oxford: Oxford University Press, 2005), 223.

23 Gordon, "Simulation without Introspection," 56.

the pair's connection. Indeed, he proclaims despondently that her death has made him "the first nothing" (l. 29). He elects to remake his being into nothingness by seeking out an existence in this world that simulates that of death. He identifies with the darkest day of the year, St. Lucy's Day, as a reflection of his beloved's sadness in leaving this life. Using such melancholic images to structure his perception of the netherworld aptly displays an other-oriented view and recasts his feelings of absence into an illuminated possibility of reciprocity.

In addition, he laments that he is the epitaph of winter's withered landscape that is "Dead and interr'd" (l. 8). Such a complaint matches the desolation of death and the accompanying feelings of sorrow and loss. By perceiving his beloved as a person who can still respond to him, he creates a scenario that links his state of mind with hers. The scope of simulation revolves around her alone and what he imagines it is like to be in her situation, focusing on the body's noticeable absence to ascribe specific mental states to her. The potential to perpetuate this relationship springs from mentalizing how her present state affects him and functions as an "elixir" to refine his perception of her state of being (l. 29). He may claim that "I am none," but the continuum of knowing generated by this simulation fosters an empathy that is "a form of inner or mental imitation for the purpose of gaining knowledge" of her mind.[24] It validates his ability to grasp her distinctiveness, cherish these differences, and promote a closeness that can cross onto another plane of existence.

The poem's very premise centers upon the speaker assessing how his beloved's passing redefines his person in relation to hers. The emptiness caused by her death has taken away any joy that he feels in this world, distilling him down into nothing. Yet, by relinquishing what makes him human, he draws nearer to her and becomes "love's limbeck" (l. 21). It is not simply a matter of identifying with her current state, but restructuring his feelings of nothingness so that they do not culminate in sadness but surety in sharing this moment with her. He attunes himself to the qualitative dimension of her death "which word wrongs her" and what it signifies (l. 28). His bleak outlook reflects a certainty informed by his response to her passing: "If I an ordinary nothing were,/ As shadow, a light, and body must be here" (ll. 15–16). Her absence adversely affects his sensory vitality to such a degree that he forgoes consideration of any physical concerns. As the quintessence of primordial nothingness, he is left to ponder what form their coupling now takes. Balancing these feelings with a cognition of what constitutes their love prevents his complaint that he is "every dead thing" from slipping into maudlin sentiment (l. 12).

---

24 Karsten Stueber, *Rediscovering Empathy* (Cambridge, MA: MIT Press, 2006), 28.

Pursuing a kind of knowledge that defies empirical proof shows that empathy is not determined solely by reason's dictates. It debunks the idea that a high-level simulation—one which ultimately assesses the other's motives and beliefs—relies upon a confluence of intellective and affective means of knowing. A sensitivity towards the other's condition in conjunction with a conscious volition to sustain this condition attests to his facility in adapting to the differences between them. By receiving and decoding her feelings (or lack thereof), he acclimatizes to this unique situation, which preserves both his sense of self and their union. Being no longer entranced by the pulse of life's sensuous bounty that once coursed through his veins, he has an affinity with the sun's dimming light on the shortest day of the year, "the year's midnight" (l. 1). This looming darkness actualizes her experience. When he becomes "the grave/ Of all, that's nothing," the sensations and actions underlying this metamorphosis illustrate that bodily impulses have become subdued as if he is experiencing the very same nonaction of his beloved (ll. 21–22). Simulating the phenomenological character of death determines his epistemic approach to her passing and the world around him. Mary Zimmer observes that his "exclusive devotion to her in life, [causes him to refuse] to acknowledge a sun, or source of light and being, greater than she."[25] His perception of the world and himself thus redefines what constitutes a meaningful form of communication.

As the sensory perception of his beloved's emotions directs his own affective responses and sensations, he realizes that simulation is a necessary rather than a sufficient condition for establishing an empathetic rapport. It empowers him to participate, at least vicariously, with her experiences and use this awareness to maintain his connection by deepening his understanding of her person. Facially, the idea of imitating a dead person's condition may seem fantastical or, worse, presumptuous, but its purport dramatizes its impact upon his very being. This method of coping depicts with verisimilitude the mental response system to the loss of a loved one. Twenty-first-century neuroscience shows that direct face-to-face interaction is not necessary for the neural networks to trigger the mind's mirroring mechanisms. They do not fire randomly, but differentially depending upon the situation's immediacy and intimacy.[26] His embodied synchrony thus attests to the power that her ardor still wields over him. The yearning to reciprocate it transcends physical stimuli, utilizing feelings from the past as well

---

25 Mary E. Zimmer, "'In Whom Love Wrought New Alcimie': The Inversion of Christian Spiritual Resurrection in John Donne's 'A Nocturnall upon S. Lucie's Day,'" *Christianity and Literature* 51 (2002): 558.
26 Marco Iacoboni et al, "Grasping the Intentions of Others with One's Own Mirror Neuron System," *PLoS Biology* 3 (2005): 529–39.

as the present to construct a viable imitation. He recollects how "we two wept, and so/ Drown'd the whole world" to substantiate and validate his current twinning of emotions (ll. 23–24). Even when they had chosen to redirect their attention to care for other things, this brief separation deprived them of the life-giving sustenance of each other's love. It caused their souls to withdraw and "made us carcasses" (l. 27). Memory and sensory deprivation comprises a vital element in an inviolable imitation that informs his perception of her present condition. It drives him to welcome "dull privations, and lean emptiness" (l. 16). Although this descent into melancholy may ruin him to others, his nothingness discloses a mental process that is structurally akin to hers and redefines what constitutes the space between couples.

The abyss between life and death ensures that he does not lose sight of those boundaries containing his person. He points out the transience of corporeal life. His sun will never renew, for love has made him the distillation of the nothingness out of which the universe was created (l. 15). Yet, even in this state, he is still very much alive. If he merged his identity with hers, their bond would erode into a monism that corrupts the underlying purport of the imitation.[27] Individuality underpins the originality of this exchange and the immanence of the self and other. Respecting these differences, the speaker bemoans his forlorn but still sentient state of being:

> The general balm th'hydroptic earth hath drunk,
> Whither, as to the bed's feet, life is shrunk,
> Dead and interred; yet all these seem to laugh,
> Compared with me, who am their epitaph. (ll. 6–9)

Within the dead of winter, the natural world no longer generates life; it is a barren landscape. Despite the barrenness of its landscape, it, according to the speaker, cannot compare to his disconsolate grief. His beloved's passing has undone his state of calm and brought him to the brink of death. This imagery has been traditionally interpreted as indicative of alchemy, which produces gold out of a base metal being reduced to nothingness.[28] An alchemical metaphor, how-

---

27 As the preeminent philosopher on nothingness, Jean-Paul Sartre warns that any merging between two identities would cause one to slip into an unwieldy solipsism. See Jean-Paul Sartre, *Being and Nothingness: An Essay in Phenomenological Ontology*, trans. H. E. Barnes (London: Routledge, 2003), 293–94.

28 See, for example, the work of Edgar Hill Dunce, "Donne's Alchemical Figures," *English Literary History* 9 (1942): 257–85; Joseph Anthony Mazzeo, "Notes on John Donne's Alchemical Imagery," *Renaissance and Seventeenth-Century Studies* (1964): 60–89; Kate Gartner Frost, "'Pre-

ever, does not fully explain the fact that he elects to use this nothingness to mirror the beloved's condition. As Jennifer Nicholas observes, "the movement toward regeneration that the reader expects from this metaphor appears nonexistent. At the end of the poem, the speaker seems to stand in the same despairing darkness in which he began."[29] Standing in the same place, however, is not a failing, but an affirmation that a bold line of demarcation separates his imitation from her essence. His entire being may resonate with the emptiness reflective of the netherworld's consumption of life, but it cannot fully match her condition.

Despite the trauma induced by her loss, maintaining this distinctiveness enables him to employ an objective basis when structuring his response to assess her reality. The inclination to mimic and synchronize his sensations and feelings with hers does not spring from a false belief that they can converge emotionally, but a stark realization of the impenetrable distance between them. As the night continues to darken, this realization refines his perception of her and how best to simulate what this year's midnight signifies. Consequently, the darkness at the poem's end differs drastically from its earlier description. Instead of being the time when the "world's whole sap is sunk," it is a time for celebration (l. 5). Here, "she enjoys her long night's festival" (l. 42). The effectiveness of his simulacrum makes her as real to him as possible. Though it cannot traverse this world's bounds, it individuates him from other living humans. While nature dies and buries itself, he is "their epitaph." By identifying so closely with the social construct that commemorates the moment where the biological is subsumed into stone, into writing, he finds a way to articulate how his melancholy delineates him from the rest of creation yet aligns him with her. His inscription metaphorically demonstrates an ability to adopt a state of mind attuned to the void caused by death, which connects him in some manner—no matter how limited—with her plane of existence.

As he strives to relate as fully as possible with her death, the boundaries of his objective self do not become too porous, making him overly involved with her person, but remain clearly demarcated. In effect, his empathy creates a new sense of self. He perceives himself as something rebegot of absence, darkness, and "things which are not" (l. 18). Embodying those affections and mental states attributed to his beloved imprints an indelible mark upon his being. It prompts him to ponder the machinations underpinning this recently evolved identity:

---

paring towards her': Contexts of *A Nocturnall upon S. Lucies Day*," ed. M. Thomas Hester (Newark: University of Delaware Press, 1996), 149–71.

29 Jennifer L. Nichols, "Dionysian Negative Theology in Donne's 'A Nocturnall upon S. Lucies Day,'" *Texas Studies in Literature and Language* 53 (2011): 352.

> For I am every dead thing,
> In whom Love wrought new alchemy.
> For his art did express
> A quintessence even from nothingness. (ll. 12–15)

Love's alchemical reaction signifies the transmission of feelings from the realm of the living to that of the dead. The passion that flourished when she was alive has engendered an affective consciousness of her otherworldly existence. His "nothingness" underscores the intention to re-secure their attachment and construct a means to share in an experience that is both foreign and real to him. Simulating "every dead thing" shows that the effort to mirror the beloved's state supersedes a mere involuntary reaction. It is not an instance of emotional contagion where he "automatically catches another individual's affective state [and] recruits interpersonal body representations."[30] Rather, he wants to know her in this present state and the best way to do that is become a living mirror of death. In his study of how people cope with the loss of loved ones, cognitive psychologist Jean Decety explains that "the perception of others in painful situations constitutes an ecologically valid way to investigate the mechanisms underpinning the experience of empathy."[31] In his estimation, empathy is a construct to account for a sense of similarity in feelings experienced by the self and the other without confusion between the two individuals.[32] For the speaker, this sense of similarity sparks the desire to imitate the beloved's deceased state, which illustrates how a simulation of absence can transform feelings of distress into something artful, "A quintessence even from nothingness."

Being able to claim "I am none" establishes a communion that completes itself neither through total transcendence nor through physical satiation (l. 37). Rather, it signifies a brief period of simulation lasting no more than one night. Ramie Targoff maintains that what gives Donne's poetry "its tremendous vitality derives to no small degree from his desire to seize this moment and not the next, to isolate and then luxuriate in a particular instance in time, to be all there in body and soul."[33] Being consumed by the bleakness of "the year's midnight" underscores the affective actuality of their relationship that allows him to transition from an "ordinary nothing" into someone extraordinary (ll. 1, 35). No matter how transient, the purport is not to relive what once existed, but to draw closer to her essence and draw a connection with its ineffability.

---

30 De Vignemont, *Mind the Body*, 129.
31 Decety and Lamm, "Empathy versus Personal Distress," 199.
32 Decety and Jackson, "The Functional Architecture of Human Empathy," 71–100.
33 Targoff, *John Donne, Body and Soul*, 23.

In the final lines, he returns to the metaphor of the shortest day to affirm the emotional verity of their bond. As opposed to the bleakness of the darkness permeating the first stanza, he now expresses a much more optimistic view of the night and her situation. He does not see her in a world where "the sun is spent," but rather in a "long night's festival" where she feels joy and engages in activities (ll. 1, 42). This positivity invites him to join in the celebration, transmuting desolation into exhilaration.

> Since she enjoys her long night's festival,
> Let me prepare towards her, and let me call
> This hour her Vigil, and her Eve, since this
> Both the year's and the day's deep midnight is. (ll. 42–45)

Night illuminates his nothingness and prepares him for her, for she is both the vigil and the eve. He re-centers his cognitive map, recognizes how this dimension allows him to express an empathic affection for her being in this "deep midnight." Even if the end goal is not fully realized, his semblance refines his aptitude for grasping her perspective. It strengthens his belief in her love, offering vital sustenance for his being, proving that his imitation is neither futile nor uni-dimensional. Hence, recasting the value of night and day, darkness and light, creates a conduit for empathy to flow freely so that she remains an integral factor in his life.

Whereas grief causes the speaker to conform his thoughts and feelings with his beloved's state of being, an all-consuming love enables the speaker in "A Valediction Forbidding Mourning" to resonate the fullness of the other's affection. Safeguarding its sanctity generates an emotional surety that allows them to withstand any separation that they must endure. He urges her to make no show of their joy being together or distress when they must part ways. Conforming one's decision-making with the other enables them to become mirrors of one another. This intellectual and emotional harmony results in being "Inter-assured of the mind" that their bond can transcend external pressures and physical parameters (l. 19). While its essence stems from what causes this like-minded thinking, the decision to exercise this mode of consciousness and cultivate a reciprocity of affection and belief in each other's commitment gives shape to their empathic expression. The interplay between body and belief fosters a psychic identification that proves more powerful than an emotive response and enables their spirits to thrive, unconstrained by time and space. As such, there is no occasion for sorrow or grief. This farewell to mourning depends upon the speaker and beloved to align their affection and being in the same direction so that the movement of their souls goes in the same direction. As opposed to the bodily impasse faced by the speaker in "Nocturnal upon St. Lucy's Day," the challenge facing these lovers does not revolve around the physical as much as the intellectual in that their decisions must coincide with one another. Essentially, this noetic resonance keeps their bodies aligned with one another which enables them to maintain a metaphysical connection. Given its complexity, this simulation depends upon directing the whole of their being towards the other's thoughts and feelings, while remaining faithful to its intimacy. Although it plays a lesser role, the physical operates cooperatively with the mental powers. Hence, they achieve a synchrony that heeds the other's motion—whether it be cognitive or corporeal—and fosters a loving understanding of what motivates the other's self.

In the first two stanzas, the speaker lays out a simile to point out that any kind of separation from friend or lover must be done without complaint and drama. For the virtuous man, the sanctified state of his soul fills him with a surety that salvation lies within his reach. Consequently, he has little worry about his imminent death and, in turn, breathes so calmly and quietly that some of his friends say "The breath goes now," and some say "No" (l. 4). The friends' inability to understand the depth of his virtue and, in turn, replicate such equanimity illustrates that they lack the familiarity and insight necessary to access his reality. The speaker, however, knows first-hand what comprises his beloved's emotive state and directs her to "make no noise/ no tear-floods, nor sigh-tempest move" so as to preserve the intimacy of her affection towards him (ll. 6–7). By urging her to duplicate his silence, he provides a means to intensify their passion and gain an equal appreciation of what the relationship means to each of them. This shared understanding establishes the integral role that the body plays in elevating their love to a higher plane. Their embodied synchrony enables them, as Goldman notes, "to generate further mental states" and create a bridge between their expressivity that allows the speaker to access her mind.[34] It produces the affectionate knowing necessary to link him with her with such force that no separation threatens the surety of their bond.

This muted display of sublime happiness exalts them above the dull sublunary "laity" (l. 8). Ultimately, it frees them from becoming dependent upon sensory knowledge: "Care less, eyes, lips or hands to miss" (l. 20). Recognizing the limitations of the physical empowers them to appreciate the transcendent quality of their affection. The conformity of their souls manifests itself through the couple's mimesis. Copying each other's movement discloses not simply the other's perspective, but affirms that it reflects one's own. Their love can therefore withstand separation, expanding "Like gold to aery thinness beat" (l. 24).

---

34 Goldman, *Joint Ventures*, 177–78.

While this auric melding suggests that one merges into the other, they maintain a self-other distinction because each relies upon the other to mirror the other's movement. Duplicating the beloved's movements and emotions may draw attention to her subjectivity, but witnessing these acts first-hand makes the lover uniquely aware of his humanness. Even though he can never wholly lose himself in her person, this absence of knowledge, as Emmanuel Lévinas notes, is exactly his presence as other.[35] It underlines the self-other delineation central to empathy, for what he sees and who he simulates is neither an object nor an analogue. Her distinctiveness and volition is necessary for the simulation to be meaningful and enhance the depth of their love. It gives rise to an authentic experience that provides the grounds to discern what comprises her desire to be with him. Reciprocity thus affirms both their devotion and individuality. It transmutes their emotive correspondence into a metaphysical connection where they know with certitude the other's state of being. As John Freccero explains, "the earthly gold of the two lovers is refined into the immortal and incorruptible gold of the glorified body and soul."[36]

Since the interplay between the couple now occupies two planes, Donne uses his famous conceit of a drawing compass to illustrate how their souls work in concert. While the two arms move in two distinct directions, each depends upon the other mimicking the other's movement. The first line drawn by the compass charts a linear path from the center to an outlying point and returns to the center.

> And though it in the center sit,
>> Yet, when the other far doth roam,
> It leans, and hearkens after it,
>> And grows erect, as it comes home. (ll. 29–32)

No matter how far apart the two may move away from one another, the beloved's soul faithfully follows the protagonist's motions. That it "leans and hearkens after" the his movements confirm the importance of mirroring in order to place oneself in the proper position to apprehend the profundity of the love expressed. This movement also illustrates the distinctiveness of each one's role in this simulation. As Amy Coplan states, empathy is a complex process "in which an observer simulates another person's situated psychological states while main-

---

35 Emmanuel Lévinas, *Le temps et l'autre* (Paris: Fata Morgana, 1979), 89.
36 John Freccero, *In Dante's Wake* (New York: Fordham University Press, 2015), 196.

taining clear self-other differentiation."[37] The intensity of their focus springs from a selfless devotion that appreciates one's indebtedness to the other.

Yet, this ethereal link, which he openly admits "ourselves know not what it is," does not exclude the value of the body (l. 18). When the souls come together, it prompts a primal, physical response on the lover's part. His desire becomes aroused and seeks to consummate their ardent affection. This provocative interchange between the flesh and the spirit prompts Targoff to note: "Just as he [Donne] regards his body and his soul as simultaneously connected to each other and as discrete beings, so he regards the individual lovers in their ideal state of union as essential to each other's existence and as inherently distinct."[38] Indeed, the compass's two arms joined by a fulcrum highlight both their singular existence and their shared experience. This combination engenders an internal awareness of what distinguishes self-knowledge from that acquired through a fully realized love. Although the breadth of shared knowledge may lie beyond their comprehension, the compass's second movement assures the couple that it exists and lies within them. Here, in the final stanza, it draws a circular motion that expresses not only the synchrony between their two souls, but also the indissolubility of their transcendent connection.

> Such wilt thou be to me, who must,
> Like th'other foot, obliquely run;
> Thy firmness draws my circle just,
> And makes me end where I begun. (ll. 33 – 36)

The protagonist's path may run at a different angle from everyone else's, but his beloved's soul follows his in kind. This movement facilitates each one's ability to grasp the other's state of mind. Their revolutions create a continuum of knowing founded upon mirroring the other's passion. Otherwise, this compass would fail to produce a fully round circle. Her "firmness" emphasizes how value is determined by what each sees in the other. It enables him to grasp her thoughts and align his accordingly. This constant awareness engenders a heightened appreciation of their relation to one another, which allows him to see himself from her perspective. Nancy Selleck's observation about early modern discourse supplements this view: the "Renaissance conception of self lies in the importance of being the object of the other—the sense that even the subjective self originates in

---

37 Amy Coplan, "Understanding Empathy," 5.
38 Targoff, *John Donne, Body and Soul*, 51.

that other's experience."[39] This insight gained through this harmony of movement surpasses what each could see on his or her own. Its reflexivity reveals a distinct avenue of knowing that depends upon them being selflessly attentive to each other's motions.

Via the compass's circular motion, they track each other's movements all the while maintaining a passionate awareness of what they value above all else— each other.[40] This mimicry heightens each one's consciousness of the another, proving that "empathic responses occur more readily vis-à-vis individuals who are salient, currently perceived . . . or bear greater resemblance to us."[41] Their mimesis is not simply a collateral effect of love, but a concerted focus upon the other's significance to the relationship. Its function is not to simply apprehend her commitment to him, but recognize that her experiences occur specifically to her.[42] These movements fulfill the protagonist's creative design as a caring, attentive person. His mirroring may not resonate with a precision that offers an absolute surety of what his beloved is experiencing, but it highlights the depth of his interpersonal knowledge. The decision to attune himself to her singular motions is a freer act than simply mourning their separation because it looks beyond his personal needs and takes into account what she is thinking and feeling. The emotional transference conveyed through the simulated acts valorizes the shared understanding. This shared understanding is not bound by bodily constraints but both affirms and strengthens the symmetry of their affection.

The harmony achieved between the lovers in "A Nocturnal upon St. Lucy's Day" and "Valediction: Forbidding Mourning" allows them to traverse physical bounds in order to maintain a metaphysical connection. Paradoxically, this connection shows how the body plays an integral role in empowering the lovers to enhance their empathic potential. In "The Ecstasy," however, the purpose of imitation does not center upon staying connected when separated. Instead, it strives to develop the link between body and soul without jeopardizing their distinctive-

---

39 Nancy Selleck, *The Interpersonal Idiom in Shakespeare, Donne, and Early Modern Culture* (New York: Palgrave, 2008), 165.
40 In a study by Natalie Sebanz, Gunther Knoblich, and Wolfgang Prinz, the results showed that people routinely track the mental states of others in their immediate environment. This tracking is done by representing the other's actions in a functionally equivalent way as one's own actions, just as simulation theory predicts. See Natalie Sebanz, Gunther Knoblich, and Wolfgang Prinz, "Representing Others' Actions: Just Like One's Own?," *Cognition* 88 (2003): B11–B21.
41 Goldman, *Simulating Minds*, 297.
42 De Vignemont examines how the bodily content drawn from interpersonal contact, even if not self-specific, ultimately grounds the sense of bodily ownership (*Mind the Body*, 137).

ness as they ascend to heavenly heights. The speaker consistently emphasizes their synchronization: "Sat we two, one another's best," "our hands," "our eye-beams," "our eyes" (ll. 4, 5, 7, 8). Each supplements the other so that neither loses sight of what he or she contributes to the relationship. This mutuality causes the lover, in Graziani's words, to "speak with his mistress, not to her."[43]

When looking into her eyes, the speaker increases the passion and attentiveness to her perspective: "Our eye-beams twisted, and did thread/ Our eyes upon one double string" (ll. 7–8). The ocular twisting indicates an active engagement where the lovers must first envisage the other's emotional state and then duplicate the accompanying behavior. The congruence between their movements and expected consequences makes them both agents and objects. This innovative model of perception and cognition enables the constitution of a meaningful interpersonal space.[44] Their bond is informed, not constrained, by their joint physical expressions, which are attested to by the repeated use of the collective pronouns, "we" or "our." Instead, their individuality comes to the fore at the onset of their ecstatic experience. As their souls prepare to ascend to their ethereal state, they "hung 'twixt her and me" (l. 16). This is the only place where the poem distinguishes the lovers' heterogeneity. This singularity of their souls must determine how best to attain a "love refin'd" (l. 21); it elevates the self-other delineation to another realm. The resolution rests with letting the love flowing through their very being "interanimate" them. As Targoff notes, "interanimation conveys a sense of motion, a forward thrusting of soul into body in a manner that the ordinary term 'animation' lacks."[45] Akin to the simulation topos, each must initiate the necessary action to strengthen the connection, yet this soulful act must resonate with the affection central to the other's passion. Although each feels the same kind of love, both must recognize that a difference exists because the result is the creation of a "new soul" and this can only occur via the unique contribution of each one (l. 45).

As stated earlier in this chapter, the speaker must distinguish his consciousness from hers. If not, he would suffer from an egocentric bias, erroneously believing that she feels and thinks the very same way as him. The self must exist on its own and in relation to the other, for the moment exists because of each one's singularity. While explicating the specificities of the simulation remains difficult to articulate because of the soul's ineffability—it is a "mixture of things they

---

43 René Graziani, "Donne's 'The Extasie' and Ecstasy," *Review of English Studies* 74 (1968): 136.
44 See Gallese, "Neoteny and Social Cognition," 307–32. Gallese studies the notion of embodiment from a neuroscientific perspective by emphasizing the crucial role played by bodily relations and sociality for the development of distinctive features of human cognition.
45 Targoff, *John Donne, Body and Soul*, 55.

know not what"—the couple needs the body both to provide a concrete basis to illustrate the mutuality of their expression and to fulfill the soul's design (l. 34). Just when they are at the highest point of awareness, their souls descend back into their bodies. At first, the prospect of reanimating these "sepulchral statues" causes them to question this return: "But oh, alas, so long, so far,/ Our bodies why do we forbear?" (ll. 49–50). They have yet to realize the inextricable tie between the body and soul, for it is the body that first gives form to their love.

While they may complain that their spiritual state houses "Th'intelligences," the body "the sphere," the need to apprehend that the whole of their person proves inclusive of all these states (l. 52). Donne himself writes in a letter to Sir Henry Goodyer that "we consist of three parts, a Soul, and Body, and Minde: which I call those thoughts and affections and passions, which neither soul nor body hath alone, but have been begotten by their communication."[46] When they recognize how the body "Yielded their forces, sense, to us," however, they come to realize its epistemic value and that in order to maximize their sensory expressions of ardor, they must work in concert with the other (l. 55). This realization proves accurate in light of modern scientific findings: "Observing others acting or experiencing emotions and sensations elicits our sensorimotor and emotion-related resources as if we were acting, or experiencing similar emotions and sensations."[47] These cognitive processes depend upon the body for their content and structure, which enable the speaker to attribute the proper mental states and emotions to the beloved.[48] Putting into praxis this mimetic ability shows that sensory knowledge drawn from the other elicits a reciprocity that is not "dross to us, but allay" (l. 56).

As these sensations, gestures, and acts cause similar bodily reactions, they enhance the lover's facility to ascend, for the soul must "to body first repair" (l. 60). Through the body, the speaker and his beloved come to realize what binds them to one another. Alastair MacIntyre writes, "empathetic awareness allows us to understand others in the same way."[49] By mirroring holding hands or looking into each other's eyes, the lovers cultivate a loving empathy that reveals a horizon of unfolding meaning that allows them to expand beyond the corporeal and attain transcendent heights of being. It thus extols the intrinsic value of being human and lauds the body as the locus of knowing.

---

46 John Donne, "To Sir H.G," in *Letters to severall persons of honour* (London: Printed by J. Flesher for Richard Marriot, 1651), 70.
47 Gallese, "Neoteny and Social Cognition," 320.
48 See Lawrence Shapiro, *Embodied Cognition*, 2nd ed. (New York: Routledge, 2019), 10–32.
49 MacIntyre, *Edith Stein*, 86.

Only by recognizing the correspondence between the soul and the physical can this couple fashion a semblance that reflects the wholeness of the other.[50] The affective and cognitive congruency enables them to perceive accurately each other's perceptions and desires. The speaker readily shares this knowledge when he concludes the poem with a précis of his epiphany:

> And if some lover, such as we,
>> Have heard this dialogue of one,
> Let him still mark us, he shall
>> See small change when we're to bodies gone (ll. 73 – 76).

The emphasis lies upon "dialogue of one," with the speaker talking to himself. Even though he and his beloved have experienced an ecstatic coupling, the core truth centers upon the dual yet intertwined parts of his being. Charles Mitchell notes, "The self gives voice to both its body and its soul in order to bring them to terms with each other."[51] Each one's body gives shape to their congruency and facilitates their ascendancy via their attentiveness to the other's distinct qualities. Lianne Habinek stresses that the desired understanding between the two lovers depends upon "how each individual lover's soul is connected to his or her body."[52] Its purport exceeds the stimulus for desire and becomes the operative means to assess their own potential and use this power to strengthen the bond.

In all three poems, the beloved's presence is the focus and animating center of the speaker's perspective. Whether stemming from a passionate embrace or a silent devotion, a trying separation or rapturous ascension, their intimacy prompts the speaker to decenter himself from a self-oriented state to an other-oriented one. From this position, he forges an interpersonal link that can transcend this world's bounds. No matter the distance between them—physical, spiritual, or existential—, he assiduously follows her movements, whether real or perceived, to gain an incisive view into her person. Pursuing such an end, no matter how challenging, enables him to express an empathy that grasps that the beloved's mindedness involves resonance phenomena at various levels of

---

50 Martin Schulte-Rüther, "Mirror Neuron and Theory of Mind Mechanisms Involved in Face-to-Face Interactions: A Functional Magnetic Resonance Imaging Approach to Empathy," *Journal of Cognitive Neuroscience* 19 (2007): 1354 – 72.

51 Charles Mitchell, "Donne's 'The Extasie': Love's Sublime Knot," *Studies in English Literature, 1500 – 1900* 8 (1968): 101.

52 Lianne Habinek, "Untying the 'Subtle Knot': Anatomical Metaphor and the Case of the *rete mirabile*," *Configurations* 20 (2012): 259.

complexity. Whereas physical imitation aligns his person with hers, which establishes his devotion, imitation of thought and decision-making produces a keen insight into her state of being. This process of knowing radically differs from the conventional view that empathy is simply a tool for alleviating distress. Striving to match the beloved's state of mind refines the appreciation of each other's distinctiveness and elevates their relationship to an inviolable, dignified state.

Crashaw's Religious Heroines and Their Life in Thought

As a poet concerned with spiritual matters, Richard Crashaw uses a different approach than Donne in depicting a lover's ability to break through corporeal constraints and ascend to a higher plane of interpersonal knowing. Donne's lovers mirror the movements of each other with such dedication that the ensuing insight reveals how the body and ineffable love can co-exist and, in turn, create a bond that can withstand any external force attempting to disrupt the intimacy. Crashaw's lovers, on the other hand, privilege the soul above all else and use their bodies to express such a conviction. Their total devotion to God in "The Weeper" and his Teresian poems, specifically "The Flaming Heart," involves an innovative and highly personal use of the body to simulate a selfless understanding of His compassion and sacrifice for humankind. Crashaw does not focus on the vulnerabilities and physical challenges facing human lovers, but rather employs lavish conceits to relate how Mary Magdalene and Teresa of Avila model divine virtue through their actions in order to foster a relationship that transforms each one's very being. The sheer intensity of their ardor highlights their extraordinary commitment and flourishes within this world by focusing on the next.

Imitating God's infinite care is by its very design limited by reason's bounds. Yet, as creations of His beneficence, humans are imbued with the ability to recognize and put into praxis the goodness emanating from above. Magdalene's and Teresa's thoughts and feelings mirror the decision-making and compassion manifested by Christ's actions. In "The Weeper," Magdalene's tears flow as "parents of silver-forded rills!/ Ever bubbling things!" that are "Still spending, never spent" (ll. 2–3, 5). Their endless flow mimics the effusive outpouring of love from on high. For Teresa, her transverberation graphically confirms a honed ability to embody virtue to such a degree that His solicitude interpenetrates this world. Neither woman relies on their intellect alone to ascertain the beloved's state of mind because God's wisdom far supersedes mere human reason. His solicitude for humankind, however, establishes an everlasting link with us. Consequently, both understand that what defines His goodness is His infinite love and conform their behavior accordingly. Refined by faith, their simulation of charity and humility allows them to participate in a dynamic, visceral experience with Him.

Whether portrayed through a rhapsodic lyric detailing Magdalene's hyperbolic crying or a poetical recounting of Teresa of Avila's rapture, these heroines pattern their lives upon the dominant tenets of Christianity and, in the process, construct a knowing that binds them to the divine. Despite the divide between the Godhead's perfection and their humanness, these women pierce the divine veil through a selfless consciousness of Christian benevolence and cultivate an intimacy that impacts their very body. For Teresa, a pointed dart hurled by a seraph strikes her heart, thus proving the purity of her mind. For Magdalene, a deluge of tears rises upwards towards heaven, resonating with Christ's suffering. That both events cause joy and sadness attests to the complexity of modeling one's thoughts upon divine virtue. Still, their efforts allow them to express and experience the transformative power of love. Attaining this state of mind establishes the immediacy of Christ and reverberates with a profound empathy for His affection for humankind. Whereas Donne's speakers copy the beloved's behavior with a passion that envelops body and spirit, Crashaw's heroines are consumed with a spiritual yearning that modifies their bodies and behavior into instruments of knowing shaped by divine love.

As Magdalene's tears rise upwards, they encounter an array of spiritual or allegorical figures and demonstrate a remarkable ability to adapt to a wide range of experiences. Depicted as emotive and conscious, this river of lachrymosity shows how much one must give themselves unto the divine in order to fashion a kinship. The description underlines this protean capacity: "Heavens thy fair eyes be,/ Heavens of ever-falling stars" (ll. 7–8). Comparing her eyes to heaven illustrates an innate connection to the supernal. The source of their creation transmutes their human significance into a spiritual one. She uses her own attributes to create a path for communication. Although this celestial metaphor does not explicitly identify what transpires in Magdalene's mind, these tears represent her belief system and desire to connect more completely with the divine.[53] More-

---

53 Richard Rambuss observes, "Crashaw's tour de force tear text renders acute affect absent psychology. Here the lachrymosity is all surface special effects" (Rambuss, "Crashaw and the Metaphysical Shudder; Or, How to Do Things with Tears," in *Structures of Feeling in Seventeenth-Century Cultural Expression*, ed. Susan McClary [Toronto: University of Toronto Press, 2013], 259. Austin Warren also laments that "Mary has no part in the poem; it should be called not 'The Weeper,' but 'Tears,'" but both scholars circumvent the metaphoric power that these tears possess (Austin Warren, *Richard Crashaw: A Study in Baroque Sensibility* [Ann Arbor: University of Michigan Press, 1957], 127).

over, they establish a commonality between her and Christ's humanity that generates a "basic empathy."[54] This empathy, as Karsten Stueber notes, is a pre-reflexive ability to recognize others as rational beings who are fundamentally like us. While Christ's person certainly holds powers that far surpass hers, Magdalene's willingness to shed tears and feel compassion establishes a link between them so that she can perform higher-level cognitive tasks, such as adopting the proper perspective when following Him "where'er he strays" (l. 109). As they flow from these fair sweet eyes, they fall into a whirlwind journey where they transmogrify into pearls hanging around Sorrow's neck before turning into wine for angels (st. 7, 12). These metaphoric transmutations affirm that the sacred is not relegated to a recondite existence, but accessible to her mind. They thus empower Magdalene to realize a spiritual potential and participate in a reality that both includes and transcends this world.

The first figure whom her gravity-defying tears visit is a singing cherub who thirstily drinks them: "And his song/ Tastes of this breakfast all day long" (ll. 29 – 30). That her tears rise up into this realm and serve as a creamy repast shows that they are not passive, but seek a sacralized universe. Their movement and ability to satiate heaven's thirst discloses her mindfulness of God's creative goodness and this vision fulfills what Goldman labels as a high-level simulation: "It is to imagine a scenario, not merely in the sense of 'supposing' that it has occurred or will occur, but to imagine being immersed in, or witnessing, the scenario."[55] Magdalene through her tears engages angels who come with crystal vials to "draw from these full eyes of thine/ Their master's water: their own wine" (ll. 70 – 71). Its biblical allusion to the wedding at Cana shows that she employs various forms of knowledge to inform her simulation, such as Scripture, past experience, as well as imagination.[56] Via these forms, she can infer mental states of a complex nature, such as the desire to sow charity and the will to do so, and construct a semblance between her perceptions with those of Christ.

---

54 Stueber, *Rediscovering Empathy*, 145 – 49.

55 Goldman, *Joint Ventures*, 102.

56 Goldman's conception of high-level simulation calls to mind the enactment simulation of "self-projection" as advanced by neuroscientists Randy Buckner and Daniel Carroll. They examine how the individual can draw from past experiences and envision future scenarios so that he or she can align his or her thoughts with the other's state of mind as fully as possible. In effect, these abilities "rely on a common set of processes by which past experience are used adaptively to imagine perspective and events beyond those that emerge from the immediate environment (49)." See Randy L. Buckner and Daniel C. Carroll, "Self Projection and the Brain," *Trends in Cognitive Science* 11 (2007): 49 – 57.

Even though the essence underpinning these states lies beyond her capabilities, her tears effectively mirror the celestial wellspring of His affection.

Encountering limitations does not signify a failing on her part, for it occurs in any simulation. Ian Apperly observes that "we do not have direct access to what other people know, want, intend or believe, but must infer these mental states on the basis of what they do and say."[57] Inference can provide an incisive awareness of what drives the other person, which in the case of Magdalene enables her to model herself upon His virtue. Hence, when the cherubs drink her tears, it allows her to realize that her affection corresponds in kind to that of Christ's. The tears' metamorphosis into wine demonstrates not only a mimetic awareness of His compassion, but also the importance of the authenticity of one's commitment, for only through the very best efforts can one aspire to mirror divine virtue. Timothy Burns explains that simulation "is neither a parlor trick nor does it belong in the domain of dubious, self-proclaimed psychics. Simply put, it is the act of attributing mental states to other individuals."[58] Mastering this ability requires a sensitivity to Christ's perfection and humbleness in pursuing this course of action. Still, the cherubs' thirst confirms Magdalene's proficiency to carry out this simulation and match—to the best of her ability—His perspective.

To hone this similitude further, her tears respond to the eternal abundance of His mercy by continuing to be shed in surplus. They do not fall in drops, but erupt in "springs" and flow as "milky rivers," creating "fair floods" (ll. 1, 21, 99). Their effluence creates an excess that underscores that their overflow exceeds earthly bounds and pours into the empyrean. Expressing her affection in such copious amounts fittingly copies Him being the *fontalis plenitudo*, for the essential productivity of His creative glory is to show itself and to communicate itself. As the Seraphic Doctor, St. Bonaventure, explains, "The divine perfection produces outside itself images which bring it no more increase than does a mirror to the substance of the object which it reflects, but which are in themselves reflections of glory projected into the obscure depths of the void, participation in the eternal self-happiness and the infinite goodness of which the life of God is properly constituted."[59] Magdalene's tears draw attention to His loving perfection and, in the process, establish the distinctiveness of her body.

---

57 Ian Apperly, *Mindreaders: The Cognitive Basis of "Theory of Mind"* (Hove, Sussex: Psychology Press, 2011), 1.

58 Timothy A. Burns, "Empathy, Simulation, and Neuroscience: A Phenomenological Case against Simulation-Theory," *Phenomenology and Mind* 12 (2017): 209.

59 Etienne Gilson, *The Philosophy of St. Bonaventure*, trans. Dom Illtyd Trethowan and Frank J. Sheed (Paterson, NJ: St. Anthony Guild Press, 1965), 181.

No matter how radical the journey becomes, her tears reflect His goodness and, as a result, the speaker extols her eyes for giving them life and her cheeks for giving them a place to rest.

O cheeks! Beds of chaste loves
By your own show'rs seasonably dashed.
Eyes! Nests of milky doves
In your own wells decently washed (ll. 85 – 88)

By looking at Magdalene's features from a third-person perspective, the speaker comments directly upon the authenticity of her desire to emulate His goodness. Her cheeks are "chaste loves" and her eyes are "decently washed." This purity affirms the value of the body in cultivating a substantive connection. While her tears show that she is attuned to the pain that He endured as well as the joy consequent from His sacrifice, capturing the affective tonality of His bodily experiences, her "nests of milky doves" illustrate her qualitative difference from others and the emotions expressed by them define her person. In Frédérique de Vignemont's study on the relation between mind and body, she points out how the particular features and spatial boundaries of one's body have "a special significance for the self."[60] Magdalene's tears foster an empathy founded upon an awareness of how Christ's experience in this world impacts both of their lives. Although His dual nature differentiates them, it prompts her to lead a virtuous life so that she can empathize with His person more completely. The onrush of tears synchronizes with His virtue, generating a familiarity founded upon His overflowing font of mercy. Empathy thus transforms her body as a signifier so that it reflects a heightened understanding of divine love's hierarchical import and, in the process, establishes her individuality.

While critics often struggle to appreciate the excess of emotion, I maintain that the passion functions as a particular mode of discourse, one unbound by linguistic constraints and, as such, mirrors the heartfelt, effusive love of the divine.[61] Her actions empower her to bridge the human with the divine. Tom Lutz

---

60 De Vignemont, *Mind the Body*, 166.
61 A sampling of critics who struggle to afford Crashaw credit as a poet worthy of praise include Ruth Wallerstein, who writes that his poems "comprehend passages of the worst taste, not merely in rhetoric, but in spirit, to be found in the whole range of English poetry" (*Richard Crashaw: A Study in Style and Poetic Development* [Madison: University of Wisconsin Press, 1959], 112; C. A. Patrides states bluntly, "Reprehensible as theology and intolerable as poetry" (*Figures in A Renaissance Context*, ed. Claude J. Summers and Ted-Larry Pebworth [Ann Arbor: University of Michigan Press, 1989], 141; and, Joan Bennett laments that "Crashaw loves to elaborate sensations . . .

notes that crying is a human universal and that weeping is exclusively human, thus making it "a kind of language, a primary, and often primal form of communication."[62] Shedding tears on "beds of chaste loves" articulates a knowing affection that simulates the goodness flowing from the divine whether in the form of Christ's immanence or God's mercy. They imitate to the proper degree of the emotional purity of the supernal and signify an active choice to pursue this mode of consciousness. Like the act of love, the empathy that they express cannot be compelled and involves Magdalene's whole person in perceiving what underpins divine virtue and its accompanying belief system. In effect, they function metonymically as an ability to form a bond with a being who possesses an infinitude of compassion and understanding.

Her tears enable her to reach the fruition of her being and produce an empathy that defies conventional notions. Though commonly described as shared emotional response designed to allay the other's distress, such a definition cannot apply to the Godhead. Even though Christ's crucifixion subjects Him to great hardship, this suffering culminates in a joyous, salvific resolution. In this instance, a properly expressed empathy does not seek to alleviate the other's pain, but gain a greater insight into His redemptive power. This realization instills a greater appreciation of her individual import and need to conform her actions in line with what the divine embodies, namely charity and selflessness. Augustine, whom Crashaw explicitly acknowledges in the preface to *Steps to the Temple*, explains how this pursuit serves as the paradigm for Christian action since it demonstrates gratitude for being created and the ability to know the truth of being.[63]

> The grace of God could not have been more graciously commended to us than it was. For the only Son of God, remaining immutable in Himself, put on humanity and bestowed upon mankind the spirit of His love through the mediation of a Man. Through this, it was made possible for us to come to Him."[64]

[but] his sensations are peculiar and sometimes repellant" (*Five Metaphysical Poets: Donne, Herbert, Vaughan, Crashaw, Marvell* [Cambridge: Cambridge University Press, 1966], 94.
62 Tom Lutz, *Crying: The Natural and Cultural History of Tears* (New York: Norton, 1999), 21.
63 Augustine, *Confessions*, 13.11.12, www.newadvent.org/fathers/1101.htm. Although the preface is not written by Crashaw, its sentiment makes clear that this book of verse is intended to inspire grander thoughts than those fixated upon material ones: "Think ye, St. Augustine would have stained his graver learning with a book of poetry had he fancied their dearest end to be the vanity of love-sonnets and epithalamiums? No, no, he thought with this, our poet, that every foot in a high-borne verse might help to measure the soul into that better world" (*Steps to the Temple* [1646], 5).
64 Augustine, *The City of God*, 10.29, https://www.newadvent.org/fathers/120110.htm.

As evident by her tears, Magdalene exercises such humbleness and puts it into practice when she falls before "our Lord's feet" (l. 186). This action mirrors the humility of the Incarnation in which the divine willingly expresses a spirit of submissiveness by becoming human. By forgoing His hierarchical rank, He shows that love of the good supersedes all mundane matters. Just as God's presence in and through creation is a kind of incarnation, Jesus's is creationally interrelated to this omnipotence and, as such, affirms Magdalene's effort to forge a connection with the divine. Her emotive expression displays a devotion that makes their relationship more than supplicant-lord. He is her beloved. As such, she structures her life upon the tenets that He personifies: forgiveness and charity. Prioritizing this endeavor above any social or worldly obligation valorizes the attempt to simulate His virtue. Her tears are thus a part signifying the whole, for they indicate a personal link to Him.

The lyrical outpouring of tears matches God's expansive state of compassion as personified by Christ's humanity. It attests to a devout belief in His presence and its signification.

> 'Twas his well-pointed dart
>   That digged these wells, and dressed this vine;
>   And taught the wounded heart
>   The way into these weeping eyn.
> Vain loves avaunt! Bold hands forbear!
> The Lamb hath dipped his white foot here. (ll. 103–8)

His sacrifice instructs her how to relate what the wounded heart knows through her crying. It gives her a first-hand grasp of what drives Him onward. His love both intercedes on humankind's behalf and intersects with our being. In order to bear fruit, a branch of a plant must be organically connected to the vine, through which it receives life and nourishment. We are part of the vine and when dipping "his white foot here," the Lamb establishes indisputably that He will live in us and we will live in Him. Her weeping rejoices in this fact and seeks to express in kind the love extended to her. It is not an external sign of some inner thought or feeling. It *is* the inner thought and feeling. Shedding a tear is intelligible as a part or aspect of the happiness that she shares in common with Christ. Her "weeping eyn" thus exemplifies more than zealous devotion; it indicates a conscious awareness of their bond. Whereas some claim that this hyperbole either does not depict human reality or is "not exaggerated enough" to describe the divine's ineffability, its purpose, I submit, is not to reference one state and not the other, but rather both of them.[65] Even though the Godhead ontologically encompasses far more than the human mind could comprehend, the feelings incited by Christ's sacrifice validate Magdalene's response and its ability to forge a deeper understanding of their intrinsic connection.

Crashaw's use of emotion to interlink the human and divine permeates his poetry, which results in the recycling of images to stress the interpersonal power of affection. It shows that differing perspectives can culminate in the same conclusion. For example, Magdalene's "nests of milky doves" in stanza 15 become supplanted by Christ's "full nest/ Of loves" in "Vexilla Regis, the Hymn of the Holy Cross." Despite the dramatic change of personage, the outpouring of love still enables the two realms to work into concert with one another:

> Lo, how the streams of life, from that full nest
> Of loves, thy Lord's too liberal breast,
>   Flow in an amorous flood
>   Of water wedding blood. (ll. 6–9)[66]

The streams do not merely flow, but flood humankind revealing an unbounded ardor. He is not simply the Creator—omnipotent and omniscient—but committed to our person, for His blood purifies our person and its confluence with the body's water washes away sin. This act, like that of the bride and groom exchanging vows, attests to His all-embracing care for humankind. Juxtaposing seemingly disparate elements, such as water and blood or love and tears, conveys a sense of drama, movement, and tension to depict the unconventional interplay between sensory and spiritual modes of perception.[67] Images like these and those found in "The Weeper" consistently emphasize the incontrovertible link between Christ and humanity.[68]

---

65 Michael McCanles, "The Rhetoric of the Sublime in Crashaw's Poetry," in *The Rhetoric of Renaissance Poetry: From Wyatt to Milton*, ed. Thomas Sloane and Raymond Waddington (Berkeley: University of California Press, 1974), 192.

66 "Vexilla Regis, the Hymn of the Holy Cross," *Carmen Deo Nostro*, in *The English Poems of Richard Crashaw*, ed. Rambuss, 194–95.

67 When addressing how Christ bridges these two realms in the sacrament of Eucharist, Kimberly Johnson believes that "whatever carnal implications may follow from the presence of the body of Christ in the Eucharist, what seems to exercise Crashaw most strenuously is the bald imperceptibility of Christ's body in the consecrated elements" (Kimberly Johnson, *Made Flesh: Sacrament and Poetics in Post-Reformation England* [Philadelphia: University of Pennsylvania Press, 2014], 120).

68 Gary Kuchar believes that "Crashaw's excessive straining of the two aspects of the sacramental vision—the surface, corporeal aspect and the underlying pneumatic, spiritual perspective— runs the risk of diffusing the very union of divine and mundane orders that it inscribes" (*Divine*

Magdalene uses this link to foster an empathetic communion, which affirms the divine's presence in her life. Ryan Netzley avers that this presence "does not entail crossing a limit or leaping over an aporetic gulf between devotees and God, but rather attending to a divinity indistinguishably present in immanent sensations."[69] God's goodness suffuses her entire person so that her senses can respond in kind. As a result, she patterns her thoughts and feelings to construct a heightened attentiveness to His charity and creative power. Since her tears can never capture His essence, however, an egocentric bias does not color her perception or simulation of these virtues. The superabundance of emotion attests to her facility in apprehending God as both present and ethereal. Thematizing this surfeit underscores how feelings enable her to explore different perspectives of His omnipresence, which is evident by the tears' changing appearance. As stated earlier, they first appear as crystal clear waters flowing off snowy hills before turning into cream in stanzas four and five. Subsequent transmutations include, among others, being melted into silver currency in stanza twenty-one and being made into a perfume from warm roses in stanza twenty-seven. Each incarnation discloses a singular means of responding to and imitating the effusiveness of His love, for even if they mirror only a small degree of His nature, it confirms the intersection between the two planes of existence.

A simulation can never produce the exact specification of the original, nor should it. An empathetic act strives to understand the other person to the best of one's ability. The end result is to draw closer to that person, not become them. Perhaps, the clearest example of how her tears pursue this end is when they assume the form of two walking baths and follow Christ.[70] They place her in a position to reciprocate His love immediately. They illustrate in a most vivid way that affection—no matter how unrestrained—serves as the foundation of their bond. After all, the Son of God's decision to become man, to walk among "the Galilean mountains," stems from His love for humankind (l. 110).

Subjection: The Rhetoric of Sacramental Devotion in Early Modern England [Pittsburgh: Duquesne University Press, 2005], 112). This worry, however, remains unfounded since the spiritual never loses its identity no matter how close the two realms come together. Their contiguity may establish their inextricable connectedness, but it urges the aspirant to embrace the divine's distinctiveness and what it signifies.

69 Ryan Netzley, *Reading, Desire, and the Eucharist in Early Modern Religious Poetry* (Toronto: University of Toronto Press, 2011), 67.

70 Edmund Gosse writes, "If language be ever liable to abuse in the hands of a clever poet, it is surely outraged here. These are the worst lines in Crashaw" (Edmund W. Gosse, "Richard Crashaw," *Cornhill Magazine* 47 [1883]: 432). For a survey of critics who struggle with Crashaw's hysterical intensity, see Richard Rambuss, "Sacred Subjects and the Aversive Metaphysical Conceit: Crashaw, Serrano, Ofili," *English Literary History* 71 (2004): 498–500.

And now where'er he strays,
Among the Galilean mountains,
Or more unwelcome ways,
He's followed by two faithful fountains;
Two walking baths; two weeping motions;
Portable, and compendious oceans. (ll. 109–14)

The key element of the image rests with the action, not the object. These "two weeping motions" testify to a deep-seated yearning to align herself with Him and that they will follow every step of Christ as He strays from the mountains to "more unwelcome ways" underscores a willingness to adapt to every context and circumstance. As He began His ministry in Galilee, teaching in the synagogues and preaching the gospel of the kingdom, He welcomed Magdalene into His coterie of followers.[71] At His death, her presence is explicitly mentioned: "There were also many women there, looking on from afar, who had followed Jesus from Galilee, ministering to him; among whome were Mary Magdalene, and Mary the mother of James and Joseph (Mt. 27:55–56). Witnessing a wide spectrum of experiences increases her understanding of His state of mind. This exposure, other than simply joining the company of thirsty cherubs and other blissful creations, brings to light His humanness and the steady interaction allows her the opportunity to grasp as fully as possible the many different avenues via which He expresses mercy.

By intentionally putting herself in His shoes (or sandals), her tears represent a distinct mode of consciousness that surpasses adoration. These tears demonstrate a finely attuned awareness of His person. Even though simulation theory does not arise until the late twentieth century, the idea that mirroring another's state of mind becomes an integral facet of empathy and how one aligns one's mental state with another's motivations and belief system. Indeed, Immanuel Kant presents its central tenets two centuries earlier:

> It is obvious that, if one wants to have an idea of a thinking being, one must put oneself in its place and thus substitute one's own subjectivity for the object which one wanted to consider (which is not the case in any other kind of investigation).[72]

---

71 The gospel of Matthew charts his movement throughout the region: "So his fame spread throughout all Syria, and they brought him all the sick, those afflicted with various diseases and pains, demoniacs, epileptics, and paralytics, and he healed them. And great crowds followed him from Galilee and the Decap'olis and Jerusalem and Judea and from beyond the Jordan" (Mt. 4:24–25). All passages from the bible are taken from *The Didache Bible* (San Francisco: Ignatius Press, 2006).
72 Immanuel Kant, *Critique of Pure Reason*, trans. N. K. Smith (London: Macmillan, 1953), 353.

Magdalene's tears selflessly follow Christ's path and their superfluity attests to the commitment invested in knowing Him better. By being ready to share in the same emotional state brought on by those "unwelcome ways," she enters into a process of "responsively knowing."[73] While these tears can in no way fully comprehend the magnitude of how this suffering weighs upon His mind, this kind of knowing reveals, as Susan Feagin describes, "the structural similarities between the simulator's mental process" and that of the other person.[74] Replicating the structural processes underpinning a difficult emotional situation reveals a commonality that validates her efforts.

Even though critics chastise Crashaw for leaving Magdalene herself out of the poem, the explicit reference to the Galilean mountains stresses her presence in Christ's life.[75] The poem, as aforementioned, may not explicitly probe Magdalene's mind, revealing her fears and joys, but the tears do not appear out of nowhere. They signify her desire to refine her intimacy with the divine. Recounting in broad strokes her biblical actions emphasizes her reality and unique insight into the person of Christ. She with a handful of other women accompanies and ministers to Him.[76] She stands at the foot of the cross and sees Him laid in the tomb.[77] These events instill in her a steadfast belief in His divine nature, which accounts for why she is at His tomb on the third day: "When Jesus rose early on the first day of the week, he appeared first to Mary Magdalene, out of whom he had driven seven demons" (Mk 16:9). Being attendant to His resurrection as well as being the recipient of His powers of exorcism make her more at-

---

73 G. T. Barrett-Lennard, "The Empathy Cycle: Refinement of a Nuclear Concept," *Journal of Counseling Psychology* 28 (1981): 92.

74 Susan L. Feagin, "Empathizing as Simulating," in *Empathy: Philosophical and Psychological Perspectives*, ed. Amy Coplan and Peter Goldie (Oxford: Oxford University Press, 2014), 150. The context of Feagin's argument centers upon the ability of the reader to empathize with a fictional character. Even though she focuses on figures that stand apart from face-to-face encounters with other humans, the core of her argument applies readily to our interaction with the Christian deity. Some facets of His person may communicate themselves through corporeal acts, but other parts exist in a realm beyond our direct experience. Thus, Feagin's emphasis upon simulating the structural processes enables us to recognize a commonality between ourselves and the Creator. We realize that we can mirror a particular mental state without knowing everything about His person.

75 Even though today's champion of Crashaw's heroine, Richard Rambuss, states that the poem "offers no narrative of Mary Magdalene's conversion, or who she is or how she entered into the state of extreme, world altering feeling that here has so consumed her" (Rambuss, "Crashaw and the Metaphysical Shudder," 257). Also see, Warren, *Richard Crashaw*, 127; Gosse, "Richard Crashaw," 432.

76 Luke 8:2–3.

77 Mark 15:40; Matthew 27:56; John 19:25; Luke 23:49.

tuned to His abilities and nature than the average person. She knows first-hand what makes Him both fully human and divine. It produces a fortitude that makes her singularly determined to respond personally to Christ's dual nature.

Borne out of her extraordinary experiences, this weeping recalls her time with Christ and how His actions affected her so profoundly. It increases the scope and intensity of her feelings, focusing her ability to communicate with Him. By envisioning situations and ideas about His person, she expands her view of what defines Christ's earthly and spiritual qualities. That her tears can respond knowingly to both of these qualities comes to light in stanzas sixteen and seventeen where the language of paradox displays its power to overcome contradictions. Whereas tears most commonly signify sorrow or shame, they do not fall because of some pain or failing, but rather because she wants to love like Christ does. Despite the inherent limitations, her efforts display a conscious need for fulfillment and belief that grace intersects with nature, no matter how flawed by her humanness: "O sweet contest; of woes/ With loves, of tears with smiles disputing!" (ll. 91–92). Her tears conjoin sorrow with joy. Their imbrication empowers her to recognize both the similarities and differences between herself and Christ.

> But can these fair floods be
> Friends with the bosom fires that fill thee!
> Can so great flames agree
> Eternal tears should thus distill thee! (ll. 97–100)

That the fire to draw closer to Christ works in concert with water to refine her affection underscores how love combines opposites to express its force. Its interchange impels one to act and let oneself be acted upon. Although she initiates the tears, His fires distill their purity. This conjoining of disjunctive elements conveys the transcendent power of this state of being, whether that transcendence be envisioned or eternal. While these fair floods continue the movement which began with divine creation and culminated in His resurrection, they still require the flames of divine love to approximate and mirror His actions.

Fire not only divinizes her tears and what they represent, but also increases the intensity of the activity. It adds momentum to what is already moving, resonating with His affection. Rosalie Colie discusses the impact of this paradox: "Love heightens awareness of the body and consciousness of one's self as an experiencing being; paradoxically, by this physical intensification love induces the sensation of *ecstasies:* the articulation of the body's most intense sensations results in the sensation of bodilessness, of physical as well as emotional transcendence."[78] Magdalene's tears lift her beyond her bodily concerns, allowing her to focus intently upon the divine and how Christ's humanity also lifts those who follow Him to greater heights. Her expression of love is the ultimate simulation of Christ and its bounty generates the kind of inter- and intrapersonal knowledge necessary to grasp His commitment to her. Whereas some critics, like Robert Ellrodt, believe that the paradoxes and seeming ambiguities that run throughout the verse melt into each other, fostering confusion or, at least, ambivalence, such views do not appreciate how the tears' interaction with elements that oppose their own properties undoes a framework of absolute presuppositions and illustrates an adaptability to comprehend the complexity of the divine's nature, which both heeds and supersedes reason.[79] The continual changing properties of tears—from pearls to wine—underline this facility to adapt to the ever-effusiveness of divine love.

By increasing her understanding of Christ's virtue, Magdalene transcends herself. Her agency via these tears, which are "Heavens of ever-falling stars," reflects the light from above with such brilliance that it causes the "earth to counter-shine" (l. 11). The positivity inherent in this flood underlines the character of her simulation and separates her from her literary counterparts. By situating Magdalene among her contemporaries, her distinctiveness comes to the fore, accentuating the significance of her action and what it signifies. Crashaw's florid depiction stands apart from his metaphysical compeers by emphasizing the positive aspirations of Magdalene's tears. George Herbert, whose collection of poetry *The Temple* (1633) antedates *Steps to the Temple* by thirteen years, wrote a short poem, "Marie Magdalene."[80] Drawing from the gospel of Luke 7:37–39, he poeticizes Mary's washing of Jesus's feet with her tears: "Why kept she not her tears for her own faults,/ And not his feet? Though we could dive/ In tears like seas, our sinnes are pil'd" (ll. 9–11).[81] Instead of extolling the goodness coursing

---

78 Rosalie L. Colie, *Paradoxia Epidemica: The Renaissance of Paradox* (Princeton, NJ: Princeton University Press, 1966), 96–97.

79 Robert Ellrodt, *Seven Metaphysical Poets* (Oxford: Oxford University Press, 2000), 219–20.

80 Despite the facial similarity between the two collections of poetry, Crashaw does not attempt to place the aspirant in God's temple, but places them on a path towards this holy state. For a fascinating account of these different approaches, read Richard Rambuss's introduction in *The English Poems of Richard Crashaw*, specifically xxii–xxxiv. He writes, "Indeed with respect to genre—hymn, ode, metrical psalm, paraphrase, epigram, epitaph—Crashaw's *Steps to the Temple* has more in common with Milton's *Poems* (1645) than it does with Herbert's *The Temple*" (xxxv).

81 George Herbert, *The Temple* in *The Complete English Poems*, ed. John Tobin (New York: Penguin Classics, 2004), 163. The difficulty of this allusion lies in the fact that it misattributes the

through her person, Herbert uses the tears to stress the sins of humankind, thus failing to appreciate a willingness to forge a heartfelt bond with Christ. In 1681, Andrew Marvell lets his pen detail the travails of Mary Magdalene. Although he does not dedicate an entire poem to her, he references her in "Eye and Tears."[82] At the beginning of the poem, he extols Nature for granting the eyes the power to "to weep and see" so that they can express properly "the true price of all my joys" (ll. 2, 12). He then discusses how Magdalene's tears become "liquid chains" that "fetter her Redeemer's feet" (ll. 31, 32).[83] Like Herbert, the emphasis centers upon the repentance, weeping in sorrow at what the sins of this world have caused. In line with the poem's overall theme, her eyes and tears work in conjunction with one another to heighten the emotive significance of this moment: "And each the other's difference bears; These weeping eyes, those seeing tears" (ll. 55–56). By pointing out their supplemental rapport, Marvell invites a broader, more liberal dimension of meaning to develop. It recognizes them as co-dependent, adding depth to her sadness.

Henry Vaughan, however, chooses a different avenue to highlight. He describes Mary's weeping as an "art" that transforms sorrow into religious devotion. In "St. Mary Magdalen" found in *Silex Scintillans II* (1655), the speaker proclaims that she is one "Who loved much and much more could move" (l. 50).[84] She uses her creative imagination to produce an affection that reflects the substantive joy provided by Christ's sacrifice. Yet, instead of exploring how this artistry could enrich her relationship with the divine, Vaughan keeps her bound to this world. He focuses on her biblical travails and censures the Pharisees for remaining blind to her steadfast faith. When he addresses her former profession, he stresses the proselytizing power of her conversion:

Whose pensive, weeping eyes,
Were once sins loose and tempting spies,
But how are fixed stars, whose light
Helps such dark straglers to their sight (ll. 22–25)

---

woman being described as Mary Magdalene. Properly speaking, Luke only references "a woman who had lived a sinful life in that town" (7:37). The confusion arises in the sixth century when Pope Gregory I declares that Mary Magdalene, Mary of Bethany, and the sinner in Luke are one person. See Susan Haskins, *Mary Magdalen: Myth and Metaphor* (New York: Harcourt Brace, 1993), 16.

82 The poem is found in Marvell's 1681 posthumous *Miscellaneous Poems.*

83 Andrew Marvell, *The Complete Poems*, ed. Elizabeth Story Donno (New York: Penguin Classics, 2005), 52–53.

84 All citations of this poem are taken from *Henry Vaughn*, ed. Louis L. Martz (Oxford: Oxford University Press, 1995).

Although the imagery anticipates Crashaw's verse, the starlight is to lead others onto the right path. While conscious of what Christ's sacrifice offers humankind, the tears do not strive to increase intimacy with the divine. All three portrayals uniformly stress the metaphoric import of the tears by having them reverberate with reverential respect. They are not an involuntary reaction, but illustrate a humble awareness of His humanness. Still, these tears fall downwards and water this realm.

Along with these metaphysical poets, a number of other writers address Magdalene's historical and religious significance, yet the closest parallel to Crashaw's Magdalene is Robert Southwell's meditative prose work, *Marie Magdalens Funeral Teares*.[85] Southwell also has two short poems addressing this saintly figure, "Mary Magdalens Blushe" and "Marie Magdalens Complaint at Christs Death," but these works dwell upon the shame and sorrow associated with the sin that chains us to this world. The former concludes by stating in no uncertain terms that "sence is not free from synne," (l. 35) and the latter bemoans existence if one rejects Christ's love: "All that live, and not in God,/ Couche their life in deathe's abode" (ll. 5–6).[86] The prose work, however, readily has the tears speak for her; they are "issued in lieu of words."[87] When Christ speaks to her outside His tomb, she utters only one word, "Rabboni," before letting her tears convey the fullness of her belief:

> Love would have spoken, but feare enforced silence. Hope frameth the words, but doubt melteth them in the passage: and when her inward conceits strived to come out, her voice trembled, her tongue faltered, her breath failed. In fine teares issued in lieu of words, and deep sighes in stead of long sentences, the eie supplying the mouths default, and the heard pressing out the unsillabled breath at once.[88]

---

85 Contemporaneous with the anonymous *Magdalens Lamentations* (1601), Nicholas Breton wrote two works, *Mary Magdalen's Love* (1595) and *The Ravish't Soul and the Blessed Weeper* (1601). Two sonneteers include William Alabaster and his "Upon Christ's Saying to Mary, 'Why Weepest Thou?'" (1633) and Henry Constable whose *Spiritual Sonnettes* (1592) presents three Magdalene poems. All these works laud Mary as a devout penitent whose sorrow authenticates her love for Christ. For a discussion of Mary Magdalene as an exemplar of piety in later seventeenth-century poetry, see W. Leiner, "Metamorphoses Magdaléenes," in *La metamorphose dans la poésie baroque française et anglaise* (Paris: Éditions Jean-Michel Place, 1979), 45–56.
86 Robert Southwell, "Mary Magdalens Blushe" and "Marie Magdalens Complaint at Christs Death," in *Collected Poems*, ed. Peter Davidson and Anne Sweeney (Manchester: Carcanet Press, 2007), 29 and 40.
87 Robert Southwell, *Mary Magdalen's Funeral Tears* (1591), ed. W. J. Walter (London: Keating & Co., 1822), 72.
88 Southwell, *Mary Magdalen's Funeral Tears*, 75.

The body responds in awe to Christ's sacrifice—tears and sighs—but the stimulus is "feare" more than affection. Words cannot articulate this feeling of being overwhelmed. The idea of fostering a connection founded upon similarities lies beyond the horizon of possibilities. A mixture of dread and wonder constrain her to this world. As a result, the bond formed is a rigidly, hierarchical one. Gary Kuchar may assert that "the absence of the physical, literal object results in a deepened spiritual relation with it," but this relation revolves around the hope for salvation.[89] The tears are "signes of shame that stayne my blushinge face."[90] They mark a bold line of demarcation between the two realms, negating any possibility of something more personal, more in line with our innate connection to our Creator.

Crashaw's Magdalene, however, embodies the capacity to break free from her corporeal existence and interact fruitfully with the divine. Fear does not control her actions. For example, while some disparage the idea of Christ being followed by two faithful fountains akin to portable oceans as a high form of campiness, they ignore the constructive interplay between them.[91] The tears move in concert with Christ's movement. They illustrate an adaptability that readily puts into praxis His actions and the goodness imbued in them. The image's richness, though cognitively effortful, is contextually situated and looks beyond itself in order to enter a world both inclusive of and distinct from her past experiences.

In the final two stanzas, these tears assume the power of speech and announce how they seek not the worldly fortune of precious gems, but to fall in adoration to Christ's glory. They praise neither nature's beauty nor adorn earthly crowns, but "go to meet/ A worthy object, our Lord's feet" (ll. 185–86). Where His mercy refines her person, the effort to copy His goodness affirms her distinct value. This characterization distances itself from the grief-stricken depiction of Magdalene imposed by Crashaw's contemporaries and the stereotype of the divine as an authoritative judge. Rather, the affection exchanged between them draws upon each other's interior worth to generate an empathic rapport, establishing the simultaneous presence of the one and the other. This understanding subverts the traditional, delineation of human and divine, inviting a broader, more liberal dimension of meaning to develop. It recognizes them as co-existing,

---

89 Kuchar, *Divine Subjection*, 64. Deborah Shuger observes, "The idea here is that only in being abandoned and forsaken does one generate a genuine intimacy with Christ" ("Saints and Lovers: Mary Magdalene and the Ovidian Evangel," *The Bucknell Review* 35 [1992]: 142).

90 Southwell, *Mary Magdalen's Funeral Tears*, 77.

91 Alice Fulton, "Unordinary Passions: Margaret Cavendish, the Duchess of Newcastle," in *Green Thoughts, Green Shades: Essays by Contemporary Poets on the Early Modern Lyric*, ed. Jonathan F. S. Post (Berkeley: University of California Press, 2002), 212.

underscoring their dynamic interaction. A hierarchical divide may exist, but it neither deters nor dismisses her attempts to "meet" Him.

> Much less mean we to trace
> The fortune of inferior gems.
> Preferred to some proud face
> Or perched upon feared diadems.
> Crowned heads are toys. We go to meet
> A worthy object, our Lord's feet. (ll. 185 – 86)

Assuming such a humble place before the Lord attests to her willingness to forgo any attachment to this world. It calls to mind her historical experience with Christ as the one who stands alone outside His tomb. Her tears recollect and re-enact a scenario that strives to match the intensity of Christ's affection for humankind. Whether envisioned through familiar feelings or imagined constructs, they possess an epistemic purpose by employing various avenues of knowing to produce a sensitive understanding that evokes an empathic concern for His humanness. The goal, therefore, is not overcoming the barrier separating the two realms, but to mediate the distance between them. The effort extended in bridging this distance links her with Christ on a personal basis.

Whether their interactions occur in heaven or on earth, these tears apotheosize Magdalene's ability to identify with Christ's person. The surfeit of tears underscores her power to access the supernal. As a natural mode of affection and concern, the tears champion her facility to attune herself to and mirror divine beneficence. As a metonymic tool, they empower her to realize what constitutes His being as fully as possible. The knowledge generated by their falling and rising parallels an insistent, steadfast ardor. They are "Waters above th' heav'ns, what they be/ We're taught best by thy tears and thee" bring to light an existent and evolving interconnectedness between the two realms (ll. 23 – 24). The tears may be only part of an empathetic whole, but they conform and affirm a reality founded upon love. Informed by an emotive and cognitive awareness, Magdalene's response discloses an effective means to apprehend the extent of her possibilities, fulfill her creative design as a caring person, and draw closer to the divine.

Teresian Poetry

As opposed to Magdalene's gravity-defying tears, Teresa of Avila bridges the earthly with the empyrean via a rapturous vision. Moreover, her emotive intensity does not stem from a prior interaction with Christ, but rather from a keen awareness of her own spiritual state as it reflects the divine's sublime goodness. Crashaw directs his focus upon this event and what it reveals about her state of mind in his poem "The Flaming Heart." His argument revolves around the inadequacy of pictorial representations to penetrate the deepest recesses of her heart and mind. They cannot convey her sensitive attentiveness to the divine nor impart the wisdom that her autobiography relates about this occasion. Crashaw champions language's power to poeticize a love that exceeds what can be known through either reason or the senses. As stated in Susan Stewart's critique of the poem, "the words are the event or expression; they twist, torque, and turn the reader about and summon the mind to heavenly aspirations in the ways bodies careen through Baroque architectural spaces."[92] Just as Magdalene's tears make the "field's eyes" wish their tears were like hers (l. 179), Teresa's words—whether written in her autobiography or versified by Crashaw—disclose a simulation so complete that "all of him" fills her being and, as such, inspires the reader to restructure his or her life accordingly: "I unto all life of mine may die" (ll. 106, 108).[93]

In "The Flaming Heart," Crashaw distinguishes the artistry between painter and poet, elevating the latter because of metaphor's unbounded ability to describe the ineffable. He creates a figurative-laced paean to Teresa's love that Louis Martz describes as baroque by virtue of its "multiplication of sensory impressions, to exhaust the sensory and to suggest the presence of the spiritual."[94] As expected from the wildly sensuous portrayal of heaven in Magdalene's vision, the unexpected pairing of opposites, such as "Heav'n's great artillery" and "suff'ring seraphim" in conjunction with the synesthesia of "sweet incendiary" and the titular "flaming heart" create a canvas of images that break free from the chains of literal meaning (ll. 56, 64, 85).[95] They extol Teresa's ability to pierce the veil of the divine and forge an intimate understanding.

To spotlight this achievement, the speaker critiques an artist's rendering of her transverberation. Although the exact painting that inspired Crashaw remains

---

92 Susan Stewart, *Poetry and the Fate of the Senses* (Chicago: University of Chicago Press, 2002), 185.

93 All passages from the "The Flaming Heart" are taken from *Carmen Deo Nostro* in *The English Poems of Richard Crashaw*, ed. Rambuss.

94 Louis L. Martz, *From Renaissance to Baroque* (Columbia: University of Missouri Press, 1991), 206.

95 The "flaming heart" signifies, according to Davidson, "the baroque symbol *par excellence*, expressive of the ardours and affects, the interpenetration of temporal and divine love, a metaphor visualized so habitually that it becomes part of international language" (Peter Davidson, *The Universal Baroque* [Manchester: Manchester University Press, 2007], 166).

unknown, the poem describes a diminutive seraph plunging a fiery dart into her heart. Such a scene recollects Teresa's ecstatic experience:

> It was our Lord's will that in this vision I should see the angel in this wise. He was not large, but small of stature, and most beautiful—his face burning, as if he were one of the highest angels, who seem to be all of fire: they must those whom we call cherubim. . . . I saw in his hand a long spear of gold, and at the iron's point there seemed to be a little fire. He appeared to me to be thrusting it at times into my heart, and to pierce my very entrails; when he drew it out, he seemed to draw them out also, and to leave me all on fire with a great love of God. The pain was so great that it made me moan; and yet so surpassing was the sweetness of this excessive pain that I could not wish to be rid of it. The soul is satisfied now with nothing less than God. The pain is not bodily, but spiritual; though the body has its share in it, even a large one. It is a caressing of love so sweet which now takes place between the soul and God, that I pray God of His goodness to make him experience it who may think that I am lying.[96]

Despite the artist's accuracy in describing the proper proportions between the saint and the seraph, the speaker finds fault in the painting's inability to capture Teresa's sensory awareness of the celestial hierarchy. The saint's vision brings to light something more brilliant or magnanimous than what she could conceive in this world. Because of what she sees and feels, she does not look upon God as inaccessible, but rather as a vital figure in her life. As the angel thrusts the spear into her viscera, her body and subsequent pain confirm the purity of her devotion. The transverberation allows her to feel pain, but one which paradoxically produces joy, for it infuses her with an otherworldly love. The details of this moment consume her entire being and mirror the inflamed desire necessary to perpetuate this link between "soul and God." The interlacing of intellect and emotion, flesh and spirit, underlines the potency of His mercy and her enlightened state of mind.

The speaker, however, claims that the painting of this scene is static and fails to convey the dynamic central to this epiphany.

> Had thy cold pencil kissed her pen
> Thou couldst not so unkindly err
> To show us this faint shade for her. (ll. 19–22)

The speaker insists that he should supplant the painter because he can prioritize more effectively Teresa's position in relation to the celestial hierarchy. Figurative language capably describes the unknown and how this celestial interaction in-

---

96 Teresa of Avila, *The Autobiography of St. Teresa of Avila*, trans. David Lewis (Rockford, IL: Tan Books, 1997), 266–67

duces an admixture of supernal consciousness and yearning for self-preservation: "At other times I am in such a state that I do not feel that I am living, nor yet do I desire to die."[97] Although past experience and empirical reasoning have little bearing here, she forgoes neither her sense of self nor a willingness to contribute to this event. She is mindful that others need to share in the "sweetness of this excessive pain."[98] If the artistic medium struggles to highlight this realization, then it chills the heat of her passion. Her vision embraces His affection with her whole body and mind. Deneen Senasi believes that the speaker is not flatly dismissing the artist's "rude design" as much as staying true to the "the visual implications of Teresa's writing" (l. 39).[99] Insisting that the scene must be rearranged by giving the angel the veil and her the dart facially may recast the emphasis between agent and recipient, but his words serve a purpose that far surpass the interplay between these two characters. Just as she does in her autobiography, the speaker stresses, particularly in the final thirty lines, how she ensures that her heart's desires correspond to divine virtue. This pattern of knowing fills her with "thirsts of love more large than they," which culminates in her embracing Him with the fullness of her being (l. 98).

Embodying Christian virtue transmutes her reproductive ability so that she can now theoretically conceive on another plane. She is now "the mother seraphim" (l. 16). That she could perfect her spiritual biology to engender a "Nest of new seraphims here below" indicates the success of her ability to mirror the principles of divine love (l. 46). No picture or sketch can wholly capture that this capability not only accords her a level of knowing rarely realized by humans, but also strengthens her connection with the divine. In effect, her empathy produces a mental state which, as Gregory Currie notes, "counts as a particular type of simulated state because of the cognitive, affective, and behavioral functional roles that it plays, i.e., what outputs it produces."[100] It enables Teresa to achieve symmetry between herself and Christ's being. The structural similarities between her process of knowing and that defined by Christian virtue generate a reciprocity of affection: "By the full kingdom of that final kiss/ That seized thy parting soul, and sealed thee his" (ll. 101–2). This mystic embrace refines her being and, in turn, functions as an exemplar to the aspiring laity.

Leading such a devoted life requires an inner strength proving that she is no "weak, inferior, woman saint" but the "mistress flame" (ll. 26, 17). The affect

---

97 Teresa of Avila, *The Autobiography*, 416.

98 Teresa of Avila, *The Autobiography*, 267.

99 Deneen Senasi, "A Matter of Words: Aesthetics of Reading and Embodiment in the Poetry of Richard Crashaw," *Religion and Literature* 36 (2004): 15.

100 Gregory Currie, *Arts and Minds* (Oxford: Oxford University Press, 2004), 183.

charge of this fiery symbol signifies her link to the divine. Its import is not in overcoming the barrier separating the two realms, but in cultivating the inherent bond between them. Her empathy supersedes the general definition of sharing in another's feelings to help fortify that person's sense of self. Rather, it involves putting into praxis a purified love. As empathizer, she must initiate the action to model herself upon His virtue to gain the most accurate understanding of His affection. The dart piercing her heart proves her success. While some believe that it illustrates a "form of joy because it is a prefiguration of her future heavenly state," the fact that she presently feels this "sweet incendiary" discloses the immediacy of His presence (l. 85).[101] Whatever sensations arise from this event, no matter how foreign to human expectation, they signify a loving openness to what the divine offers: "Love's passives are his activ'st part," for there is no "nobler weapon than a wound" (ll. 73, 74). This wound places her in direct relation to His person. Jayme Yeo observes that "the wounds that Christ inflicts mimic the wounds of the crucifixion; the pain of Christ is the original pain of love. By foregrounding mutual pain in his sacred poetry, Crashaw establishes reciprocity between the lover and the beloved."[102] The pain inflicted by these wounds (or its noticeable absence) underscores Teresa's volition to fashion her mind and body in any way necessary to parallel the divine. While her endeavor is unique in that the subject of her focus is perfect, the process of knowing attests to her maximizing her abilities. As Goldman points out, animals may have mental states, but "having a mental state and representing another individual as having such a state are entirely different matters."[103] These mental states are acts of overt behavior or dispositions to behave in certain ways and, in this instance, are an effusive love. Teresa's wounds and burning heart thus convey a knowing compassion, illuminating the import of her body. It is not simply a vessel whose meaning stems solely from a rich interiority, but serves as a conduit to reflect what lies beyond the realm of reason.[104] Its sensations affirm the Godhead's presence and affection.

Addressed in an apostrophe, her chaste heart walks "in a crowd of loves and martyrdoms" (l. 83). The metaphoric quality of this description underlines language's distinct capability to resonate with a truth that lies beyond its own

---

101 Jan Frans van Kijkzhuizen, *Pain and Compassion in Early Modern English Literature and Culture* (Woodbridge, Suffolk: D.S. Brewer, 2012), 151.
102 James M. Yeo, "Political Theology in the Poetry of Richard Crashaw," *Literature and Theology* 25 (2011): 397.
103 Goldman, *Simulating Minds*, 3.
104 Although the pain she experiences from witnessing the divine is principally spiritual, "the body has its share in it, even a large one" (Teresa of Avila, *The Autobiography*, 267).

power of articulation. This "crowd of loves" refers to those living in heaven, for they have cultivated a devout faith and epitomize the willingness to die for its tenets. The very concept of love lends itself to paradoxical rhetoric. Although it is universally sought by every person, its meaning applies to a wide range of relationships, including romantic lovers, friends, and spiritual devotees. Moreover, each of these bonds can flourish outside the parameters of socially constructed reason. Love provides the alogical illustration of those choices underpinning interpersonal fulfillment. Consequently, the idea of dying for love may seem contradictory, but if its principles—in any of its iterations—are jeopardized by mandated social or religious conformity, then death appears as a plausible option. For martyrs, defending their belief in the divine's salvific power supersedes any loyalty to this world.

Teresa strives to explain this line of reasoning in her book and the speaker extols its wisdom by explicitly mentioning how its readers become "love-slain witnesses of this life of thee" (l. 84). Within this enlightened state, she explains how the conventional notions of what determines splendor and joy cannot express the wonder of envisioning the celestial. As stated in her autobiography, "fine and beautiful things, such as water, fields, perfume, music, etc., I think I would rather not have them, so great is the difference between them and what I am in the habit of seeing, and so all pleasure in them is gone from me."[105] A chaste heart allows her to conform her beliefs with the divine and, in turn, move beyond this world. Language has the unique capability to point out its inability to relate the precise value of cherished relationships and realizations that lie beyond the terrestrial realm. As a result, comparison by negation provides a means to apprehend sensations of transcendence.

While love enables Teresa to know the divine, she gains a greater self-awareness that elevates beyond earthly concerns. To capture the intensity of this moment and inherent limitations of logos, the speaker launches into a series of paratactical phrases that move from concrete to abstract imagery.[106] The implicit need to explicate these metaphors underlines the inexpressibility of her achievement and, paradoxically, lauds it as one worthy of imitation.

> By all thy dow'r of lights and fires;
> By all the eagle in thee, all the dove;
> By all thy lives and deaths of love;
> By thy large draughts of intellectual day. (ll. 94–97)

---

105 Teresa of Avila, *The Autobiography*, 429.
106 It should be noted that lines 93–108 were appended to the poem in the 1652 edition.

Addressing her as a dowry of "lights and fires" underscores the intimacy of her mystic connection with the divine. The brilliance and heat reflects her facility to generate a kindred affection, much like that of a wedded couple. Each spouse is fully cognizant of why he or she loves the other, and this love permits each to peer into the other's heart. For Teresa's mind and body to reflect divine principles, she must exercise a remarkable blend of conviction and mildness. Symbolic of the eagle and dove, respectfully, she emulates Christian virtue, but from this tangible referent point, the speaker employs a conceptual allusion of how her intellect has exceeded its rational bounds. The "draughts of intellectual day" enable her to envision this ethereal wonder. In effect, this hypothetical colloquy identifies the full spectrum of her talents in modeling herself upon His love. A passion burns within her that ignites a force that overcomes any extraneous distractions and rejoices in whatever His response may be—no matter how indescribable it may be.

The concluding lines recall the wedding imagery in the previous lines by drawing attention to the power of a kiss to sanctify one's commitment to the other: "By the full kingdom of that final kiss/ That seized thy parting soul, and sealed thee his" (ll. 101–2). Although occurring on a spiritual plane, it shows that Teresa is qualitatively different from others because she has created a pathway for mutual communication. Her actions have stayed true to her innate goodness, for she is an imprint of His love who exercised her natural aptitude to conform to it. Without being selfless, this insight cannot consider either how divine love differs from worldly virtues or how empathy occasions it. By increasing the means to apprehend the extent of her possibilities, empathy engenders a self-knowledge that reveals a facet of her person that, without this vision, would remain beyond her grasp. This kiss brings to light the intimate relation between her humanity and its ineffable origins. Its poeticizing discloses both the sublime nuances of divine love and the resolute commitment to persevere in this pursuit. Her simulation thus removes any sense of isolation and allows her to participate in an experience that produces an expanding dynamic of inclusivity, for "By all of him we have in thee" (l. 105).

Moved by the words in Teresa's autobiography as attested to by his own florid use of figurative language, the speaker charges himself as a reader to restructure his perception accordingly. Like Teresa, he must "Leave nothing of my self in me" (l. 106). If he attunes himself to her person, then he places himself in a position to achieve a similar end. Understanding her words, however, requires that he accept the epistemological paradox that loving the divine equates with dying to this world: "Let me so read thy life, that I/ Unto all life of mine may die" (ll. 107–8). Striving to imitate those actions described in her autobiography means that he must recognize the ultimate insufficiency of language; no rational construct can articulate with precision that which exists beyond the mundane. Yet, the words that he writes become a metaphor for intense experiences, particularly spiritual ones. These metaphors produce a consciousness of the self and designate what lies within its parameters of knowing. By attempting to describe an emotional transcendence, Crashaw's lexicon simultaneously conveys the divine's immediacy and distance from the aspirant. Hence, "The Flaming Heart" exalts not simply Teresa's achievement, but how she becomes a paragon for others to pattern their lives upon.

In each of their respective poems, Mary Magdalene's and Teresa of Avila's simulation possesses an epistemic value that empowers them to express an empathy that resonates with the proper kind of love and understanding. Constructing similar states of being, however, does not mean that these two women experience the same kind of emotional bond. One fashions a relationship designed to convey her extraordinary willingness to mirror Christ's every move; the other directly shares in the pure love that she has emulated up to this point in her life. The defining feature is how each elects to use the knowledge culled from their simulation to align themselves with the divine's mode of being. Each uses first-person experience—whether physical or visionary—to transform their lives as they recognize the necessity of conforming their will to the divine. As a result, no matter how radically their journeys veer from conventional acts, their experiences reveal the accessibility of sacred space and realize how to structure their lives upon divine love. By responding cooperatively to His goodness, they forge a connection that expands the bounds of human potential.

Epilogue

Throughout this book, I examined different ways that one can construct a meaningful rapport with another. The very diversity shows that expressing empathy with familial, fraternal, or other intimate relationships are not bound by social conventions or directives. It possesses its own kind of originality. While these literary authors understood the tenets of empathy long before science coined the term, their portrayals have something to teach the modern day scientist and psychologist. They illustrate not only the uniqueness of its expression, but also how to put it into praxis when facing overwhelming obstacles. While neuroscientists may offer insight into the physiological response system of the brain when aligning one's thoughts with another, a study of literature brings to light the myriad of situations that arise when trying to implement this act. No matter how precise an analytic knowledge of its science may be, it cannot describe with such verisimilitude how the intricacies of external forces impact an empathic bond. In effect, literature creates a reality that accentuates the subtle nuances of social interplay and the fundamental human desire to connect with another.

This interchange between disciplines, however, is not one-sided; it strives to show how modern thought—whether philosophic or scientific—illuminates the motivations and desires between the characters. It is my hope that this study encourages a more open transference of understanding between these disciplines. By considering the perspectives of literature, science, and philosophy, one comes to appreciate a higher strain of empathy, one which employs the full spectrum of what it means to be human. The emotional, intellectual, physical, and even spiritual factors come to light in these literary portrayals and, in turn, underscore the imperative of honing one's interpretive skill. Grasping the interpersonal import of another's words and gestures reveals the plurality of thought necessary to explicate this process. While these non-literary disciplines explain the empathic consciousness and what circumstances prove most conductive to this act, literature shows how the individual recognizes its value as an act that possesses epistemic surety. When, as Bakhtin states, "I must empathize or project myself into this other human being, see his world axiologically from within him as *he* sees this world," these literary characters illustrate how this indelible yet delicate interlacing between two minds comes to life.[1] Just as the empathizer must choose to prioritize the other's subjectivity and align their own thoughts and feelings with that person,

---

[1] Bakhtin, "Author and Hero in Aesthetic Activity," 25.

https://doi.org/10.1515/9781501515460-006

the student of empathy must make a conscious decision to consider the salience of the different approaches to this process and how they can supplement one another.

Index

https://doi.org/10.1515/9781501515460-007

CPSIA information can be obtained
at www.ICGtesting.com
Printed in the USA
BVHW040604131022
648904BV00002B/16